MW00395883

Hopi Animal Stories

Narrated by Michael Lomatuway'ma,

Lorena Lomatuway'ma,

and Sidney Namingha

Compiled

and edited by

Ekkehart Malotki

With an introduction by

Barre Toelken

Illustrations by Ken Gary

University of Nebraska Press
Lincoln and London

⊚

Library of Congress Cataloging-in-Publication Data
Hopi animal tales. English
Hopi animal stories / narrated by Michael Lomatuway'ma, Lorena Lomatuway'ma,
and Sidney Namingha; collected, translated, and edited by Ekkehart Malotki; with an
introduction by Barre Toelken; illustrations by Ken Gary.
p. cm.
ISBN 0-8032-8271-0 (pbk.: alk. paper)
1. Hopi Indians—Folklore. 2. Tales—Arizona. 3. Animals—Folklore.
I. Lomatuway'ma, Michael. II. Lomatuway'ma, Lorena, 1933– . III. Namingha,
Sidney, 1935–1983. IV. Malotki, Ekkehart. V. Title.
E99.H7H66513 2001
398.2'089'9745—dc21
00-050937

This book retains the same pagination as the original, bilingual edition, *Hopi Animal
Tales*, in which the Hopi and English pages face one another. Because the English
version of the stories required less type, the page lengths of this single-language
edition now vary considerably.

Contents

Preface

Throughout the ages, animals have populated the narrative landscape of humankind, and Hopi folklore is no exception, as is evident from this collection. Nor is this the first time that I have published Hopi stories featuring animals. Indeed, of the eighty-nine narratives that to date have appeared in books and articles of mine, fully sixty-one, or two-thirds, either deal predominantly with animals or contain significant episodes devoted to them.

Coyote figures prominently in Hopi animal stories, as is also true in the oral literature of a number of other Native American tribes. For this reason, I previously concentrated on Coyote in two separate publications. *Hopi Coyote Tales*, co-authored by Michael Lomatuway'ma, was published in 1984 by the University of Nebraska Press. A year later followed *Gullible Coyote*, which featured an introductory segment detailing all the available ethnographic facts surrounding this colorful character.

Preserving as much of the priceless treasures of Hopi oral literature as possible became a prime objective of my fieldwork from the late 1970s on through the mid-1980s. In collecting these narratives I never employed a systematic approach. As a rule, I eagerly recorded whatever story my Hopi consultants spontaneously volunteered to my ever-ready microphone.

Although the concept of *istuwutsi*, "Coyote story," is firmly anchored in the Hopi language, in general my assigning Hopi narratives to a particular thematic category and expressing this in the title of a particular story collection is essentially arbitrary. Still, I have applied this principle of thematic grouping with several of my previous story compilations. Some of the narrative materials that were published under such titles as *Stories of Maasaw, a Hopi God* (Malotki and Lomatuway'ma 1987), *Hopi Ruin Legends* (Malotki ed., 1993), or even the generic tag of *Hopi Tales* (Malotki 1978) could equally well have been clustered under such titles as "Old Spider Woman Tales," "The Adventures of Pöqangwhoya and Palöngawhoya" or "Hopi Witchcraft Stories."

Hopi Animal Stories, the title of the present collection, has no conceptual counterpart in the Hopi language. Anyone consulting the English-Hopi word-finder list of the *Hopi Dictionary* (Hill et al. 1998) will readily discover that no equivalent exists in Hopi for the abstract English notion of "animal." The phrase *himu taytaqa*, which denotes "living creature," is an attempt to capture the concept of "animal," but its makeup betrays its recent origin. Furthermore, the scope of the phrase is so broad that it would also subsume "human beings." Hopi operates with more concrete concepts such as *tuuvosivi,* "game animal," *pok'at,* "domesticated or possessed animal," and *laayi,* "herding animal." Words for "insects" or "reptiles" are equally absent from Hopi vocabulary. Creatures belonging to these and other groupings must be named individually.

All of the tales gathered for this collection constitute original Hopi source materials that have not appeared in this form in any previous publication. They were contributed by four Hopi friends of mine—three from the Third Mesa community of Hotevilla, one from the Second Mesa village of Shungopavi—who, in the course of the more than twenty years that I worked with them, freely shared them in the hope that they would be preserved for posterity. In the original hardcover edition, *Hopi Animal Tales,* the stories were presented both in English and Hopi, not only to assure cultural sensitivity and authenticity, but also to preserve these linguistic treasures of a moribund storytelling tradition for future Hopi generations. In this paper edition the Hopi versions are omitted to make the book more affordable and accessible to a general audience.

Sadly, only one of these four "story rememberers," as I like to call them, Lorena Lomatuway'ma, is still alive. Hailing from the Third Mesa village of Hotevilla, where she spent most of her life, she narrated nearly one half of the stories contained in this collection: "How the Coyotes Celebrated the Bean Dance," "The Chipmunk Girls Who Ground Pinyon Nuts," "Crow and Hawk," "How Coyote Became Infatuated with Girls," "The House Mice and the Boy from Huk'ovi," "Coyote and the Lice," "The Deer Mice," "How Coyote and Hummingbird Satirized Bat in a Song," "How Weasel Befriended the Moon," "Why the Pocket Mice Staged a Dance," "Coyote and Badger as Food Robbers," "The Crying Cicada," "The Gambling Boy Who Married a Bear Girl," and "Wren and Bullsnake." An active member of the Maraw women's society, Lorena now resides in Flagstaff, where she has been assisting me in my research on Hopi language and culture since 1982. In addition to the fourteen animal tales, many of the ethnographic insights in the glossary are hers. Lorena's outstanding command of her native language and her thorough familiarity with Hopi culture also qualified her to become one of the most valuable contributors to the comprehensive Hopi Dictionary Project, on which I worked with her and my colleagues Emory Sekaquaptewa, Kenneth Hill, Mary Black, and others at the University of Arizona from 1986 until 1996.

Already deceased is the man from the Second Mesa village of Shungopavi, who preferred to remain anonymous. Endowed with a nearly encyclopedic knowledge of his culture, he was an authentic *tuwutsmoki,* or "story bag," the Hopi term for one who could draw on an almost inexhaustible repertoire of tales, legends, and myths. From his memory readily sprang "How Field Mouse Helped the People of Mishongnovi," "The Firefly," and "The Flood at Wuukopaqlö."

Also deceased are Lorena's husband Michael Lomatuway'ma and her brother Sidney Namingha Jr., both also from Hotevilla. Sidney's tragic and unnecessary death robbed the Hopi of an extremely talented song poet. Blind from an early age like his sister, he had a marvelous memory. To this memory "The Boy Who Wanted to be a Medicine Man," "Coyote and the Ducks," "How the Ants Initiated Their Children into the Kachina Society," "How Mockingbird Took a Wife," and "The Owl that Made Off with a Little Child" owe their existence.

Michael, finally, contributed a total of eight narratives to this collection: "The Man and the Ants," "Medicine Man Badger," "The Mistreated Cats," "Coyote and Bee," "How the Hopis Got Fire," "The Cicadas and the Serpents," "Sand Cricket," and "The Antelope Kids." During the early and mid-eighties, when I amassed the largest portion of my body of Hopi oral literature, Michael was my research assistant at Northern Arizona University. In this capacity he especially helped me in the laborious task of editing my field recordings from the perspective of his native language.

The English renderings of the tales and glosses are entirely mine. They attempt to steer a middle course between too close and too free a translation. In this task, Michael's wife, Lorena, again provided invaluable assistance. While I consulted her in all instances where I had translation difficulties, I alone must be held accountable for any errors in the final English versions.

The four Hopi contributors to this volume must be the prime recipients of my unreserved gratitude. They all gravely lamented the wholesale erosion of their language and the rapid loss of their oral traditions. Interested in true cultural preservation, they therefore not only readily agreed to my tape-recording of their tales, but also wholeheartedly endorsed my intentions to commit them to print.

Next, I need to express my sincere thanks to Barre Toelken, professor of English and history at Utah State University. As one of the foremost authorities on folklore in the American West and a leading specialist in the field of Navajo oral literature, his essay "Folklore and the Hopi Animal Tales" brings a unique analytical perspective to the present work. His main idea is that while some aspects of cultural worldview may always elude us, there is enough dramatic representation in any story to give us a strong suggestion of cultural values and worldview. As an antidote to seeing the story as childlike and "primitive," this idea applies not merely to *Hopi Animal Stories* but to all my previously published collections of Hopi narratives.

My efforts to preserve as much of Hopi oral literature as possible, carried out in the field from the late seventies through the mid-eighties, were supported in part by Organized Research funds from Northern Arizona University. I thank all my colleagues who were members of the various Organized Research Committees in those years and who considered my efforts worthy of funding. I am equally grateful to Henry Hooper, now Associate Provost at Northern Arizona University who, as chair of the Organized Research Committee in those days, not only strongly backed my scholarly endeavors then but has remained a solid supporter of my research activities until the present day. He also approved camera-ready preparation of the manuscript, which was carried out with admirable competence and professionalism by Louella Holter, editor at the Ralph M. Bilby Research Center.

Finally, thanks for stylistically touching up my English translations and therefore greatly improving their readability are due to my friend Ken Gary of San Diego. In addition to these editorial services, Ken rose to the challenge of creating some striking illustrations, as he had previously done for *The Bedbugs' Night Dance and Other Hopi Sexual Tales* (Malotki 1995). His black-and-white drawings once again reveal not only his talent as a gifted artist but also his intimate familiarity with Hopi material and immaterial culture.

References

Hill, Kenneth C., Emory Sekakwaptewa, Mary E. Black, and Ekkehart Malotki (eds.)
  1998 *Hopi Dictionary/Hopìikwa Lavàytutuveni: A Hopi-English Dictionary of the Third Mesa Dialect with an English-Hopi Finder List and a Sketch of Hopi Grammar*. Tucson: University of Arizona Press.

Malotki, Ekkehart
  1985 *Gullible Coyote - Una'ihu: A Bilingual Collection of Hopi Coyote Tales*. Tucson: University of Arizona Press.

  1978 *Hopitutuwutsi - Hopi Tales: A Bilingual Collection of Hopi Indian Stories*. Flagstaff: Museum of Northern Arizona Press.

Malotki, Ekkehart, ed.
  1995 *The Bedbugs' Night Dance and other Hopi Sexual Tales: Mumuspi'yyungqa Tuutuwutsi*. Narrated by Michael Lomatuway'ma, Lorena Lomatuway'ma, Sidney Namingha Jr., Leslie Koyawena, and Herschel Talashoma. Lincoln: University of Nebraska Press.

  1993 *Hopi Ruin Legends: Kiqötutuwutsi*. Narrated by Michael Lomatuway'ma, Lorena Lomatuway'ma, and Sidney Namingha Jr. Lincoln: University of Nebraska Press.

Malotki, Ekkehart and Michael Lomatuway'ma:
  1987 *Stories of Maasaw, a Hopi God*. American Tribal Religions series, edited by Karl Luckert, vol. 10. Lincoln: University of Nebraska Press.

  1984 *Hopi Coyote Tales. Istutuwutsi*. American Tribal Religions series, edited by Karl Luckert, vol. 9. Lincoln: University of Nebraska Press.

Introduction: Folklore and the Hopi Animal Stories

Folklore comprises the customary expressions and beliefs that arise from and articulate the day-to-day associations of closely related people, whether tribal or bureaucratic, rich or poor, young or old, literate or aliterate. Folklore is the living, performative dimension of every culture and can be said to include—in addition to day-to-day customs and culture-based beliefs—food lore, gestures, cultural proxemics (culturally based "rules" for human proximity), orally transmitted stories and songs, traditional arts (rather than those requiring formal training), regional dialects, games, and handicrafts: that is to say, all those continuing expressive devices that we learn orally, by imitation, or in performance and that remain in use without formal instruction or institutional direction because we simply continue to use them.

Some folk expressions, like some forms of living language, are always changing and dying out while others take their place. In northern Europe, most people do not orally transmit the wonder tales that once were so highly prized by collectors like the Grimm brothers, but they do tell jokes—especially political jokes—in great abundance. One kind of folktale continues to exist, fossil-like, in children's books, while the other kind persists in the everyday conversations of living people, without the need of print. Legends about saints are not as common as they once were, but legends about startling modern events (like the poodle exploding in a microwave or the woman cooked in the suntan parlor) are almost impossible to avoid.

One of the most interesting genres of folklore is the folktale, a brief, fictional narrative that focuses on a single event and that is passed along orally among people for whom the continual "performance" of the story for each other constitutes an important way of expressing culturally shared values, attitudes, and concerns. Calling a folktale "fiction" implies not that its meanings are false but that a story line has been created by someone as a dramatic vehicle for a set of cultural abstractions that may ring very true to the listener—true enough to be worth passing on as a story. And it is this passing onward through and among the members of a culture that creates the distinctive shaping process that eventually erases the distinctive marks of the originator, replacing them with the constant revisions and reinterpretations of those who continue to tell the story. In this sense, we can look at a folktale as a dynamic means by which a culture continues to experience, explore, and critique a set of associated human issues.

A closely related genre in folk narrative is the legend. In contrast to the fictional tale (which may use an opening formula like "once upon a time" to announce that listeners are not expected to see the story as a collection of data), the legend is presented as the account of a factual event usually verified by the word of "the friend of a friend." Often such stories account for the origins of place-names or tell of strange-but-true events in the world around us. Although myths are also presented as true, they are characterized by a larger—usually sacred—compass: how the world was created, how death came to be, or who the gods are.

While these genres are fairly well distinguishable in Euro-American culture (because these terms are based on the observable characteristics of traditional narratives from European origins), they often do not account for the realities of Native American traditional stories. A story that may seem fictional—perhaps due to the way it describes animals talking to each other—may also be presented as a story that accounts for actual features in the local landscape or details the activities of deities. As readers will see in the present collection of stories from Hopi country, there is a constant interaction of sacred and worldly dimensions, fanciful and starkly realistic settings, animal and human worlds, fictional and biological issues, and dramatic and scientific principles. At first this might seem confusing to the careful reader, but it should not remain so. The Hopis' cultural worldview assumes a living interplay between agriculture and religion, the real and the fanciful, the animal and the human. Their stories do not fit neatly into Euro-American categories precisely because they dramatize a different set of assumptions and premises about the world and about the cultural processes of living in and expressing that world.

Rather than trying to force Hopi stories into non-Hopi categories, let us stand back a few paces and consider the larger question: what do Hopis do in their traditional narratives (whatever their generic characteristics) that serves to dramatize shared attitudes toward their world? How do their narratives work? There are observations we can make about any narrative, and we should begin there.

A narrative—in contrast to an anecdote or a faithful account of some event—is a created structure that is first of all characterized by a plot. Something "happens" in a narrative, and the function of the plot is to furnish the logical relations that provide cultural meaning to that created event. In the full description of an event in nature, our focus is on the details and their accuracy. In a narrative, our focus is on the connections between the foregrounded details chosen by a narrator as especially meaningful in the articulation of an important theme. In folk narrative, that theme and its various meanings come from the rich associations of the culture, and the connective sinews are nurtured and savored by generations of narrators through whose minds and mouths the story has passed. In this process, the distinctive styles and agendas of particular narrators become softened or muted, and the ongoing values of the culture are refined and preserved. A story will not get very far in oral tradition unless it is good enough, interesting enough, and meaningful enough for people to continue telling it and listening to it.

The plot, in other words, can be described as a constellation of interrelated references to culturally important ideas. The word "constellation" suggests that plot details are not simply strung together like beads; rather, they reflect on each other, respond to each other, and interact with each other in such a way that a plot is capable of expressing far more than what is said in the actual words and expressing it in a far more complex way.

But how can ideas be said to interact with each other in any identifiable way? Postmodern critics have recently invented the term "intertextuality" for this phenomenon; but it is not the texts that interact but the shared values and assumptions within a culture that come together richly in any folk articulation. A narrative plot usually uses characters whose actions epitomize or suggest the enactment of culturally recognizable abstractions. For example, the familiar story "The Three Little Pigs" is clearly not about pigs or pig behavior, even though the words of the story never admit that. We know that pigs do not build houses, but we know that humans do. So we could say that the story is about people. But people do not normally build houses of straw or sticks, either, so the story must be doing something more than creating ethnographic metaphors about house building. If we see the story as one that focuses on culturally validated assumptions about hard work, planning ahead, protecting the family from outside threats ("keeping the wolf from the door"), and constructing stable housing, we see emerging from this simple narrative a set of abstract values that are well known in northern Europe and in Euro-America. Yet nowhere in the story do we hear terms like "work

ethic" or "family obligation" or "foresight." Abstractions like these
are not in and of themselves very interesting; but acted out in dramatic fashion by actors who themselves suggest an ample food supply (plenty of ham), planning ahead (piggy banks), and good luck
(real and candy pigs appear in European shop windows in abundance at New Year's to suggest the idea of fortune and plenty in the
coming year), then we have a good example of a cultural constellation
that is so meaningful in its nuances and so obvious to people in its
culture that no one would think it necessary to explain these matters
to anyone. Yet someone from outside the culture might well complain
that this is all projection or imagination, that we are reading something into the text. To the contrary, what we are doing is reading as
much out of the text as we can simply by noting how these concrete,
palpable images (houses, pigs) are cleverly brought together in a dramatic enactment of relationships between human action and cultural
stability. Even in such a superficially simple tale as "The Three Little
Pigs," the dramatization sets off our recognition of a not-so-simple
cultural concept without overtly saying so.

 Our task in looking at these Hopi tales, then, is to examine the
culturally constructed plots and, using what we know of Hopi folk
custom and belief, ask "What is being acted out here?" We will not be
rewarded by any sudden, grand insight into Hopi culture, but we
will be able to understand more fully what these stories mean and
how they are more than simple entertainment. Yet entertaining they
must be—or no one would tell them in the first place, much less continue to tell them. Our obligation as readers is to look seriously at as
many facets of the stories as we can identify—from entertainment
value to cultural nuance—as we keep in mind that there is seldom
only one reason for anything, let alone one thing that makes a great
story. We will consider Hopi cultural style, custom, and assumptions
about nature and distinctive moral issues along with the idea of culturally constructed drama: "actors" bringing abstract concepts into
palpable form in "loaded" constellations.

 When we note in these stories that both the bear and the mouse
are considered healers and conclude that healing power is not related
to size, we can watch for the processes and attitudes that do constitute the basis for healing. If we know that Hopis have depended on
fertility of plants for their very survival, we will not be surprised to
encounter fertility in all its aspects (including sexuality) as an expression of the life force. If we know that corn plays a religious role for

the Hopis, we will more easily see how corn can embody or suggest sacred relationships in the logic of a story. Since rain is a part of Hopi sacred equations, we will appreciate that the encouragement or thwarting of rain indicates something more complex than the daily weather forecast. If we know that the marriage ceremony not only unites a couple but also creates reciprocal family relationships, we can read marriage in the stories as a dramatic establishment of a kinship bond central to the plot. To the non-Hopi reader it may not be immediately apparent that such equations and relationships are built into several levels of every Hopi story. For that reason, in this essay I refer to some stories several times to show the various levels and registers of folklore that interact to produce the full set of nuances that in turn provide unstated meaning to the stories.

In addition, during the process of establishing the cultural nuances of these stories, the reader is urged to consult the glossary on a constant basis, for its discussions of words and terms come directly from two of the Hopi storytellers from whom these texts came, Michael and Lorena Lomatuway'ma. Not only do they provide in their glossarial notes Hopi translations and cultural understandings for animals, place names, deities, and rituals, but they also illustrate the particularized customs and assumptions of Hopis from the village of Oraibi, where most of these stories are centered. This sense of place is important to the cultural function of the narratives because the particular place names, directions, and distances mentioned are recognizable to the Hopis of that area as the immediate environmental bearings in which they live—thus giving the stories an immediacy for the Hopi listeners that is quite the opposite of the European formula "Long, long ago, in a land far beyond the sea. . . ."

In recent years, some Hopi cultural leaders have expressed concern—in some cases outright disapproval—over the way non-Hopis have discussed Hopi materials, especially those connected with religious rituals and obligations. Indeed, many outsiders, from serious students of Native culture to New Age enthusiasts to "wannabe Indians" to desperate guru-seekers, have made use of Hopi stories, arts, and dances in a number of ways quite foreign to the Hopis' own concepts of propriety. Even the present book, which provides translated oral stories in printed form, might be considered unnecessary by traditional Hopis who would rather hear these tales narrated by friends and relatives in their own homes than to see them fossilized in a book. Are we intruding on the Hopis, then, by presenting and discussing stories in this format? I think not. To begin with, these are all story texts freely shared by their narrators, who did feel it was as important for them to be documented as for them to continue being told. And, importantly, publishing a story in print does not in any way prevent oral storytellers from continuing with important performative traditions. Further, the folkloristic approach today is an empirical one, based on what we can actually observe; it does not involve prying into ritual secrets or intruding into domains no one wants to discuss. Rather, in this case it is the study of what Hopi people customarily have said and done openly, and we use the cultural contexts of those expressions to extend the abilities of Hopis and non-Hopis alike to appreciate more consciously the richness of these classics of human articulation.

Luckily, someone wrote down the *Iliad* and the *Odyssey*, German and English wonder tales, *Beowulf*, the Irish myths and sagas, and the Yugoslavian epics. Luckily, dedicated scholars like Ekkehart Malotki have recorded the classic stories of the Hopis; indeed, world literature would be the poorer today if these wonderful narratives had been ignored. In the case of the Greek and Anglo-Saxon materials, however, there are no living cultural contexts available for us to use, no living narrators for us to ask for clarification, no living groups who might enjoy such rich literary experiences in their own everyday lives. The Hopis, fortunately, are still here, and though the storytelling tradition has virtually lapsed, some of them do still tell these tales at the proper time of year: in Kyaamuya, approximately December. We can dismiss their stories as primitive, childish fancies if we want to—and indeed that will be our impression if we read them superficially as droll accounts of talking animals. If we take Hopi custom and lore seriously, however, we will be treated to the rich feast of a literary imagination guided by cultural depth and by a culturally shaped sensitivity to the nuances of the natural world.

Traditional Hopi Style and Narrative Logic

On Third Mesa, all stories (sing. *tuuwutsi*; pl. *tuutuwutsi*) begin with the formulaic phrase *aliksa'i*—to which the listeners traditionally respond "*Oh*." In other villages on other mesas, the storyteller might start with "*ituwutsi*," literally "It is my story." And the stories customarily end with a phrase like "Here my story ends." Such formulas demarcate a narrative in terms appropriate to its content and function (for example, personal anecdotes and reminiscences are not so framed) and thus foreground the text as a discrete articulation of a cultural drama. In a similar way, opening phrases such as "once upon a time," or "when I was young," or "by the way," establish the tone and cultural assumptions about the content of the English-language story to follow.

Combined with a regular audience response (*"Oh"*)—which continues throughout the performance of a Hopi story—this customary device serves to engage the narrator and audience not only in a lively moment of entertainment but also in an interactive experience of Hopi values as well. In addition, the initial setting in these stories usually establishes a condition of stable habitation in that important geographical "home" locale ("People were living at Oraibi and all across the land people were settled in villages") in which the story-telling performance takes place, creating still another level of personal involvement and living cultural context. And this orientation is extended still further in many of the stories that name certain known places in the real landscape and that describe the actions of characters in terms of those key directions ("He went northeastwards around the mesa") actually used by the listeners in their own daily travels in their home territory.

The structure and development of these stories also follows Hopi traditional assumptions about cause and effect as well as cultural expectations about the sequence of actions. Forgetting or ignoring standard Hopi religious practice or worldview inevitably leads a character into embarrassment, death, confusion, or failure; proper application of Hopi custom produces well-being, stability, fertility, and community success for the characters. In some stories, an irony grows from a discrepancy between these two sets of assumptions, as in "The Antelope Kids," where a couple prays successfully at the appropriate shrines in order to have children but then treat their twins improperly and lose them to the antelopes. In a few stories, the device of interdiction/interdiction violated—much more common as a logical premise in European stories—sets up the inevitability of plot direction. For example, in "The Owl That Made Off with a Little Child," an owl warns people that the kidnapped child must be kept in a room for four days, and no one may look in. This interdiction is broken (as it must be for the story to proceed), and the child turns into an owl. In "Sand Cricket," the protagonist's grandmother fastens hair to his head with pitch and tells him not to go where it's warm and not to lie down, but since he is going courting, and Hopi courting included sleeping overnight with the young lady, the interdiction is impossible to obey. Here, as in all stories, if the structuring of the story's logic is not consonant with the culture's assumptions about normal actions, the story will not make sense and will stand much less of a chance of being passed along in the oral tradition.

Folktales usually describe sequential repetition in numbers that reflect the culture's assumptions about the meaning and direction of narrated human actions. In Euro-American stories, the number of actions is usually three, with the third position being the most important ("The third time's the charm"), suggesting that the scene is lineally arranged, the first two actions preparing us for the third, decisive move. In Northwest Coastal tribal stories, the number is usually five and seems to suggest not a sequence but a stable gathering or a complete number (perhaps analogous to the five fingers on a hand). Among the Navajos, the number is usually four and is often used in conjunction with the four cardinal directions and their distinctive colors. These Hopi stories favor four as well, and while there is little to indicate a reference to the surrounding directions, there is a symmetrical effect achieved by this convention. In "How the Hopis Got Fire," for example, four creatures (two birds and two animals: two who live in the sky and two who live on the ground, a predator, a carnivore, an herbivore, and a scavenger) collaborate with humans to obtain fire. In "How Field Mouse Helped the People of Mishongnovi," Field Mouse uses a sequential trick that causes a hawk to impale himself on the fourth dive.

Characters—whether animal or human—observe the proper Hopi greeting formulas when entering someone's home or when meeting each other: "Are you here also?" or "So you've come" or "This is where you are, then." These greetings, parallel to those used in all Pueblo societies, are acknowledgments of other people's positions or actions and are more complex in their way than the word "Hi!" Someone entering a pueblo dwelling from the roof expects to hear an invitation from within; the interchange between visitor and visited thus actually dramatizes their relationship at that moment as much as it functions like a knock on the door. And when animals follow these same formulas, we can assume that the Hopi listeners are envisioning a narrative drama in which all parties observe the niceties, the proprieties, and the conventions of relationship that underlie the assumed meanings of everyday deportment in the Hopi community.

Incidentally, while the stories presented here are furnished with titles, they are seldom given formal titles by Hopi narrators in their home contexts. Naturally, if someone in the family wants to hear a particular one, some phrase akin to a title might be used: "Tell us that one about the mouse at Mishongnovi," for example. These narrators were asked what they would call their stories if they had to refer to them by title, and their suggestions are utilized in this collection—for the convenience of a culture that stores its narratives in books rather than preserving them by continual performance.

Traditional Content

As is the case in every culture, these stories are phrased in terms of customary behavior; so it follows that an awareness of Hopi custom is essential to our understanding of normal events in the plots. Because Hopi culture is matriarchal and matrilocal, we should not be surprised to see women playing decisive roles in these stories. Older people, regarded as wise, often function as advisors. Dancing—both social and ritual—enjoys a high priority in Hopi life; practicing dance steps, composing dance songs, and the extensive preparations for dance events, all of them important, community-centered aspects of life, are used prominently in these stories to evoke the human and social issues in tales that use animals as actors. Relationships among humans, between humans and animals, and between humans and the natural environment are made visual and palpable in the dances and ceremonies. These customary scenes in a story go far beyond the realm of social entertainment or the superficial possibility that animals might act in a cute fashion.

The custom of purifying oneself in a sweat lodge is probably the most widespread single cultural feature shared by Native American societies. It functions not only as a physical steam bath, but as a spiritual and psychological purification often accompanied by ritual songs and prayers. Tribes joke about who has the hottest sweat, who knows how to do it "right," and often disagree on what kinds of behavior are allowed inside the cramped quarters of the lodge. But the Hopis have never used the sweat lodge, which may be one of the motivations for the sequence of events in "The Firefly." Both Navajos and Hopis tell jokes about each other; this tale suggests that the Navajos do not understand the physiology of the firefly (fireflies do indeed contain a corrosive fluid and also go through a process of maturation in which the insect emerges from a pupa) and that they bungle their sweat lodge custom by making the steam so unnaturally hot that it destroys rather than purifies.

Kivas—as well as many older dwellings—are entered by ladder from an opening in the roof. Not only are certain invitations and greetings associated with this entryway, but the custom of *descending* into someone else's living space (giving a real sense to the phrase "dropping in") provides a dramatic enactment of how centrally a visitor is placed in certain social scenes. On the other hand, a visiting suitor who has not yet won the favor of a young woman's attention is described as lurking outside the ventilation hole of the room where she grinds corn; architecturally marginalized and conversationally limited, the youth must whisper and peek through the small hole until he's dismissed, rejected, or invited in.

Having been invited in, the suitor sleeps with the young woman until the couple determine that the bond is acceptable and will last, at which time they are essentially considered married. Obviously, the placement of characters in customary scenes is an index of the nature of the relationship being dramatized. A character's misuse, abuse, or ignorance of the cultural norms can thus be the occasion for laughter and derision (reminding the listener to observe the "rules" carefully) or the signal for a character's failure to achieve a goal.

These rather "open" courtship rules might strike the outsider as promiscuity enfranchised, but the cultural logic behind them actually animates much of the life, survival, and value system of all Pueblo societies: fertility is central to the life of the community and is celebrated in all its aspects, human, animal, agricultural, and ceremonial. Stories like "The Gambling Boy Who Married a Bear Girl" dramatize the custom of a girl inviting a boy to sleep with her; in "Sand Cricket," much of the action consists of preparing an unlikely suitor for the realities of staying overnight with a very attractive young woman. While such plots may well be sexually suggestive, it is within a cultural context where sexuality is not smothered but promoted. Indeed, open expressions of human sexuality—often foregrounded by explicit antics of the clown societies during ceremonies in the plaza—are considered no more "X-rated" than the rituals that bring rain to the plants. Of course, early missionaries and government agents saw these expressions as proof that the base nature of the savage needed reconstruction. But these eloquent stories provide the narrative dramatization of larger relationships and parallels between humans and nature than those reformers could have dreamed.

The Hopi stories are also full of proverbial wisdom, both drama-tized (as in "How Coyote and Hummingbird Satirized Bat in a Song," where the serving of stolen meat is depicted as despicable) and overt-ly stated (as in "The Man and the Ants," where the story both drama-tizes and states the precept "Don't promise the ants 'your meat' or they'll come for you"). A similar combination of enactment and com-ment is presented in "Coyote and the Lice," where we hear "Don't eat only meat; it will make your behind itch."

Some stories provide dramatic models of how (and how not) to raise children, conventions about planting and animal husbandry, information about the eating and hunting habits of animals, medici-nal properties of plants, seasonal behavior of reptiles and birds, and developmental stages of insects. In "How Field Mouse Helped the People of Mishongnovi," chickens are described as becoming sick from fright because of a hawk: they stop laying eggs and lose their feathers, an accurate depiction of chicken behavior built into the story. Later in the same story, Field Mouse suggests hanging the dead hawk on a pole to scare away other predators, an accurate depiction of human assumptions about animal psychology. In "Crow and Hawk," customs and assumptions about food proprieties and birds' eating habits are established.

The connections between animals and healing dramatized in "The Deer Mice" certainly remind us today of the role of deer mice in the recent hantavirus epidemic; long before scientists had discovered the role of deer mice in the problem, Hopis and Navajos were recal-ling that older traditions required the burning of all bedclothes if peo-ple noticed that deer mice had run over them at night.

These stories display a tremendous range of customary content: from folk science (the traditional account of the development of the firefly from pupa to adult, for example) to cultural attitudes toward songs, sex, and environmental relationships. Clearly, the "work" of a Hopi tale, what it accomplishes in its home context, goes far beyond the immediate entertainment of a few friends and relatives. Rather, it functions as a living library of culturally constructed observation, information, and attitude.

Traditional Philosophy and Worldview

The themes and motifs discussed in the previous section can be called the building blocks of Hopi stories—meaningful vernacular elements placed into the structural framework of a plot because they encapsulate ideas that make a difference, that elucidate or bring to the fore important attitudes being explored by the narrative. Some of these customary ideas are so systematically interlaced with larger assumptions about life that they can be profitably discussed as dramatizations of cultural worldview. While I attempt no thorough exposition of Hopi worldview, I nonetheless point to a few larger clusters of assumptions that lie behind the logic and the aura of deep urgency we feel in most of these stories. In their fullest sense, these ideas are very general and abstract and are probably not articulated overtly anywhere (unless in the training and ritual activity that goes on in the kivas under the direction of special mentors). It is through the stories that these ideas become dramatized in specific, concrete, local terms.

Relationships. Instead of the individual being the central concern of the culture, for the Hopis it is the group—usually an interactive family or a functioning village. Such a focus requires not simply that there be more actors, but that they be presented as a collection of interdependent entities whose continued existence and reality depend on the group dynamic, even when the actions of only one member of the group are emphasized. Appropriately, then, the stories stress the importance of reciprocal relationships between and among all members of the group. Everyone is expected to give, share, give back, supply, teach, and respond to everyone else. Moreover, this mutual responsibility goes beyond politeness or form and seems to be an equation for proper, moral behavior in the world. Selfishness and aggressive individual competition appear as problems and moral weaknesses.

When the youngsters in "The Antelope Kids" are mistreated by their human mother, for example, they are rescued and nurtured by the antelopes until they slowly become antelopes themselves—and thus become part of the food supply that eventually nurtures the village of their cruel parent. *Of course* antelopes furnish us with their bodies: they are our relatives, and that's what relatives do, in spite of the shortcomings of individual people.

In "How the Hopis Got Fire," it is significant that we are not told that fire was "discovered," but that it was sent for and obtained through the coordinated efforts of Owl (a flying predator), Gopher (an underground herbivore), Coyote (a four-legged carnivore and scavenger) and Vulture (a flying scavenger), who all risk themselves to supply the Hopis with an essential element of human, not animal, life. In "The Gambling Boy who Married a Bear Girl," the boy is

watched over by animals who later ask him to make prayer sticks and
feathers for them when he gets home, to "help sustain our lives,"
clearly an articulation of the concept that human prayers are one
aspect of a reciprocal system that asks the animals to provide food,
medicines, powers, and guidance in return for human ritual acts of
renewal. When the boy neglects to perform these obligations, he
learns a still deeper lesson by being killed and then resurrected by the
animals. He then spends the rest of his life as a healer.

In "How Field Mouse Helped the People of Mishongnovi," Field
Mouse helps rid his area of a bothersome hawk that is killing the
domesticated chickens of local humans (who must have inadvertently
supplied much of Field Mouse's food). In thanks to Field Mouse and
Old Spider Woman for their help, the people make prayer sticks. In
"The Man and the Ants," a lazy man promises meat to a village of
ants if they help him weed his fields. They do the work and he pays
them in piki the first time but continues to exploit them without
further reciprocation. In an apt and powerful scene, the ants devour
him from inside, suggesting among other things that laziness, selfishness, and abandonment of reciprocal obligations are self-destructive
qualities that will eat you up inside. "The Crying Cicada" dramatizes
the reciprocal—and ritualized—relations between the cicadas, warm
weather, and food. A cicada laments that humans have been cooking
and eating cicadas without regard for the fact that it is they who bring
the warm weather for crops. The cicadas move away and next summer, warm weather does not come; the situation is resolved by a man
who makes prayer feathers for them and in his prayer articulates the
human need for cicadas. Our food supply and our weather are nego-
tiated from both sides; the cicadas, assured that they are needed and
valued and that they will receive prayers, accede to sacrificing themselves.

Gender. The focus on female attractiveness, sexuality, and matriarchal identity suggests the power of females in the area of fertility.
The model is expressed in these stories in many ways, from the ever
present (but not always articulated) matriarchal, matrilocal system to
female-controlled courtship to open admiration of women for their
erotic power. The firefly in the story of the same name is looking for
"Women, big women," and in many of the stories, courtship entails
that the young man be invited by the young woman to stay overnight
with her to explore sexual possibilities. Matriarchal power exerts
negative functions in the stories when it is misused: for example, in

"The Antelope Kids," although it is the man's prayers that succeed in obtaining children for the barren couple, it is the mother's inability to treat them right that results in their departure. The mother, not the father, beats the children; but since it is her home, they must leave. In "The Owl That Made Off with a Little Child," even though the child is cranky beyond measure, it is the mother who throws the child out where it is rescued by an owl and raised in the owl's nest. The story ends with a warning not to cast out a child who cries at night (the time when, of course, one normally hears owls).

Agriculture. Hopi assumptions about agriculture include the belief that human behavior and morality have a direct influence on the welfare of growing things and thus on the greater good and continuity of the community. The careful maintenance and grooming of fields, prayers for rain, and encouragement of growing plants are all seen to be moral and religious activities as well as horticultural and are relevant to the life of the whole community and not just the successful harvest for a single farmer.

A particularly dramatic demonstration of an abrogation of the normal relationship between rain and survival is provided by "The Flood at Wuukopaqlö," in which a community decides to celebrate its increased population by praying that rain will *not* come. The cloud chiefs, angered at this sacrilegious petition, focus all the rain on that one spot and cause a flood that drowns most of the inhabitants.

Ritual. While these stories do not delve deeply into ritual detail, they nonetheless refer to ritual activity, and several of them actually describe some rites. Since rituals are considered a physical enactment of prayer, these scenes stand as vivid examples of the idea that a narrative drama can give shape and definition to an otherwise abstract reality. Hopi custom sees prayer not as abstract but as a dramatic expression of a desired condition. In some ways, then, ritual is not so much a petition for sacred results as it is the accomplishment of a sacred act. The stories that contain ritual scenes provide something far more detailed and powerful than local color.

Of course, the most powerful rituals of all are those enacted by the kachinas and various societies during the annual round of Hopi ceremonialism. These striking and extremely moving events are not fully detailed in the stories here, and rightly so. But several of the stories do refer to the rituals and their styles. In "Why the Pocket Mice Staged a Dance" and "How the Ants Initiated Their Children into the Kachina Society" (as well as in several other tales) the actual preparations, celebrations, and behaviors associated with ritual dances are integral parts of the story and provide ongoing though vicarious experience in matters that become more fully realized during the actual rituals in which people take part. In "How the Coyotes Celebrated the Bean Dance," kachina behavior is imitated, but the level of impersonation is ridiculous. For those who know proper ritual behavior, such stories employ the humor of hyperbole to highlight propriety and ritual know-how by making fun of those who do not know or fail to observe the rules.

Orientation. According to many Hopis, their past has included periods of migration over vast areas followed by the intentional choice of settlement in their present location. Over time, as disputes and ritual variations arose (some of them as recently as the 1930s), groups of Hopis have moved away to establish new villages. In each case, there is a highly developed sense of centering local realities and rituals on the village and on its kivas. Solstitial directions, formations on the horizon, nearby and distant mesas and canyons, and the movements of sun and moon establish a rich context of orientation and identity with the home place (mostly the vicinity of Third and Second Mesa, from which the narrators hail). This quality comes through vividly in the stories as characters experience their adventures in an intimately known, intensely local world. Characters in these stories are not only associated with certain places that are announced in the formulaic opening statements, but their movements within the stories are carefully delineated in locally meaningful directions: sunwise or counter-sunwise, northeastward around the mesa, down off the mesa, out toward a certain canyon, and so on. The listener familiar with the local geography recognizes where the action of the story takes place, and the Hopi listener in particular has the sense of inhabiting the same immediate world as the characters dramatized in the stories.

Emotion. All emotions are significant, not only in and of themselves as motivators of characters' actions, but as informal indicators of stability or instability in the psychological "scenery" of the story. Rattlesnakes are avoided, our glossary notes, not because they might bite, but because they might be angry and thus bite. Good thoughts promote good hunting, and bad thoughts inhibit the necessary intersections with game animals (for example, in "Medicine Man Badger," we hear that hunting was good in the old days because back then no one had bad thoughts). In "The Mistreated Cats," the cats prepare and stage a community dance but become openly angry when the unwelcome frogs insist on attending (visitors from others places normally attend Hopi dances and enjoy Hopi hospitality). The cats in their anger compose and sing a song that ridicules the frogs, provoking the frogs to get angry and start singing their own song, which causes a downpour that drowns the cats. Knowing that emotions are considered keys to the story line as well as to behavior, we can watch for symptoms of emotion that suggest cultural meaning in the actions of characters and in the denouements of the stories.

Humor. Humor is of particular importance to the Hopis, as it is to all other tribes in the Southwest. For the Navajos, for example, a sense of humor is tantamount to a measure of one's intellect, and whoever makes a baby laugh for the first time is expected to give a party to celebrate the emergence of humane perception in the infant's personality. For the Hopis, laughter is seen as an important dimension of one's mental health and life expectancy. A person who enjoys laughing and making others laugh is often called *qatsiwuphoya*—literally, "life-prolonger." Humor may be aimed at someone who doesn't act properly or who is consistently foolish; several of the stories presented here feature parodic behavior, humorous reversals, and jokes played on others in ways that reflect on cultural norms and expectations. For example, in "Coyote and the Ducks," Coyote tries to steal a duck (other stories make it clear that stolen food may corrupt the eater), and when the ducks obtain permission to pray first before being eaten, they quack loudly until their owner comes and kills the would-be thief. When coyotes try to do a Bean Dance (in the story of the same name), they dress like kachinas and try to dance, but they stumble all over the place, falling on their faces. An Oraibi hunting party passes by and kills all the coyotes who are dressed like kachinas. In some stories, we can assume that simply a statement of the plot would be humorous to a Hopi. For example, when Coyote becomes infatuated with a girl and tries to collect and wear all the necessary courting gear (in "How Coyote Became Infatuated with Girls") or when Sand Cricket's grandmother glues hair to his head so he can go courting (in "Sand Cricket"), the patent implausibility must strike a humorous chord, even when the story in other respects describes the accoutrements of courtship in rigorous detail. In other stories, when animals make fun of each other ("How Coyote and

Hummingbird Satirized Bat in a Song," for example), the humor is much more openly articulated, for the medium used—parodic song— is a recognizable cultural genre of humorous critique.

Hopi humor, like all humor, is culturally contexted and is far too complex to be treated adequately in a short essay. Suffice it to say that it is characterized by a focus on cultural discrepancies, a heavy use of sexual and scatological reference, and a rich employment of puns. These are obviously rewarding areas for further consideration and enjoyment for those who have command of Hopi language and culture, but they do evade and elude full translation. The reader can be sure that these stories are far funnier for Hopis than they are for non-Hopis and that the humor has a cultural point to it.

Shamanism. A shaman (a Siberian Evenki word) is someone, male or female, who has obtained magical or spiritual powers through some traumatic personal experience with the powers of the Otherworld. Most often, this experience is described as an actual death and a resurrection, and the healing is provided by animal or spiritual helpers who then function as guides and mentors for the rest of the shaman's life. In some tribes the trauma comes from what we would call a near-death experience; in others, the spirit guide is obtained through a demanding ritual, like a vision quest or a sun dance. The process of going "to the other side" and returning, rigorous in itself, is also regarded as conferring a larger variety of attributes on the person who survives it: the shaman may thus be able to represent both male and female genders, may be considered invulnerable to normal weapons, may be thought of as both alive and dead or as both animal and human. This expansion of powers allows the shaman to find the cure for otherwise hopeless health problems or injuries, to represent a spiritual connection between community and nature, and to exercise a psychological influence on both humans and animals.

While most Hopi ceremonialism centers on the kachinas (who appear as deities animated by human "impersonators"), and most healing is done by Native doctors (often referred to in English as "medicine men"), certain people emerge as special and powerful healers in their own right, and the process by which these practitioners gain and exercise their powers is dramatized in several of the stories presented in this collection. For example, in "The Gambling Boy Who Married a Bear Girl," after the young protagonist is killed by his bear wife, the other bears dig up his grave, bring his body back to their kiva, and resurrect him. The animals teach him to cure sicknesses and he becomes a famous healer. This typical shamanistic transformation takes place in the San Francisco Mountains, home of the Hopi kachinas. In "The Boy Who Wanted to be a Medicine Man," the boy kills a deer, breaks its leg, and tries to cure it. A stranger approaches and offers to become his teacher; the mentor takes the boy on a long journey, turning into a bear in the process. When they arrive at a kiva the boy is asked to disrobe and then is seated on a woman's wedding dress. Kachinas come and whip him until he is a pile of meat. Covering him with another wedding dress, the kachinas then dance him back to life (the wedding rituals and wedding robe certainly have powerful reverberations for Hopis in particular). His bear mentor takes him home and makes him promise to be a healer without asking any pay other than food. Sometime later, the boy kills a deer (note the parallel to the opening of the story) and almost immediately hears about a small boy whose legs have been broken. Calling upon his teacher "father," he restores the boy's legs.

While bears are notable in Hopi beliefs because of their powerful size and healing abilities, they are not the only shamanistic mentors. In "The Deer Mice," for example, a young boy who is not a good hunter discovers a kiva inhabited by deer mice, who invite him into their kiva. There he watches as they first injure a mouse and then cure him; they invite the boy to stay, and after breaking his hands and legs, they restore him to health. He returns home, repairs his sister's dislocated hip, and becomes a famous medicine man (and an accomplished hunter).

Propriety. The stories also dramatize the delicate balance of customary proprieties and values in Hopi everyday life. For example, in "How Coyote Became Infatuated with Girls," Coyote's grandmother gives him exact instructions on the proper items to carry when he goes courting (bow, quiver, red yarn, buckskin leggings, dark woven shirt, and red ocher). However, to get these things Coyote must intrude into the home of a human and steal them, an action not condoned in Hopi practice. Almost predictably, Coyote gets killed in a deadfall trap; dressed in human courtship finery, he ends the story skinned and mounted as a scarecrow. The story observes that the proprieties extend beyond mere objects and into ethical behavior, suggests that the choices of an inappropriate mate may end in disaster, and dramatizes the negative results of subterfuge in courtship.

The proprieties illustrated in "How the Ants Initiated Their Children into the Kachina Society" are even more delicate. The story details the ants' extensive preparation for a kachina dance and discusses the concept of sacred impersonation, which is central to the kachina complex. The ants copy the lifestyles and values of the Hopi villagers, but in their enactment of the kachina ceremonies, they become excessively enthusiastic and get carried away. After the ant kachinas whip the initiates almost to death, nearly severing their abdomens, they decide not to have any more initiations into the kachina cult. The tiny waists of ants today provide a contemporary reminder of the necessity for moderation in kachina ceremonies.

Another set of cultural proprieties finds expression in "How Coyote and Hummingbird Satirized Bat in a Song." When Bat invites his two friends over for a feast he feeds them stolen jerky and piki from the nearby village of Oraibi. Upset that they have been served stolen food by Bat ("he who can't kill on his own") and probably feeling guilty that they have partaken of it and have thus been potentially affected by eating the stolen food (which might cause holes to appear in their bodies), they make up a satiric song and dance about the experience, humiliating Bat and destroying their mutual friendship.

Despite the many levels of cultural nuance we have been able to discuss through the folkloristic approach, it should be evident that we have only been able to scratch the surface of meaning in these tales. Nonetheless, several important dimensions of Hopi storytelling and its function in the Hopi cultural world should have become very clear. For one thing, like most folk narratives, these stories function as dramatic intensifications of Hopi traditional values, and they provide a means by which the Hopis (and we, more distantly) can reexperience, examine, and even debate values and assumptions that come directly from the vernacular heartbeat of the society. The everyday perspectives on Hopi reality available to us from their folklore add a priceless dimension to the official histories, ethnologies, demographies, religious studies, and literary anthologies; indeed, through a serious consideration of the Hopis' everyday folk traditions, we obtain valuable insights into a realm of human expression we are not likely to encounter in any other form.

Barre Toelken
Utah State University

The Stories

The $ylvan

The Man and the Ants

Aliksa'i. They say people were living in Shungopavi as well as in
other places across the land. These people were farmers, so they
sustained themselves by growing crops. In those days it used to rain a
lot, which meant that all sorts of things ripened in the fields in great
abundance. But while the rain caused these things to grow in large
quantity, alas, it also produced many weeds. So those tending the
fields had to make daily trips to the fields to weed them.

At Shungopavi lived a man who was married. Like everybody
else he had his plot of land where he planted, and just like all the
others he had a huge amount of weeds growing there. Most men
knew full well that there was no other way but to toil hard if they

wanted to bring home a harvest, and so they worked their fields industriously. This fellow, however, was sort of lazy, so he would ponder how to rid his field of weeds without putting out much effort.

Each day upon returning from his field he would head right to his bedroll and prop himself against it. Usually, it was not until he and his wife were going to have their meal that he would get up again. Day in, day out, he repeated this routine. Each day he mused over his weed problem until one day some beings came to mind. So he said to his wife, "I believe I can find some beings to weed my field for me."

"You won't be able to find anyone. All the men and boys around here are busy," she commented.

"Those are not the ones I have in mind," he replied. "Just give me three or four of your rolled piki before I leave for the field tomorrow," he requested.

He now told her what beings he had in mind. They were the ants. There was a large colony of them living in the middle of his field. The man knew that ants can devour things very rapidly, and that's why he thought of them. Perhaps they would eat the unwanted weeds for him.

The following morning when he was about to set out again, his wife handed him four piki rolls. With these he proceeded to his field and, upon his arrival, headed directly to the anthill. After reaching his destination, he saw a few ants scurrying about outside of their home. To these he said, "Whatever it is that you are doing, let it go for a minute. I want to ask a favor of you." All of the ants stopped what they were doing and listened.

"All right, what is it?" they inquired.

The man then presented his request. "If you destroy the weeds for me, I will give you my meat." The ants readily agreed.

Next, the man walked about his field crushing the four rolls of piki and scattering the flakes all round. He thought that if the ants went about eating the piki flakes, they would do the weeding at the same time. Sure enough, before long the ants started on their task. Upon emerging from their belowground home they went about cutting down weed after weed, gobbling up the piki crumbs at the same time. Apparently, the colony of ants living there was huge, for a great many of them appeared. So many came out, in fact, that one side of the field became thick with them. That's where they were going to start.

As a matter of fact, the ants were cutting down the weeds. While this was going on, the man informed them that he had grown thirsty. He laid down his hoe and went to the place where he had a field hut. There he took a drink of water. Not wishing to return to work in the heat of the sun, he lay down in the nice cool shade of the lean-to. There he soon fell asleep.

The ants continued chopping down the weeds on their own. Quite a while later, towards evening, after waking from his sleep, the man looked about, inspecting his field. Much to his amazement, it was cleared of all the weeds. Not a single one was in sight. He nearly swooned when he discovered that the ants had rid the entire piece of land of weeds.

Without bothering to approach the ants the man returned home. He felt happy for he knew that he would now be able to control the weeds. As soon as they began to sprout again, he would right away clear them off. After his arrival at home he shared this news with his wife, and she also felt happy for him.

From that day on the man certainly did not put as much effort into working his field. He failed, however, to pay the ants their due. Each time now he worked in the field, he was able to cope with the weeds, and when it became too hot, he simply retreated to his field hut and took a nap.

This went on for quite some time. Then one night, as he was still asleep, a pain appeared on his back, much as if something had stung him. When he told his wife about it, the two got up and went to the firepit. There they stoked the fire until huge flames leaped up. The man turned his back to the light and, much to their surprise, the two noticed an ant crawling along there. His wife said, "This ant obviously bit you. That's what caused the pain. I can see a red spot there." With that, she grabbed the ant and flung it into the flames.

From that moment on the man felt ill. The red spot became larger and larger and the pain too grew more severe. Eventually, the bite became infected, with pus oozing out. According to the man his back felt as if it was teeming with little creatures.

Indeed, the man's back had become a real ants' nest. Ants were actually swarming throughout it, devouring it. At some point, they had eaten his entire back. As a result of this the man died.

The man had offered himself as the source of meat to the ants. Thus, according to what the Hopi say, one must not promise ants "You can have my meat" or "I'll give my meat to you." This one must not promise them. For when they grant you your wish and accomplish what you have asked of them, they will do this in return for your flesh. Those who are wise teach us to refrain from this.

And here the story ends.

How Field Mouse Helped the People of Mishongnovi

Aliksa'i. A few Hopis were living in Mishongnovi. In addition, there were people settled in villages all across the land. All these people owned lots of chickens and were able to have eggs with their meals on a daily basis. Once in a great while a family also killed a chicken and ate it with great gusto.

One day people noticed that a few of their pets were missing. At first they had no idea who was stealing them, so they set up their children as guards on top of the chicken coops, where they stood watch with bows and arrows.

In doing this they discovered that a hawk was the culprit. It was killing the poor chickens. Hawks are extremely swift birds. So while a chicken was walking here and there thinking of nothing in particular, the hawk would swoop from the sky with tremendous speed, grab its prey in its talons, and fly off. Hawks are also very skilled and clever hunters. They usually make one kill, stash it somewhere, and then return a second time, taking off another one. This hawk too always carried off two chickens.

Each time the hawk came, one of the guards would shoot at the bird, but it was so fast that the arrow always missed. So the children failed to destroy the hawk, and meanwhile the number of chickens shrank rapidly.

When the chickens themselves became aware of the hawk, they never left their coops any more. Finally, they became sick from fright and stopped laying eggs. They began losing their fluffy feathers, and in the end they were walking around with featherless tails.

When the children guarding the flocks noticed this, they told the villagers about it. They now tried all sorts of schemes to get rid of the hawk, but when all of their efforts proved fruitless, they informed the village chief. He assured them that he would consider the matter for them.

That same night he left his house and, late though the hour was, descended the southeastern flank of the mesa. His destination was the home of Old Spider Woman. Upon arrival at her place he looked inside. There was an opening at the top, but it was extremely small. The chief was still standing there wondering what to do when a voice bade him enter. The old woman was evidently at home. Being endowed with greater than human powers she had of course heard him coming. So she shouted up to him, "Come in, stranger."

The chief replied, "I don't know how to get inside. This hole is too small."

The old woman down below said, "Just turn your heel over the opening. It's bound to get larger then." The chief did as bidden and, true enough, the opening became large enough for him to enter. The old woman welcomed him and said, "There, have a seat, stranger." She then had a ritual smoke with the visitor. Only then did she inquire as to why he had come. "You must be about for a reason. No one just comes into my house for nothing." The village chief now shared with Old Spider Woman the problem with the hawk. In the end he added, "But it's not only you I sought out. I also came desiring the help of the Pöqangw brothers, your two grandchildren. If all three of you team up, you might perhaps come up with a solution for our problem."

The old woman immediately called her grandsons over, but they ignored her. That very moment they were having a big fight, oblivious to everything else. They were shoving each other around and throwing one another on the ground. Each time one of them struck the ground, he screamed out in pain, only to race back to fight his brother anew.

The old granny kept hollering at the two, but they would not settle down. "Stop it," she yelled. "There's a visitor here for you. Quit fighting and come here." The two, however, did not obey. Finally, the old woman grew so furious she went over to the vessel where the water for the house was stored. Scooping out a large amount, she approached the brothers and doused them. Now they stopped and, though reluctant to yield, they had no choice but to come over to her and the chief. Clearly, they were still angry, but they had to keep still when they saw that they had a visitor.

Pöqangwhoya and Palöngawhoya listened as the chief again related the problem with the hawk: the bird was killing all of the chickens in the village. "You two always overpower your foe, that's why I came to you for help," the chief explained.

The two brothers assured the village chief that he could count on their assistance. They would call on someone else first, though, they said, someone who was quite powerful.

"Is that so? Well, then ask him, whoever he is. It can't hurt. He may know something that can help us." The two brothers replied they would go get him right away and were gone before anyone could say a word.

Pöqangwhoya and Palöngawhoya headed southeast from their house in the direction of their race course. When they got there they ascended to the top of a kiva, where the older of the two called inside through the hatch on top, "Listen, friend, are you home?"

The owner of the house evidently was in, for a voice replied, "Yes, I'm not in bed yet. Come on down." Apparently, he knew exactly who the two callers were. As it turned out, the one living there was Field Mouse.

Pöqangwhoya and Palöngawhoya entered, and Field Mouse welcomed the two brothers. "All right, have a seat. You two really come around at just any old time. I suppose you have a good reason, though, for coming here at this time of night." Field Mouse lived with only his grandmother there, but she had already been asleep for quite some time.

"Yes, but we did not come for something concerning us," Palöngawhoya explained, whereupon Pöqangwhoya, his older brother, told Field Mouse why the village chief of Mishongnovi had come for help.

Field Mouse felt sorry for the villagers of Mishongnovi, and promised that he would definitely come to their aid. All three of them then left and returned to the home of the Pöqangw brothers, where they entered without an announcement.

Old Spider Woman made Field Mouse feel at home, and the village chief once more told in his own words of the problem with the hawk. Field Mouse quickly agreed to help and said to the chief, "Very well. Four days from now I'll go on the warpath. There's one thing, however, I need to ask you to do."

The village chief promised to do his heart's desire and asked what he wanted. Field Mouse replied, "The only thing I wish of you is to make me some prayer feathers and prayer sticks. You must color them with red ocher, though. Next, I'd like you to bag a small amount of pulverized iron ore for me. I'm small, as you know, so I won't need much. On the morning of my deadline bring those things over to me," he instructed him. The chief answered Field Mouse that he would do so.

The village chief now thanked all of them and then went home. He felt much better now as he went to bed. After all, Old Spider Woman and the Pöqangw brothers had been of great assistance.

The following morning, Field Mouse woke up early. After sharing with his grandmother the news of the night before, the two ate breakfast. Then he told his grandmother that he would go over to the Pöqangw brothers' place to have them do something for him. On his way out the old woman wished him well, and then he was off.

Upon arriving at his destination, Field Mouse entered. Both the brothers and their grandmother greeted him happily. They made him feel at home, and he told Pöqangwhoya and Palöngawhoya that there was something he wanted them to do. "Well, what is it?" both of them cried.

Field Mouse said, "Yes, I'd like you to go to a greasewood stand and get me some greasewood branches. If I want to kill that hawk, I must use the greasewood plant. It is an extremely hard wood." He also pointed out to them what size branches they were to cut.

The two brothers readily agreed and assured him that they would leave in a little while. Field Mouse was about to leave for home when he added another request: they were to bring the greasewood over to his house when they came back with it. Once more the brothers promised to do his bidding, so Field Mouse returned home.

After getting home, he decided not to do anything for the time being. He would just wait for the two brothers. He knew that they would not be coming too soon. For wherever they went, they played shinny along the way.

Sure enough, when Pöqangwhoya and Palöngawhoya set foot outside the house, they carried their shinny ball with them. Their grandmother had definitely told them not to play ball while doing the errand. After all, their friend was anxious to get those greasewood sticks as quickly as possible. But as always, they paid no heed to the old woman and left talking back at her.

They headed out in the direction of the greasewood patch. By midmorning, when the sun was already high in the sky, they finally reached their destination. They had wasted a lot of time playing shinny. So now they searched for what their friend had desired of them. Eventually they found branches the size he wanted, cut them off, and headed for home again, playing shinny all the while, of course. Instead of returning to their house, however, they made straight for Field Mouse's place. Upon arrival they shouted inside, "Hey, is the old rascal home?" Field Mouse heard them and bade the two enter, which they did. The old granny was also there, but she had not uttered any welcoming words. The poor woman had grown so old that she was completely deaf. However, when Pöqangwhoya and Palöngawhoya were inside, she cried, "Have a seat, strangers."

"But these are my friends," Field Mouse protested. "Remember, they live northwest of here with their grandmother." Now the old woman recognized the two.

The Pöqangw brothers handed the sticks over to their friend. Field Mouse was elated. "Thanks," he exclaimed, "You brought me exactly what I had set my heart on. This should do the trick. Let's sharpen the branches now."

The brothers offered their help right away. When the sticks were sharpened, they built a fire. That done, they placed each into the fire. After leaving them there for a little while, they removed them again. They did this to harden the tips.

The Mishongnovi chief, at the same time, was fashioning prayer sticks for Field Mouse. He had not been asked for too many, so he was finished by late afternoon. He carefully wrapped them up and stored them away in a safe place.

Field Mouse, meanwhile, was already gathering all his special clothes and gear. By the time he had everything ready, the eve of the set day had arrived. That same evening he dug a tunnel in a south-westerly direction from his house. As he was digging, he drilled a hole from the tunnel to the surface in four separate locations. The first was quite close to his home. The second was a little farther southwest. The third was even farther away, and the last one was the greatest distance from his home. At this fourth hole he drove a greasewood stick into the ground with its tip pointing up. Its tip stuck out just the right distance, for he had figured the length just right. Then he decided exactly how he was going to execute his plan. The only thing left for him to do the next morning would be to dress up.

When Field Mouse had completed all his preparations, he went back inside his home. It was his plan to stay up all night without sleep, as though keeping a vigil. So he settled down by his firepit and filled his pipe. Then he kept smoking. He was still doing that when a voice called in. He asked the visitor to enter, and much to his surprise, there were three visitors—the two Pöqangw Brothers and their grandmother.

Field Mouse made them feel at home. His own grandmother was already asleep and was not there when they came in, so he himself set out some food for them. As they were eating, they informed him that they had come to help him with his all-night vigil. They were aware that he would stay up that night without sleep. "Thanks, indeed," he exclaimed, "I'm glad I don't have to spend all the time till morning by myself." He was elated that the three had come without being asked.

When the visitors were done eating, all four of them sat down by the firepit, late at night though it was, and ritually smoked with Field Mouse. In this manner they helped him with his vigil. Field Mouse was very grateful to them.

Finally, daylight was approaching. The village chief now picked up the prayer items he had prepared and headed out in a southeast direction to Field Mouse's place. Upon arriving there, he immediately recognized it. He could tell by the standard that had been erected. It was obviously there because Field Mouse was involved in a ritual. Respecting the standard, the chief did not proceed on to the roof of the kiva. Instead, he simply called in, "Hey, come out and receive what I brought you." That's all he said, and he waited there for Field Mouse to come out.

Sure enough, it was not long before Field Mouse emerged from his kiva. He stepped up to the chief and took what he had in his hands. "Thanks so much for bringing me these prayer items. With their help I'm bound to succeed," he said. Then he continued, "Well then, I know when the hawk will come for your chickens. It will be sometime this afternoon. I'll be waiting here for it at that hour. You go back to your village and let your people know that if they want to watch me, they should come here to the mesa edge on the southeast side. They can look on from there. If they stay up there, the hawk can't see them."

"Very well," the chief replied. With that he returned home and ordered his village crier to make a public announcement that anyone interested should go to the mesa edge on the southeast side and watch Field Mouse from that place. He had reached the end of his four days and was ready to have a public dance. The people, of course, had no idea that the mouse intended to kill the hawk for them. No wonder they kept asking each other in the village why Field Mouse was going to perform a dance. But anyway, it was nice that he was going to provide some entertainment, so they decided to go watch him.

By noon the people were dressing for the occasion. Down below the village Field Mouse also was getting dressed. He had retrieved his bundle of ceremonial clothing from his back room and was preparing body paint by soaking kaolin in water. This white liquid he intended to use to decorate his body. Next, he took a drum from somewhere and placed it next to the firepit. In the meantime, the whitewash mix had become as watery as he liked it. But first he looked out at the sun to check if it was the right time. Apparently, it was exactly the right time, so he painted his body. To begin with, he whitened his hands and scratched the appropriate designs into the paint. Then he whitewashed his waist area, then the chin. Next, he colored his legs and chest. Last were the arms, which he painted in the same way. After that he went over to the firepit and dried himself.

When his makeup was dry he began to dress. He wrapped himself in a kilt of a kind usually worn by the Snake dancers. Then he put on a necklace of the most beautiful turquoise beads. Next, he attached two-clustered feathers to his hair and the prayer feather the chief had prepared. It was all daubed with red ocher. Red ocher he also applied on his face and above the eyes. Somewhere he had gotten a shell bow guard, which he tied to his left wrist, and lastly he hung a stone axe on his hip. This is how Field Mouse had planned to costume himself. He was really dressed up and looking stunning. Now he was ready to go out.

By the time he emerged from the kiva, the edge along the mesa was already crowded with spectators. The people were staring in his direction and when they spotted him they could hardly believe their eyes. His costume was most impressive. They were telling each other about it when he emerged. "He seems to be out. There's somebody moving about."

"Can it be true?"

"Yes, that's him," the people cried.

No sooner had Field Mouse made his appearance than he walked a few steps away from the kiva, struck his drum, and began his public performance. He was moving around in little hops, hitting his drum at the same time. It was amazing how well the little fellow was dancing. The onlookers were staring with open mouths. Even though he didn't have a strong voice, he was singing quite loud.

Just then, the hawk was on his way to Mishongnovi and happened to fly by, right above Field Mouse while he was performing there. The hawk noticed that the mouse was up to something, so instead of continuing on in the direction of the village, it circled above him for a while. Soon the urge arose in it to take the little thing along with him. Field Mouse had spotted the bird but pretended not to see it. At this time he was dancing near the hole that he had pierced from the tunnel right next to his abode.

As the hawk fell from the sky to grab him, Field Mouse took his time running away. It was not until the hawk was getting rather close that he tossed away his drum and quickly disappeared into the hole. The hawk failed to catch him. All the spectators who saw the bird were worried about the poor mouse.

After a while, Field Mouse returned from his hole and after scanning the sky, hopped back to the drum. He picked it up and began his dance routine again. The hawk evidently had not left and spotted the mouse dancing there again. So he decided to try a second time.

This time, Field Mouse had ventured a little farther from his kiva. But he stayed right next to the second hole he had dug. He did not seem to have any misgivings about his safety. Secretly, however, he kept glancing at the sky while performing his dance.

It was not long before the hawk got ready to try again. At first, as is the bird's habit, it climbed way up in the air. Then it swooped down at its prey, but as it snatched for the mouse, it missed again. Field Mouse had seen the bird and quickly entered the second hole.

With this dodge Field Mouse made the hawk angry. Now more than ever the bird was determined to catch him. He dove down a third time, but he missed once more.

By this time the spectators were full of anxiety for Field Mouse. "He should quit now," they kept saying to each other. "What he's doing is too dangerous." One of them said, "Someone go tell him to put a stop to this. We're glad he provided this entertainment. He can do it again some other day when the hawk is not around."

One person was getting up to go down to Field Mouse when another said, "I don't think you'll get there in time. The hawk is about to try again."

Sure enough, the hawk was going to make a new attempt. As before, he rose way up in the air and then came diving down at a tremendous speed. By now the hawk was sick and tired of this game and aimed at Field Mouse with its mind set on catching him. He carefully watched the mouse as it was approaching. He saw the hole that the mouse had dug there and figured that it would surely seek refuge in it. So it decided to aim right at the hole.

Field Mouse, too, was fully alert, just as before. He seemed to be dancing there without any concern for himself. All the people watching had their bungholes pulled in tight, so scared were they for the mouse. All their attention was on him. They really thought the hawk would get him this time.

The hawk had nearly reached Field Mouse when he flung down his drum and took to his heels. He barely managed to escape into his kiva when the hawk came after him.

The people watching exclaimed, "He got caught. The hawk has him in his talons. Look, he didn't fly away."

"Yes, indeed, it looks that way," some replied. They were about to return home when someone cried, "He seems to be peeping out of his kiva. Look!"

"I guess you're right," somebody else said. And they all sat down again and stared down below. They were wishing with all their hearts that it would be Field Mouse.

True enough, Field Mouse was peeping out from his kiva again. After coming out he sneaked up to the hawk and nudged it with his foot, but it did not move the least bit. Now he was convinced that the hawk was dead. With that, he stepped up to the bird and uttered a war cry. The people along the mesa edge shouted too. "Thanks, you killed it! Thanks, you survived." This and similar things they screamed.

The hawk, evidently, had not seen that it was diving directly onto the greasewood stick. Field Mouse knew that it could not see it from up there. The hawk had acted just as Field Mouse had planned. It did not spot the stick until it was almost upon it. At that point it was not able to turn in its flight, for it was approaching with tremendous speed. Thus, the tip of the greasewood pierced the throat of the bird and killed it instantly. It did not even give a jerk before it was dead.

In this manner the tiny Field Mouse destroyed the mighty hawk.

The chief of the Mishongnovi villagers now descended to the mouse and expressed his gratitude to him for helping them. Field Mouse replied, "Take the dead hawk with you and fix it to the end of a pole by the chicken coop. Then all those creatures that like to eat chicken won't pester them anymore. From this day on your pets will have sex again to produce offspring, so they will multiply once more." That's all he said, and the chief took the bird to go home. Before he left, however, he said, "We won't forget you here. And we will always remember Old Spider Woman and the Pöqangw brothers, who live near you. So you all live here happy in your hearts." With that, the chief returned home. Field Mouse, too, went back into his house.

In this fashion Field Mouse, who is endowed with great knowledge, destroyed the hawk. As he had predicted, from that day on the chickens grew in numbers again, and the Mishongnovis once more had eggs to eat.

While the Mishongnovi women were preparing food, the men fashioned prayer sticks for all those living below the mesa. This is the message they wanted their chief to deliver: "When you take these prayer sticks down below, tell Old Spider Woman and her grandsons that we are grateful for their assistance. To Field Mouse who killed the hawk say that we won't be troubled by that bird any longer." With that, they handed the prayer sticks to their chief, and he took them down below. He himself had made some prayer feathers that he also included in the offerings. As he delivered these various gifts, the recipients were elated. In this way the mortals and gods were helping each other out. From that time on, the village chief made sure that he always made prayer sticks for them. So I guess, the people there still have lots of chickens.

And here the story ends.

Medicine Man Badger

Aliksa'i. People were living at Oraibi. In addition, all across the land, other Indian groups were settled in villages.

Not only people inhabited the land. Northwest of Oraibi Badger also had made his home. He was an excellent medicine man, and the Oraibis knew him as such. So whenever one of them was sick or in pain, he sought out Badger for treatment. Since he was charged with the task of healing, he had to treat everyone delivered into his hands.

Southwest of Oraibi the field mice also were living, but no one knew that they were there. They had established their homes at a place called Wupatsmo, "Big Hill." A large number of the mice lived there.

For entertainment, the villagers of Oraibi used to perform kachina dances as well as social dances. The kachinas would typically
arrive, entertain the people until noon, and then depart again. Once
in a while they showed up as Runner kachinas, challenging villagers
to race with them. In this and other ways the people there were
entertained.

One day, one of the Oraibi men felt like putting on an event
again. He decided to organize a hunt, so he requested that the crier
chief make a public announcement about the hunt. He did the man's
bidding and announced that the hunt would take place in the area
southwest of Oraibi. When the boys and men learned about this, they
became anxious with anticipation. It was agreed that they would go
hunting in four days.

While the men looked forward to this appointed day, they
readied all the necessary gear. Some straightened their arrows and
others got their flat rabbit sticks or other hunting sticks ready. The
bowstrings on some of the bows were loose, so they had to be re-
placed. When all these things were finished, the morning of the hunt
had arrived.

Crossing the village boundary, the men headed out towards the
southwest side of Oraibi, in the direction of Tuuwanasavi. Here they
assembled at some place. When all were present, they first held a
ritual smoke, then they set out and went along hunting in a northeasterly direction.

In those days, nobody had any bad thoughts in his mind or harbored any bad intentions in his heart, so the men met lots of cottontails and jackrabbits wherever they went. Each time they flushed out
a rabbit, several others ran out from a bush. Once in a while, four or
five in all. And every time, without fail, one of the men would hurl
his boomerang or hunting stick after the rabbit. The excitement,
understandably, was great. Rabbit sticks were flying in all directions.
Every hunter threw his stick in order to kill the jackrabbit or cottontail, without any consideration that he might hit his fellow hunter.

This went on in several places until one of the hunters accidentally struck another man with his hunting stick. The injured man was in great pain, but he acted as if it was not really serious. He wanted to be part of the fun and action and strove to keep up with the other hunters. At one point, however, he failed to stay abreast of them. No one came to help him because everybody thought that nothing had happened to him. So the others paid no attention to him. At one point the men decided to go back, so they turned around where they were and, hunting along the way, slowly moved homeward.

By now, the injured man was lagging far behind. His leg was in such pain that he could only advance slowly. He was still not near the village when the sun set and it got dark. The poor man stumbled along, bumping into all kinds of obstacles. This is how he progressed. When he left with the others, it had never occurred to him that any-thing like this could happen to him, but now, because of the accident, he could no longer participate in the hunt.

The man was still dragging himself along in this fashion when, much to his surprise, he spotted the light of a fire. He thought a shepherd might have the fire going, so he decided to head in the direction of the fire for the time being. Sure enough, it was not long before he reached the spot where the light was coming from. But he spotted no one tending the fire. Still, from the light of the fire he knew that someone had a home there. He really was at a loss because no-body normally lived there.

The injured man saw a kiva and climbed up on the roof to peek inside through the hatch. What he saw were field mice that had made their home there. There were a great many of them. He was still look-ing in when one of the mice spotted him and notified the others. They all bade him enter. "There's a stranger about. Come on in," they called from down below.

The man replied that he couldn't enter because he had hurt his leg.

One of the mice, from all appearances their leader, immediately told some of his men to bring the stranger inside. So a few went out to get him. Grabbing on to his arms and legs, they brought the man in. Having done this, they placed him northeast of the firepit. The mouse leader inquired what had happened to him that he was around in this condition at such a late time of day.

The Oraibi man told what had befallen him. All the mice sitting across from him were listening to his story. In the end, he said to them, "Couldn't one of you take me to Honanyaha, where Badger is at home? He's a doctor and could help me."

The mouse leader replied, "We too possess healing knowledge, but unfortunately, humans don't know this, so they never come to be treated by us. Nevertheless," he assured the man, "there's no need for you to seek out anybody else. Just stay here with us and we'll fix whatever ails you. We may be small and ugly, but you can trust us," he assured the man.

"All right, that's fine by me. I'll put myself into your hands, for my leg hurts terribly and is throbbing with pain." Thus the man declared his willingness to let the mice be his doctors.

The mouse chief now gave orders to prepare everything to treat the patient. All the mice dashed to a point in the northeast where they entered a back room. After a while they emerged and came up to the man. Once more they picked him up and, after spreading out some sand, placed him on top of it. Then they ran back to the back room. This time, when they returned, each one had his hands whitewashed with kaolin and a prayer feather tied to his hair.

All of the mice now scurried around the man and started working on his leg. They were doing something to it that did not cause him any pain. The man was clearly aware of their treatment but experienced no pain whatsoever. Before long the mice had completely restored his leg. And no sooner were they done than they rushed back to the place in the northeast and disappeared into the back room.

The mouse leader now encouraged the man to get up. Obediently, he rose to his feet and stood without any problem. His leg felt perfectly all right. In awe the man looked at the mice. He understood now that others besides Badger could heal a person. He thanked the mice profusely for restoring his health.

Upon returning from the back room the mice came with great quantities of food. They set it out on the floor and bade their visitor eat. After he settled down to the meal the mice, too, sat down with him, and everybody ate.

When the man was satisfied, he indicated that he wanted to go on home. The mice, however, would not hear of it and invited him to spend the night with them. They explained that he couldn't go any-where in the dark. He might not step right and break his leg anew. Once again, the man consented and slept there. The following morn-ing he returned home. Since he had killed a few cottontails the pre-vious day, before he left he offered them to the mice in appreciation, hoping to gladden their hearts in a small way. He would have owed a large payment to Badger, had he healed him.

The mice, however, refused the meat. They said they had per-formed their service free of charge. They said they knew nothing of any fee and claimed that they had been charged to help people and would not take anything in return.

Once more the man expressed his gratitude to the mice and then departed for home. When he arrived in Oraibi, the people already knew that he had not made it back the previous night. They asked him why, so he explained that one of the hunters had struck him with a hunting stick and broken his leg.

The people would not accept his story. After all, he was obvi-ously in perfect health. Now he no longer concealed what had hap-pened and told them how he had entered the home of the mice at night and how they had healed the broken leg. The people still refused to believe him. However, when the man who had struck him with the hunting stick came by to check on him he confirmed the story. "He's not making this up. I really hit him and apparently in-jured him, but he did not complain. As we were returning, I suddenly remembered him, but he was no longer behind us. I thought that he had perhaps returned home right after the mishap, so I paid no attention to this any more. I'm sure he's not telling a lie. If someone believes strongly in something, it can make things right for someone," he said to them. Now the people were convinced that the story was true.

As the man was telling what had befallen him, the people listened in wonderment. Again and again they begged him to repeat his story. He complied with their wishes. He also pointed out, of course, that Badger knows the healing arts. But since he had fared so well at the hands of the field mice, he praised them all day long. In addition, he mentioned that they also declined payment for their service. Instead, they had explained that they healed a person free of charge. In this manner the man talked to all those who came to his house. The people, having listened to him, spread the fantastic tale all across the village. Before the next morning all of Oraibi was familiar with it. As a result, people decided no longer to seek out Badger as medicine man. Instead, they would go to the field mice now in case of an injury or sickness.

When Badger got word of this turn of events, he became jealous. Furthermore, he refused to accept the claim that the field mice were doctors. Knowing that he would have to visit them to check the story out, he pondered what on earth he could do. Finally, he came up with a solution. He first made his bed on the northwest side of the firepit inside his den and hid a hunting stick underneath it. Then he placed a bowl next to his bedroll and kept vomiting into it. For four consecutive days he did not eat a morsel, so on the fourth day he really did not look too good. As a matter of fact, he looked rather sick. The poor thing had no strength left at all.

It so happened that on the same day someone walked past his place, so he called, "Please, have pity with me and go to Wupatsmo for me. Talk to the field mice there and ask them if they would come here and help. I'm miserable. It seems something terrible is about to happen to me. For this reason I need them right away." The person, whoever he was, agreed to Badger's request. He headed over to Wupatsmo and related everything to the mice.

The mice did not hesitate a minute and consented to go to Badger. On their way to Honanyaha, Badger's home, they passed the outskirts of Oraibi, along the northwest. Badger of course had heard them when they arrived, so he lay there on his bed moaning in pain when they filed into his den. They had come without bringing any sort of medicine.

Upon entering, all of them stepped up to Badger and surrounded his bed. Then, together and holding each other by the hand, they started dancing. Their dancing was accompanied by singing. Badger really seemed to be in bad shape, he growled so. Moving in a procession around the place where he was lying, the mice were dancing:

Hayaa'aa'aa hayaa'aa'aa.
Over there at Honanyaha
Old Man Badger called the field mice
To doctor him.
He heard about their healing arts,
So he pretends to be hurting here.
Four days long he starved himself.
Haynaawe, haynaawe.
Haynaawe, haynaawe.

In this fashion the field mice sang and danced, parading around Badger. It was obvious that the song had been carefully composed, and when they reached the end, they filed out of the den.

Badger, of course, grasped the meaning of the song at once and saw that he had been ridiculed. Evidently the mice knew he was not really sick when he called for them to doctor him. He grew angry and, pulling out the stick from underneath his bed, struck after those mice that still remained. But because he had not eaten anything in four days, he was without strength. As a result, he was not able to beat hard. In fact, he was so weak that even though he managed to hit one mouse or the other, the blows came down in a rather ineffective manner. Many he missed entirely.

No sooner were all the mice gone than Badger rushed out of his den trying to chase after them. However, he only kept this up for a little while before he was exhausted and had to stop. So all the mice escaped without any harm.

As the mice were running off, a few of the young ones failed to catch up with the others. And since they ran for their lives, they dashed off in just about any direction. For this reason, not all of them succeeded in getting home. In this way they scattered all across the land. That's why field mice can be found everywhere nowadays.

And here the story ends.

How the Coyotes Celebrated the Bean Dance

Aliksa'i. They say people were living at Oraibi. In addition, the Hopis had founded villages all over the land that they had claimed as their own.

Southwest of Oraibi, at a place called Ismo'wala, many coyotes lived and hunted. Of course, they also ventured into the vicinity of Oraibi; therefore they knew full well that a large village existed there and that many Hopis inhabited the place. However, the coyotes also knew that the Hopis hunted them, so they never approached the village proper. When one of them happened to pass by the village, he usually did so without coming too close to it. As a rule, he took a roundabout route and then headed back to Ismo'wala if he was returning home from the northeast.

Now the Hopis had many customs and rituals, and whenever they performed any of them, it was an exciting time for the people. During the month of Powamuya (about February), they held a great celebration of which the coyotes knew nothing. But even if the coyotes had been aware of these rituals, they would never have gone there to witness them. Only one not afraid of death would have dared to approach Oraibi. However, they all treasured a long life, so they avoided the village.

One day, one of these coyotes had been roaming the area along the northeast side again and was trotting home, still early in the day. It was high noon as he neared Patangvostuyqa, "Pumpkin Seed Point," from the northeast. Here, just before reaching the mesa point, he had intended to turn northwest. But just as he was approaching this location and was about to head to the northwest, much to his surprise, he heard a noise. It seemed as if someone was weeping. To determine what it was, the coyote stopped and listened. As chance would have it, he happened to pass through there exactly during the time of the Powamuy ceremony, or "Bean dance," and what he thought was weeping was the peculiar singing of Hee'e'wuuti, "Hee'e' Woman."

During the month of Powamuya, Hee'e' Woman typically emerges from her home to sing her song. After this performance, she heads northwest to round up her children, all the various kinds of kachinas. As she progresses and reaches a certain site, each type of kachina, in turn, will make its appearance. In this fashion the kachina goes along gathering her offspring and then continues to the village of Oraibi. By the time she gets all of them gathered there, the number of kachinas has usually swelled to a great many. In the village they follow Hee'e' Woman, going from kiva to kiva. They actually make several circuits of the village. On this occasion the people present can view the many different types of kachinas. The children especially look upon them with great awe, for the assortment of kachinas is mind-boggling. Some they have never seen before, so they can't name them all. So when a child does not recognize a particular kachina, he asks an older person what type he or she might be. If he knows the answer, he will tell the child, and in this way the child is able to learn the name of all the kachinas. A few of the kachinas are always unfamiliar even to the old people. This is what these kachinas customarily do in the month of Powamuya.

So it was the song of the Hee'e'e that the coyote had heard when he had stopped to listen. He soon concluded that no one was weeping at all. Somehow he realized that it was Hee'e' Woman who was singing her song there. The coyote listened with great concentration. As he spied on her, he noticed that, after ending her song, she descended to the northwest side. Continuing in the same direction, she arrived at a place where two new kachinas approached her. Evidently, the two were a pair of Hotootos. They were the ones she encountered first. Both of them were coming along stomping their feet at a quick pace and then they followed her. Now all three of them proceeded northwest where, at some point, Söhönasomtaqa joined them. Thereupon, this small group turned southwestward.

Before long, the Red Hawk kachina made his appearance, and together all of them went along the northwest gathering up different kachinas. As they converged on Katsinwala, "Kachina Gap," they were joined by a great number of kachinas. From here the entire group headed for Oraibi, the kachinas all hooting and crying their individual calls at the same time. Some of them possessed their own songs that they sang as they walked along. The result was an amazing mix of sounds. Among them also were those who do not have any songs, such as the Hu' kachinas for example. But they in turn had their own calls that they sounded out. In this manner Hee'e' Woman was wont to escort her children into Oraibi.

The coyote was staring at Hee'e' Woman in amazement. Never before had he seen such a sight. As he was curious to learn more about the whole affair, he stealthily followed Hee'e' Woman and saw how she went along gathering up her children and accompanying them into Oraibi. It was an incredible experience for him. The kachinas who were following their mother were completely unaware that the coyote was trailing them. When the coyote had seen enough, he returned home. No one noticed him as he ran along the northwest of Oraibi towards Ismo'wala.

Upon his arrival back home, he immediately sought out the home of the coyote leader and reported to him what he had seen. He sat there with his ears perked up, listening in fascination. In the end the coyote said to his chief, "Perhaps we too ought to do something like that. I think I managed to observe those kachinas quite well, the way that they dress, what their calls sound like, and how they move about. If we also staged this ritual, we could have a great event."

The coyote chief immediately took a liking to the idea and readily gave his consent. "Indeed, we'll do that. But let's wait until we've gathered here in my kiva. When all the males are assembled here, you can tell them once more what you experienced. I don't see why they would reject the idea. It must truly be an important ritual," he said in full agreement with the suggestion. "I'll have my town crier announce the meeting of all the men and boys at my kiva." With this, the other coyote departed and returned home. There he remained until, a little while later, the town crier announced the chief's bidding for all to congregate at his kiva.

For this reason, the coyotes began amassing there. What the meeting was all about, none of them knew. A few were asking others, but apparently no one had a clue. The chief had been the first to go to the kiva and was already inside ritually smoking when the men began arriving. As each one entered, he found a place for himself and sat down. Before long all the coyotes had assembled. Only the coyote who had brought the news of the Powamuy ceremony still had not yet arrived.

When everyone seemed to have gathered, this coyote too proceeded to the kiva. The others had been inside for quite a while already when he finally made his entrance. Upon his arrival the chief spoke to him, "All right, come down to this lower level, and after we've finished smoking you can tell these others what you've seen." With that, he stepped up to the chief's side and seated himself there. The other coyotes didn't know what to make of this. Why had he been the last to enter and why was it him only that their chief invited to smoke? What news, they wondered, had he come to share with them?

While the ritual smoking was going on, the others sat in their places and waited. Finally, when the smoking was done, the leader spoke up, "Now, tell everybody here what you witnessed in Oraibi. They in turn may ponder then if they care to go along with us so that we can look into the matter." The coyote did as bidden and related to them what he had observed. No one said a word. They were so engrossed in his story that they gave him their undivided attention. Even long after he had finished his account, still no one dared to utter a sound. But when eventually their chief asked them what they thought of the idea, they all gave their consent to stage such a ritual too. They would have no trouble finding the proper costumes for themselves. No doubt, the kachinas were clothed most elaborately, but since they were great hunters, they would have no problem acquiring such items as buckskin and feathers. So they all agreed to do it and were looking forward to totokya, the eve of the event. For that reason the coyote chief set a date, which would be sixteen days from then. Their hearts filled with joy, as they now all looked forward to that day.

By the time the appointed day arrived, the coyotes had accumulated all the ceremonial clothing and things they needed. Apparently, all the coyotes at Ismo'wala had learned of the totokya and were waiting, full of anticipation. No one knew what those kachinas looked like. The one who had seen them, however, had instructed the others in every detail so that on the eve of the great event they were all donning exactly the same costumes as the Oraibis. It stood to reason that the coyote who had brought this news would take on the role of Hee'e' Woman, mother of the kachinas, himself. He therefore went a little ways northeast from Ismo'wala and began making his preparations. Before that, he had carefully instructed the others where to take up their positions so that he could come along, gathering them up as he went. Thus, they were all readying themselves along their assigned spots and were just finished at noontime when Hee'e' Woman first sounded her song. As she proceeded then, she went along gathering up her children and ushering them towards Ismo'wala. What a sight to behold! The coyote dressed as Hee'e' Woman had smeared his face with soot and, garbed just like her, resembled her completely. The entire entourage now advanced in the direction of Ismo'wala. Somehow the kachinas had gotten hold of such an enormous amount of feathers that they had overdone it when they adorned the tops of their heads. Because of this, they could not see very well, for the feathers kept falling into their eyes. Small wonder, then, that one here, another there, would trip over a rock or exposed root and fall flat on his face, only to get up again and continue on. In this fashion the procession moved onward. Unfortunately, Hee'e' Woman, their mother, had plastered too much soot on her face, and now it got into her eyes and blurred her vision. As a result, she stubbed her toes on an obstacle more than once, and three times altogether fell sprawling on the ground. Her rattle was already cracked, but nonetheless she was determined to go on.

It so happened that on this very day the Oraibi menfolk were going on a coyote hunt. Having completed all aspects of their Powamuy ceremony, they had decided to head out to Ismo'wala. They knew that large numbers of coyotes were living there and that they would have no trouble killing them. By chance, therefore, the hunters were proceeding towards Ismo'wala exactly at midday when the coyote kachinas were headed there.

The Oraibis had not yet reached Ismo'wala when, much to their surprise, they noticed that a great number of coyotes were headed towards their destination. They had no idea why, but as soon as they spotted the animals, they passed the information around. It was certain now that this hunt would be an easy one. Without making any noise, they stealthily stalked the coyotes. The coyotes, in turn, were totally unaware of the hunters and were joyfully heading towards their homes. They were sure that the kachina procession would be an enormous success. Of course, they also had along the types of kachinas who act as guards, but the latter paid no attention to what was going on behind them. Besides, they were unable to make out whether anything was following them. The feather decorations that were tied to their hair were blinding them, so they stumbled along without seeing the Oraibis behind them.

The coyotes still had not yet reached Ismo'wala when the hunters surrounded them and started their hunt. Anyone who had brought a hunting stick hurled it at a coyote. The coyotes, whose heads were adorned with thick bunches of feathers, at first were unaware of what was being thrown at them and what was causing them pain. As one of them removed his feathers, though, he realized that they were encircled by Hopis from Oraibi who were hurling their sticks at them. Instantly, he alerted the others who in turn doffed their feather decorations. Being able to see clearly what was happening, they scurried off in every direction but soon discovered that there was no place to go. Evidently, a large party of Oraibis had formed a tight circle around them. Thus, when a coyote dashed in any one direction, he was forced to make a complete turnabout and head the other way. The poor creatures were scampering back and forth, but it was only a matter of time before all of them lay dead on the ground. So these kachinas never made it to Ismo'wala.

Meanwhile, the other coyotes who were expecting the arrival of the kachinas at Ismo'wala waited in vain. Filled with great anticipation, the poor things had been waiting for a long time, but not a soul came into sight. After a good amount of time had elapsed, one of the coyotes decided to check the direction where the kachinas were supposed to appear. He still had not come upon them when suddenly he heard the shouting of hunters. Immediately it dawned on him what was happening, so without waiting a moment he turned around to alert the others at Ismo'wala. Considering it a matter of life or death, he ran as fast as his legs could carry him. The minute he was back, he quickly jumped on a rooftop and cried out his announcement. "Coyote hunters from Oraibi have met the line of kachinas and apparently killed them. That's why they have not shown up."

No sooner did the coyotes present there learn of this than they sped off, fleeing in every direction. Those with children, concerned that harm would fall upon them, dragged them along with such force that the children's feet barely touched the ground. It stood to reason that the Oraibis would come over to Ismo'wala, so they all bolted off. But the hunters had slain enough coyotes and decided to stop their hunt. And so, after telling each other that they would go back, they returned home. What a sight they presented, toting along the coyote corpses dressed up in such a queer manner. By now they had figured out what those varmints had been up to and laughed at them as they lugged them along.

This was the reason the kachinas never made their appearance at Ismo'wala. Meanwhile, those coyotes who had survived had scattered about in the area. And so now, a coyote can be found just about anywhere. As they spread out all over the land, they made their home just about anywhere. Because of these events the coyotes never completed their Powamuy ceremony. Instead they fled from their original homesite.

And here the story ends.

The Firefly

Aliksa'i. People were living here in the Hopi villages. Also, all across the land, other Indian groups were settled.

At a place northeast of here a Navajo family was at home. They had to use their water sparingly, so they had built a little hogan-type house in which they bathed. They did not use water, though, when they took a bath. Instead, they cleaned their bodies with steam.

The first thing to do when taking a steam bath is to build a fire next to the sweat lodge. Big rocks are piled on the fire and as soon as a rock is good and hot, it is rolled inside. With his clothes off, the bather then enters the sweat lodge with a little bit of water. Once inside, the opening of the lodge is sealed up tight with a blanket so the steam cannot escape. The bather next splashes water on the hot rocks, causing steam to rise up. When the entire inside is filled with steam, the bather stays a while. As soon as he is soaked with moisture, he rubs his skin to roll up the dirt on it. Finally, when all the dirt is gone and the bather is finished with his bath, he will shout, "All right, open up!" And then someone on the outside usually opens the entrance to the little hogan. Upon leaving the sweat lodge the bather, still wet with sweat, rubs himself with fine sand. This is a way of drying himself. After that he is done. In this fashion Navajos bathe themselves.

Once the Navajo man who was living there wanted to take a steam bath. So he got a fire going and sat there waiting for the rocks to get hot. As he sat he heard a voice from somewhere in the northeast. He scanned the area for the source of the voice but failed to see anything. However, whatever it was was clearly coming towards him. Before long the creature appeared from behind a little dune ridge and made straight for the man. He finally recognized what it was. It was a firefly. As it was moving closer it was singing something. Listening, the man heard the following song:

Women, big women.
Women, big women.

It was indeed a firefly that had come up to the man. Its body was round and its back was decorated with a beautiful red design.

As the firefly passed alongside the Navajo, it spotted the man, so it stopped in its tracks and by way of greeting said, "Are you here also, stranger?"

"Yes, and you likewise are about, stranger?" the Navajo replied.

"Yes, I was just heading this way. So what are you up to?"

The man now explained that he wanted to take a sweat bath. "When all the dirt is gone from your skin you feel really good."

"Is that so? Could I possibly join you inside and also steam myself? I seem to be really filthy. When I'm covered with sweat the dirt on my body is just so it can easily be rolled off with my fingers."

"I guess so. After all, you won't take up much room. As soon as these rocks are hot we'll go in together," the Navajo replied.

With that, he placed some rocks on the fire, and then the two sat there waiting side by side. Eventually, when the rocks were really hot, the man rolled them into the little hogan. Then he said to the firefly, "All right, that's all there is to it. Let's go in now." So one after the other they entered the sweat lodge.

The man sealed the entrance good and tight. Next, he spilled water on the rocks and big clouds of steam rose up, filling the entire lodge. Then the two were in there together. As they sat there the air became extremely hot. The firefly got hotter and hotter, so hot that it finally burst open.

The firefly contained a liquid that splashed on the Navajo when its body exploded. The liquid was so hot that blisters formed all over the Navajo's body, causing excruciating pain. He suffered unbearably, so much so in fact, that he died. In this way the firefly caused the death of the Navajo man.

The firefly, in turn, had not suffered any damage even though it had ruptured. Underneath its outer shell was another layer of shell. That's why nothing happened to the little thing. It simply marched out of the sweat lodge and said, "Thanks, I enjoyed my bath." And turning to the dead man it said, "You're really a gullible fool. I was bound to do this to you." The firefly then continued on in the direction of Nuvatukya'ovi, the San Francisco Peaks. On its way it once more chanted its song:

Women, big women.
Women, big women.

Now, as a matter of fact there are hot embers inside the firefly. That's why you do not kill a firefly when you encounter one. For when its hot juices splash on a person, blisters form all over his body and in this way it kills. That's the reason the Hopis don't destroy a firefly. In this fashion this tiny insect killed a Navajo.

And here the story ends.

The Boy Who Wanted to Be a Medicine Man

Aliksa'i. They were living in Oraibi. A lot of people were living there, among them an elderly couple who had one son. He was a grown up boy, but he was in no way thinking of getting married. He wanted to be a medicine man, and his mind was always on what he must do to become one. All his thinking was focused on that.

Now he also frequently went hunting, and one day he went hunting again northward of Oraibi, most likely toward Hotevilla. At that time Hotevilla did not exist, or rather, no one was living in Hotevilla yet. While he was hunting around, his thoughts were once again on his favorite topic—being a medicine man. In due course he came upon a deer and shot it. Then he went to it and purposely broke the deer's leg, and then he started working on the leg he had broken, trying to heal it again.

After he had spent a considerable length of time on it someone came up to him without him noticing it. Not until that person started speaking to him did he notice his presence. A man was standing by him. The man standing there asked him, "What are you doing?"

"Yes," he replied, "I have always had the wish to be a medicine man. So I broke this deer's leg and was now trying to fix it again."

"Oh yes?" the stranger replied.

"Yes," answered the boy.

"And is that really your desire?"

"Yes, it is."

"Well, actually I heard you and because I pitied you I came. So if you are serious about being a medicine man, come back here four days from now. Then I will tell you something else. And if you don't really want it I know you will not come," the man said.

"Very well," the boy said. He was happy. "I will definitely return on that day."

"All right," said the man. "So now don't mess around with this any more but go on home."

So then the boy went home with his prey over his shoulder. When he reached home his parents were glad. From then on he eagerly awaited that fourth day. On the third day he said to his parents, "Tomorrow I'll go hunting again but I won't be back the same day. I'll stay overnight."

"Very good," his parents replied, "we won't be expecting you then."

This is what he announced to his parents. Then on the morning of the following day he dressed and prepared for the hunt. When he was finished he started out into the area north of Oraibi. He knew, of course, where the man had met him. So he headed straight to where he had killed the deer. He was not in a hurry. Just when it was getting to be evening he arrived at his destination. The man was not there yet. So he sat down under a tree and waited for the stranger. The sun was about to set when someone came to him. It was that man again. The man said to the boy, "You have come then?"

"Yes," he replied.

"All right then, let's go. We should hurry, it's far."

So they got under way. They went westward. They had covered a considerable distance when the man said to the boy, "Stay here for the time being, I will go shit," he said.

"That's fine with me," the boy answered in turn.

The man disappeared into the forest. It was not long before the boy heard a rustling noise. What appeared in his view was not a man. It was a bear that came out towards him. The boy got frightened, but then the bear spoke to him, "Don't be afraid, it's me," the bear said to the boy. "From now on you can ride on me, because it's still far. If we travel on foot we won't reach our destination early. So climb up on me."

So the boy went up to him and climbed on him. "Now then, let's go," the bear said and started running. A bear can run extremely fast. Now they were really making some headway. In this fashion they got close to their goal. Then the bear stopped. "All right, climb down. From here on we will walk again. We are getting close."

So then the boy got down and the bear disappeared into the forest. When he appeared again he was back in his human shape. "Well, let's go," he said.

Then they got going again. Finally they arrived at a place that was lit by a fire. Evidently they had arrived at a kiva. They climbed on the roof, and the man shouted down inside the kiva. "It's customary to welcome someone."

They were then welcomed by some voices that hollered, "Come in please. We are grateful you have come." Evidently they had been waiting for them. So then they climbed in, the man first and the boy after him.

When they had entered, those inside greeted them. "All right, have a seat. We've been waiting for you."

Many people were there, all men. They made the boy sit down north of the firepit. Then they smoked. One of the men, most likely the chief, looked out at the sky, and when he came back in he said, "Now, I guess it's about time. So I suggest that you, the father-to-be, ask once more whether he still wants it."

"Very well," the father-to-be said. He went to the boy and asked him again, "Well now, are you still certain you want to be a medicine man?"

"Yes," the boy replied.

"It is settled then," said his future ceremonial father. "Take all your clothes off. When you've done that, come here."

The boy undressed, and his father-to-be spread a wedding dress out right in the center of the kiva. "Now, come here," he told the boy. The boy obeyed and then he said to him, "Sit down here," and he indicated that he meant the center of the wedding robe. So the boy sat down there. "Well," he said to him, "you really want it."

"Yes, by all means," the boy answered.

"It won't be long before they will come," he said.

So then he sat there and waited. And, true enough, it did not take long before some beings with their accompanying noises approached. Meanwhile these beings climbed on top of the roof. Apparently they were kachinas. Then there was actually one that was saying something. Upon entering, it turned out to be Hahay'iwuuti. All kinds of kachinas came in behind her. There were many. Hahay'iwuuti stepped up to the boy, and upon reaching him, said to the kachinas, "Now, use all your energy." This is how Hahay'iwuuti put strength into the kachinas. Then the kachina that was in front went to the boy. He and all the other kachinas were carrying yucca whips. One after the other those kachinas whipped the boy with their whips. Not all of them had beaten him yet when he was already cut up into pieces. Blood was flowing all over his body and after a while he was no longer aware of what was happening to him. Now the kachinas hacked the boy into pieces. Nothing on the boy, neither his flesh nor his bones, was still in one piece. When all the kachinas were finished, the boy was nothing but a pile of meat.

Then the future father of the boy said, "Thank you for being done. So don't tarry now." He then covered the boy, or rather the meat pile, with another wedding robe. Then the kachinas started dancing toward the pile. Without letup they were dancing toward what was covered up there. While they were doing this it looked as if the boy was going to come back to life. Once in a while the pile stirred a little. Then the kachinas really put all their efforts into their dancing. In this way the boy finally began to move quite strongly and eventually uncovered himself. Looking around among the kachinas he exclaimed, "Oh boy, is it hot." He was sweating.

"That's for sure," the men that were sitting there replied. "We are grateful we brought this to a successful end and you've come back to life."

"Yes," he answered. At that he got up. He was the actual boy again and nothing was wrong with him. The kachinas who had finished dancing filed out again.

When they had all left, his father-to-be went to him and said, "Come back here," signaling to the northern side of the firepit. So the boy sat down there and his father said, "Now, this is the way we learn this. You have acquired this knowledge and therefore you must now be there for the people. It was your wish to be this so now you must devote yourself to this task. You will care for the people, not in return for any payments, but only for food."

"Yes, for sure," he replied to his father.

This is how his father instructed him. "Remember these instructions I have given you. Now you can dress. We must go back now. If we leave right away we'll just get back in time."

The boy dressed again and they started out. His father again changed into a bear, and the boy rode on him from there. The sun had not risen yet when they reached their original starting place. There his father changed back to a man and said, "So if you intend to treat someone one day, you must always step out of the house first and call me. I will always hear you."

"Very well," the boy said to his father.

"And always remember what I have told you. I will go back now. Your parents are probably waiting for you."

So then they parted and went their way. The boy went home to Oraibi and his father went also to his house. Shortly thereafter the boy killed a deer and carried it home on his back. And indeed when he returned his parents were happy to see him.

So there he was living now. And so it happened one day that a boy fell from a horse and broke both his legs. When the boy heard about this he said to his parents, "Why don't I go there and see what I can do."

The parents replied to the son, "No, that's out, you don't know anything about this business."

"But I would like to try at least."

So his parents gave their permission, and he went to the home of the little boy. When he arrived the poor little fellow was lying there crying. He said to the little fellow's parents, "Let me try it."

"All right," the little boy's parents answered.

The boy, recalling his instructions, first stepped outside and called his father. No sooner had he called him than something drove into the ground right next to him. It was the wing of something, or rather, a feather. Then he thought, "This is evidently my father." So he pulled it out and put it into something. Then he went back into the house to the little boy. He sat down by him and inspected his legs. It was clear where they were broken. It seemed to him as if he was actually seeing it, that's how clear it was. So then he put the little boy's legs back together, fixing his legs on both sides. After this he went home.

And the next day, while he was sitting outside his house, some children were playing. Among them was the little boy whose legs he had fixed just the night before. He had evidently completely re-attached and healed his legs. They had apparently healed that same night.

This is how he became a medicine man. As soon as he treated anyone he got well again right there and then. When the people heard this they came only to him when they needed a medicine man. He was a most excellent medicine man. And he had to be there for the people, for at any given time someone might come and get him. I guess he's still taking care of people in Oraibi somewhere. And also whenever someone wants to pay him for his services he refuses. He only accepts food. Thanks to him the Oraibi people are still doing pretty well.

And here the story ends.

7

The Mistreated Cats

Aliksa'i. They say people were living in Oraibi, and some of them had cats for pets. All together, cats were plentiful at the village. Now, cats are naughty critters that are bound to cause mischief somewhere. For example, whenever a man was spinning yarn, a cat would approach, play with the ball of yarn, and get it thoroughly soiled and tangled. This usually made the person spinning the yarn very angry. Also when someone was cleaning the innards of an animal, a hungry cat roaming the area might show up and tug on one of the intestines. This too would anger the person, and often both sticks and curses would be hurled at the meddling cat. "Don't pull on that, you bad cat. Those aren't your innards; those are the innards of a sheep!" the person might shout, while throwing something at the cat. These cats were such a nuisance that even their owners harbored animosity toward them. Because they behaved so poorly, the cats were the object of anger and mistreatment.

The cats became upset about this and one day held a meeting. At the meeting they discussed forming their own settlement and living there as they wished. "When we have our own village, we won't be mistreated any more," they said. So then they moved from Oraibi to another place.

When the cats found a suitable place, they set up their colony and lived there according to their own rules. No longer were they mistreated, no longer did anyone curse them.

After living there for a while, they all agreed to put on a dance. They set a date for the event, and as the day approached, the cat men and cat boys went out hunting for meat for their stew. They killed a lot of mice and were elated. They now had enough food for their visitors from the far-off villages. On piktotokya, two days before the dance, all the female cats were busy preparing piki, and on totokya, the day before the event, they had large amounts of stew cooking. They were also preparing other food. Because this was the cats' first attempt at such a thing, they were looking forward to the day of the dance. The cats making up the dance group were busily gathering their costumes. The spirit of cooperation was high. When one cat could not find a particular item to wear and asked another cat for help, the other cat would quickly volunteer the item by saying, "Yes, I have that." The cats were so nice to one another that they would even offer each other items that weren't asked for. "I also have this item. You may borrow it from me if you are having a hard time finding it." Because they treated one another so amicably, they were able to provide one another with all the costuming needed for the dance.

Then the day of the dance arrived and all of the cats, full of anticipation, got out of bed very early. The new cat brides took their baked pik'ami pudding out of the pit ovens and, after everyone had eaten, the dancers emerged from their kiva for the first performance. All of them were dressed in elaborate and beautiful costumes for the grand ceremony. The dancers were all lined up in a row and they hopped about, one after the other. Even though their dance was a farce, they still put all their energy into it. They were so cute. No one knew what type of dance they were putting on, but that didn't matter. This is how their song went:

We, we
Are the little cat girls, the little cat boys.
Because of me
Your corn stack and jar of
Peaches are still safe and sound.
We would be better,
But you are mean to us,
Women and men.
Poor me, poor me, poor me.
We're dancing timidly.
Cat, cat.
Meow, meow, meow, meow.

This is how they sang. It was the only song they danced to. The poor things lacked a real composer, and that's the reason they had no other songs.

The day before the big event had not arrived yet when other cats in the vicinity heard about the dance. So they began arriving as spectators. By noon of that day, the cats had danced their dance five times, and then the females began taking food to the dancers. They hauled in tremendous amounts of food for them. Then too the local villagers invited their visitors to feast with them. The cats were inviting complete strangers into their homes to partake of the feast. As a result, the visiting cats had plenty to eat.

Other visitors began arriving before the second set of performances got under way, including, to the surprise of all the cats present, some frogs. When the villagers learned of this they said to each other, "Oh dear, some frogs have come," and they pointed to where the frogs were sitting. The frogs were unwelcome at the dance and the cats viewed them with contempt. Someone went to where the dancers were resting and told them about the frogs. This infuriated the cat dancers and they said, "Why on earth did they come? We're not putting this on for their entertainment, and now here they are." Despite these protestations, the cats knew there was nothing they could do about the frogs.

The dancers now returned to the site of their performance and, sure enough, there was a horde of frogs sitting there. The dancers renewed their performance and cats and frogs alike enjoyed the show. When the performance was over, the dancers returned to their resting place. But the cats were angry and didn't want the frogs at their ceremony. "What can we do to make them leave?" they asked one another. They had pondered this for a while when one of the cats said, "Why don't we tie them into the lyrics of our song? Maybe if we do this, they'll get angry and return home."

Surprisingly, one of the cats had already composed a song and he sang it to the others. The cats decided to use the song during the next performance. As soon as they had memorized it they returned to the plaza. Then they started dancing, and the song went like this:

Cat, cat is shaking.
Cat, cat is shaking.
He is shaking the frogs' hind ends.
He is shaking the frogs' hind ends.
Cat, cat.
Meow, meow, meow, meow.

This was how their song went.

When the frogs became aware that the cats had poked fun at them in the song, they were in an uproar and asked each other, "Why did they ridicule us in their song?" The leader of the frogs said, "Let's all croak at the same time. See what happens then." Following his instructions the frogs all croaked in unison.

Suddenly heavy, thick clouds gathered over the village and it grew quite dark. It then began to rain and soon became a downpour. The plaza began to fill up with water; streams entered the houses and the cats began to run from their homes. It rained so hard that it wasn't long before the entire village was flooded. The rain dampened the spirits of the cats, and soon the flooding had them really worried because they didn't know how to swim. Only the frogs went about swimming happily and croaking loudly.

On the eve of what should have been a very joyous event for the cats, the rains came and all the cats drowned. This was how the frogs got their revenge.

And here the story ends.

8

Coyote and Bee

Aliksa'i. They say people were living at Oraibi. In many villages, they say, people were living. Here at Ismo'wala Coyote had made his home. He had Bee as a friend, but Bee really didn't care to be friends with Coyote because he knew of Coyote's bad ways. So he didn't want to keep company with him.

Coyote had stolen Bee's honey on more than one occasion, which Bee didn't find amusing. So he intended to get even with Coyote in one way or another. However, because Coyote had no possessions of his own, there was nothing Bee could steal from him. And since Bee, poor thing, didn't have any relatives, he had no one else but Coyote to visit. Coyote was also a great liar, which was another thing Bee didn't like about him. Moreover, Coyote was very inquisitive and was always asking questions.

Sure enough, one day when they were together again, Coyote did just that. He said to Bee, "There's something of yours that I wish I had."

"Oh really? What is that?" Bee replied.

"Yes, I have seen more than once that whenever you want something to eat, you don't waste any time but quickly kill your prey and then feast on it. I've been wondering if you would teach me that way of hunting. If I came across something then, I could do exactly as you do to make a quick kill."

"Oh really? Is that what you want from me?" responded Bee.

"Yes, so won't you teach me?" Coyote pleaded.

"What are you thinking of killing?" Bee inquired.

"Well, since I eat cottontails and jackrabbits, I thought it would be good to try it out on them."

"Is that so? But rabbits run so fast you couldn't do to them what I do. I go for something that doesn't flee so fast. Only then can I make a kill," Bee said. "Maybe you can think of something else, something that doesn't run away as fast as rabbits do," Bee suggested.

Coyote mulled the idea over for a while and then said, "Well, I've just thought of another one. We coyotes enjoy the taste of badgers. Badgers can't run away so fast, but we seldom eat them because they really know how to fight and are also very strong."

"Oh yes?" said Bee." By coincidence I know of one badger that lives near here on the southwest side of the mesa. Exactly at noon he cleans his house, and during that time he is very preoccupied. I don't think he is even aware of it when someone walks past him. If you sneak up on him then, he won't notice you. So tomorrow I'll go to the greasewood patch over there to cut off a branch for you and make a stinger out of it. I usually make stingers out of greasewood for my- self. Greasewood is really hard and doesn't wear out right away, so it lasts me a long time," Bee explained to Coyote.

And because that is Coyote's nature, he believed the story, listen- ing to every word Bee had to say. And readily he consented to have Bee do what he said for him. Bee now told him that he would set out for the greasewood patch first thing next morning and that he would come back to Coyote's den after he had cut off the greasewood branch. Coyote accepted and was elated. "Thanks, please do that. I'm so grateful I have you as a friend. Because of you I'll have a real feast tomorrow night," Coyote said to his friend. He was overjoyed with Bee.

Bee now informed Coyote that he was returning home. "When I get home, I will first fix myself something to eat. If I go to bed early then I'll wake up early." With these words, Bee left Coyote's den.

On his way home he flew to Badger's home. Arriving there he called in, "Hey friend, come out for a moment, I have something very important to tell you."

Before long Badger came waddling out in his pigeon-toed way. "Why do you want me right away?" he asked.

"Yes," Bee replied, "when I was just over at Coyote's house, he asked me to show him how to hunt. But since he has already stolen my honey from me so often and that is still on my mind, I'm schem- ing to get even with him. So I told him I would go to the greasewood patch tomorrow and cut a branch off to fashion a stinger from it for him. And I thought of you when I told him this story. I mentioned to him that you usually do something here at noon and become so tied up in your work that you're not aware of anything else. That's the lie I told him. He also told me that he very much enjoyed badger meat, so I got this idea. When I bring him here, proceed with what you are doing, pretending not to notice us. When he nears you then, I'll let you know and you can do as you please with him. Of course, I planned this without asking your permission, so it's up to you," Bee said to Badger.

Badger responded with laughter. "Is that so? So you came up with that idea right away, huh? Well, certainly I'll go along with you. That old character is so wicked, I'm sure you're not the only one who is angry with him. Trust me, we'll get even with him," he said to Bee, readily agreeing to the proposition.

After hearing the good news Bee proceeded home. Meanwhile Coyote was busy gathering things at his home. Anxiously looking forward to the following day, he went to bed early that night.

Next day, Bee headed for the greasewood patch first thing in the morning. When he spotted a large greasewood bush, he cut off its biggest branch. Having done this, he sharpened it. Then he built a fire and held the stick in it. He withdrew it when it became black from the smoke. The greasewood stick now looked exactly like Bee's stinger. Then Bee flew with it to Coyote's den.

Coyote immediately noticed it when Bee arrived, for he was already waiting for him. He invited Bee to enter, so Bee went in and said to Coyote, "Well, I brought this stick for you. So let's try it out on you. I think I cut the right size. Just bend over and I'll try to fit it into your behind."

Coyote had to bend over now. Bee came up to him and started jamming the greasewood stick into his behind. Coyote was screaming, "Ouch, ouch!" Bee got very angry with him and hollered, "You must not howl like that. In the beginning this is bound to hurt you. It also happened to me at first, but then I got used to it and now there's nothing to it. It hurts like this just for a little while, then the pain quickly subsides. So don't scream like that."

Coyote had no choice but to calm down and hold still while Bee shoved the sharply pointed greasewood stick up his behind.

"All right, I think this will do. Your chances of succeeding are pretty good now. You're bound to kill something. Also, that stinger is very becoming on you," Bee added in a complimentary fashion.

Next Bee told Coyote how to sting with fatal results. Coyote listened carefully with his ears fanned out. "When Badger removes earth from his burrow he usually comes out backwards over his dirt mound. I'll be flying about the area keeping a watch on him for you. The moment I shout, 'Now!' rush him with your behind pointed toward him. As soon as you reach him, throw yourself at him with great force. But don't waste time looking behind you. Even though you can't see what you are doing, you're bound to make a kill. Also bear in mind that the stinger drives in all on its own." Coyote agreed with everything Bee had to say. "Well then, let's be on our way. Badger is probably at work by now. "

When Bee was through talking to Coyote, he helped him stand up. But because the stick was jammed up Coyote's rear, the poor thing had no way of straightening up comfortably. Finally, with some effort, Bee managed to get him into an upright position. Then they proceeded to Badger's house. The stick was causing such excruciating pain that Coyote had a hard time walking. The poor thing had to walk bow-legged and every so often he howled, "Ouch, ouch." Bee flew alongside, admonishing him: "Keep your mouth shut, for if Badger hears you, he's sure to disappear deep in his burrow. You must be quiet as we are nearing his place." With words like this from Bee, Coyote was eventually compelled to trot along in silence.

Sometime later the two approached Badger's home, so Bee said to Coyote, "All right, here it is. Walk a little over there along the south side and then move backward in this direction. When you reach Badger's burrow, hide next to the tumbleweed. And the minute I give you the signal I want you to rush backward as fast as you can." After these instructions he sent Coyote south and flew over to Badger.

Reaching Badger's burrow, Bee said to him, "All right, I've brought him along. I'm sure he'll come here from the south in a little while. So act as if you are not aware of us."

"Very well." These were the only words Badger spoke. Thereupon he retreated into his den and pretended to be very busy.

Sure enough, along came Coyote, approaching with his back pointed toward Badger's burrow. Badger acted as though he didn't see him. Meanwhile Coyote had reached the tumbleweed and stopped. Bee was flying around above Badger. Badger knew this, but not once did he lift his head.

When Bee saw that Coyote had reached his destination he shouted, "Now!" No sooner had Bee shouted the signal than Coyote pointed his rear end toward Badger and rushed toward him at full speed. At the same instant Badger rapidly turned about and ran toward Coyote. The moment he reached Coyote he quickly grabbed the greasewood stick and with all his might jammed it further up Coyote's behind. And because Badger is very strong he nearly impaled Coyote on the stick. This is what Badger did to him. Coyote could only scream "Ouch!" before he died on the spot.

This is the way Bee plotted against Coyote and with Badger's help brought about his death. After the two had killed him, they ate him. From that time on no one ever again stole Bee's honey.

And here the story ends.

9

The Chipmunk Girls Who Ground Pinyon Nuts

Aliksa'i. People were living in Oraibi and in many other villages across the land. Oraibi was heavily populated, but these people of long ago did not have an abundance of crops. They only planted enough to last them through the winter and into the warmer spring days. And because they did this, they would set these rations aside for the winter. For the same reason, during the warmer days, they would gather different wild greens that they also put away for the winter. In addition, they sustained themselves during the lean months by eating pinyon nuts. They typically went out to roast these nuts. In the past, they used their wedding robes as bags to haul things. So when they roasted a large amount of pinyon nuts still in the cone, they would fill these robes with nuts. After returning home with the nuts they would dry them out. Then, when there was nothing to eat, they would take the pinyon nuts, pound them into a paste, and have them for their meal along with some piki. So for the winter rations it was necessary to gather these nuts. Of course, they also planted crops such as watermelon, muskmelons, and squash, which they harvested in small quantities.

At Oraibi lived a man along with the others who had three daughters but no son. For this reason, this man did not produce many crops, and his family, out of necessity, gathered greens to supplement their diet.

Once again autumn arrived. Surprisingly, that year the man grew a large amount of squash. This one day he was telling his daughters that they would have to go and haul them back from the field. His field was somewhere southwest of the village. He instructed his daughters, "We'll all go and lug them back. This year there's a good amount, so we'll have to make more than one trip."

Then early one morning they all set out to harvest the man's crops. Upon their arrival at the field, however, there wasn't a good squash to be found anywhere. Evidently, some green beetles had eaten the leaves, causing his plants to dry up. When no squash worth harvesting could be found, the family became angry. The area was swarming with the little pests. What's more, they were now taunting the people. As soon as they were approached, however, they quickly scurried into the cracks that were present there. The man had planted his crop where there was a dried pond, and when the pond turned dry, the mud cracked into pieces and curled up into little crevices. Inside these little cracks the insects were living, so the man and his daughters went about stomping on the dry clay dirt.

Everybody was furious. Finally, the father said, "There is not a good one to be gotten, so I guess we'll have to go without any squash. We have no choice now but to go for pinyon nuts somewhere. We'll just have to go and pick up some nuts," he stated.

At this time of the year the pinyon nuts had already fallen out of their cones and were lying on the ground. One day, this man went southwest of Hotevilla to a place northwest of Apoonivi where there was a promontory. He went there to gather wood. It so happened that lots of pinyon nuts were to be found there. Having discovered this, he returned home and instructed his daughters to go to this place and collect these nuts. Then they would not be wasting their time by going for the squash.

So they went there, choosing a way that led past Mumurva, "Marshgrass Spring," on the northwest side. Soon they made their ascent somewhere to the rim of the mesa and when they arrived at their destination, they went about picking up the nuts. In the process, they slowly headed towards the edge of the northwesterly cliff.

Upon reaching the cliff, they went along its edge picking nuts, when suddenly they heard some noises. The girls stopped in their tracks and listened, but nothing appeared to be going on anywhere. But there certainly were sounds coming from somewhere. So the girls continued picking pinyon nuts. A while later one of the sisters said, "Listen, those are clearly voices."

"For sure," another replied, "I also keep hearing something. It seems to be coming from somewhere beyond this cliff. Let me go sneak over there," she said.

Stealthily she proceeded towards the northeast for a short distance and then went to the edge of the cliff. While she paused, some voices were speaking. Again she listened. Evidently some people were singing. This was what they were singing:

Kyo mee kil'eetsatsa.
Kyo mee kil'eetsatsa.
Pisileekil'eetsatsa mi'i ho'e.
Pisileekil'eetsatsa mi'i ho'e.

This was how the song went. The girl thought, "I wonder who is singing there."

She went to fetch her sisters, and all of them went back and hid behind a jack pine, listening. While they were still there, the voices started up again and repeated the same song. The eldest now said, "I wonder who is doing the singing."

"I don't know," one of her sisters answered. "But they're right around here."

With that, they went about searching. Upon reaching the very edge of the mesa, they followed it until, much to their amazement, they discovered some female chipmunks grinding. They were grind-ing pinyon nuts. The sisters stared at the sight. As they watched, the chipmunks were grinding and singing the same song. They were all in a row next to one another, and as they were grinding, their breasts were swinging back and forth. With their hands pressing down on the grinding stone, they sang in unison:

Kyo mee kil'eetsatsa.
Kyo mee kil'eetsatsa.
Pisileekil'eetsatsa mi'i ho'e.
Pisileekil'eetsatsa mi'i ho'e.

Upon finishing this little ditty, they would brush off their manos, take the pulverized nuts out of the grinding bins, and store them in a container.

The girls now took a closer look and noticed that the chipmunks were filling the finely ground nuts inside the shells from which the nuts had come. They had set these shells out side by side. That done, they picked up the shells and quickly descended over the edge of the mesa. Again and again the chipmunks went through the same routine. The three sisters laughed at them with delight. Meanwhile, it became late afternoon. The girls had wasted their entire time watching the chipmunks. As a result, they collected only a piddling amount of pinyon nuts. Then they left for home. After discovering these chipmunks at this location, they kept going back to the same spot to gather nuts. This is as far as the story goes. Perhaps these female chipmunks are still grinding nuts here.

And here the story ends.

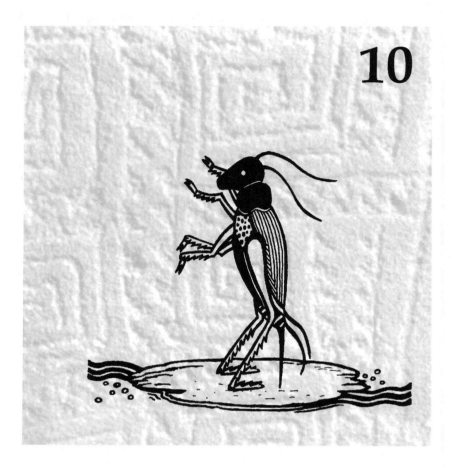

10

The Flood at Wuukopaqlö

Aliksa'i. Some beings were living in the northeast somewhere at a place near Wuukovaqavi. There, at a location known as Wuukopaqlö, "Large Pond," they had their homes. Once the leader of this settlement invited his friends, who were the powerful heads of various religious societies, to a meeting. So they gathered at the home of their chief and engaged in a ritual smoke. When one of those there suggested that the chief probably had a good reason for calling them together, he replied, "Yes, I'm very happy about something, that's why I called you here."

"All right, what is it?" someone asked.

"Well, you know, our children have greatly increased in number.

Just listen," he said to them, and then they all strained their ears. Sure enough, adults could be heard shouting, and the laughter of children could also be heard there too. "This is the way life is here now. That's the reason for my happiness, and that's why I called you together. What's your opinion?" he asked them.

"There's nothing wrong with this. We're glad that our population has multiplied. That's the reason there is so much happiness out there," they replied.

It is especially at night that the beings living there carried on in this manner. All night long their sounds could be heard. And since they were in happy spirits, their leader too was happy. Finally, he said to the assembled men, "I've got something to announce. That's the reason I asked you to meet with me. Perhaps if I tell you what's on my mind and then ask something of you, you'll feel the same way I do," he declared.

"All right, what is it?" Let us know what's been on your mind so that we in turn can give it some thought," someone said.

"Well, as I explained before, I'm elated that you, my children, our people, have multiplied. All around they are merry. So it occurred to me that from now on it should not rain for a while."

Upon discovering his wish, the males mulled it over. Finally, they said, "Very well, that's all right." They fully agreed with their chief's wish.

Once more they had a ritual smoke. When they were done, their leader said to them, "All right, I guess that's all. Return to your homes now and pray for this from the bottom of your hearts. That it will not rain for a while." This is what the chief wanted of them, and so they departed for home.

The clouds, of course, are always on the move, so the yellow cloud chief from the northwest happened to be in this area when he overheard this plea for the stopping of rain. Immediately, he summoned the other cloud chiefs of the other directions. Upon gathering at his home, he said to them, "I heard some bad news, that's why I asked you here."

"Is that so?" they inquired. "All right, what's the matter?"

"Well, I was traveling around just recently when I arrived here at Wuukovaqlö. The headman of the settlement there had just assembled his important leaders and was telling them how happy he was that their children had increased to such big numbers. At the same time, however, he also told them that he did not want it to rain for a while. That is what really angered me. He shouldn't be saying things like this. It amounts to telling us to stop doing what we must do. But rain is a task we've been charged with. By producing rain we provide moisture for people so that they may drink. Therefore we cannot stop doing that. This is the unfortunate wish I heard. For this reason I asked you to gather here. I wonder what your thoughts are regarding this matter."

"Is that so? My word, you are right. Who is this person that expresses this hapless thing?" the others inquired. "All people around here pray for rain. They depend on us, as well as others, while they live their lives. That person who doesn't want rain must be an idiot. We'll have to make it rain even though he doesn't care for it." The rain chiefs were furious as they expressed their opinions. "So four days hence we'll make it rain, but we'll release our moisture only over them. We'll see what they make of that." They all agreed. Let's set the date so that we can go there at that time," someone else proposed.

"Very well," their leader said, "I just wanted you to think this over with me. I was curious if you felt the same way as I, that we should converge upon them. Well, it's settled now, we'll go and make it rain on them."

From this point on the clouds proceeded toward the day they had agreed upon. They started preparing their lightning bolts and their canteens.

Each night those responsible at Wuukopaqlö smoked at the home of their village leader, praying that it would not rain at all. All about the place the children and the adults were happy and laughter could be heard, but even though the noise was disturbing, their leader never complained to them about it. After all, they had increased in number, and he was elated about this.

Meanwhile, four days had passed, and the agreed date for the clouds was at hand. That day, the clouds assembled at one common site, bringing their canteens along with them. Their leader then instructed them, "All right, as you recall we are going to go over to Wuukovaqlö. Let me first flash my lightning, though, from the northwest. Then you do the same. After that we'll head their way. Next, when I have made it thunder, you all do likewise. After that, I will again make it thunder, but this time twice, then we'll go shower them with rain. Let's not hold any moisture back. Not until we've poured all our water upon them will return here." This was the plan the rain chief put forth to them.

That very morning when the clouds had reached their fourth day, the leader of Wuukopaqlö stepped outdoors and looked about. Much to his surprise, he noticed that from every direction clouds were descending upon them. Without wasting a moment, he quickly called his peers together. As they entered his home, they inquired, "What is it? Why did you send for us so urgently?"

"Yes," he replied, "see for yourselves. I think those clouds are about to cause a lot of trouble. They're perched up there in every direction."

"Why on earth would this be so?" someone asked.

"I don't know. Perhaps if we fashion a charm, we can stop them somehow," their leader proposed.

By now, the clouds really looked threatening. They were probably going to cause havoc. Therefore, the leader asked his crier chief to make the following announcement: "I guess you, my people, are out there. It looks like the clouds are going to cause trouble, so be ready. If they are not too violent, we may survive somehow. Just do as I do when the time comes." This was the message of the announcement. Now the poor things were very concerned.

Meanwhile, the clouds began closing in on Wuukopaqlö from every direction. When they neared their destination, the chief from the northwest produced a thunderclap and the others followed suit. When they actually reached the place, the northwestern cloud chief made it thunder twice, whereupon it began to sprinkle. After this, all the other cloud leaders did the same and then, following their leader's example, dumped their moisture upon them. Apparently, the rain was not going to cease soon. As a result, it poured all day.

Because of the heavy rain that night, no one could be heard making a sound at Wuukopaqlö. The children and the grown-ups were not hollering and shouting with laughter. Instead, it was dead silent. Everyone was saddened by the fact that it had rained so much. As the hours passed, the pond began filling up. The residents, not wanting to perish by drowning, climbed up on all sorts of things. Many were clinging to dried crownbeard flowers, one behind the other. As it turned out, the people living there were crickets. They had prayed against rain because they did not wish to drown from all the water. The force with which it rained that day would surely destroy them.

For this reason they did not want it to rain. The rains, however, did not let up. The crickets, having climbed up on everything in sight, were clinging to these things, freezing terribly. When the pond was completely full, some of them, poor things, fell into the water and floated about in it. In the end, these unfortunate ones simply drowned, while the others just froze to death. In this way, all the crickets were wiped out. A few, however, arrived in this part of Hopiland from elsewhere, and so now they live here again.

And here the story ends.

11

Crow and Hawk

Aliksa'i. People were living at Oraibi. Over at Masaatuyqa, Crow had made his home and southeast of Mungya'ovi, in the vicinity of a butte, lived Hawk. The two birds hunted by flying back and forth in their own separate territories. Crow, of course, has a habit of gobbling up just about anything—snakes, grasshoppers, lizards, and stinkbugs. Hawk, on the other hand, likes prey that is rich in meat, so he goes for cottontails, jackrabbits, chipmunks, and rock squirrels. He really relishes these creatures. That's the reason he goes in search of them.

One day, Crow and Hawk had a chance encounter. Since they are always on the wing hunting for something to eat, it so happened that both of them were headed for the same place northeast of Oraibi, along the southeast side of Tsa'aktuyqa. It was here that they met and flew along side by side. Somewhere they landed and looked about. Birds typically do this wherever they land. Then they can see quite clearly where a cottontail or jackrabbit is located. These birds really know the business of getting their prey. Crow turned to Hawk and said by way of greeting, "Hey, are you also here?"

"Sure," Hawk replied. "What's up?" he asked.

"Come over here to me."

"What for?" Hawk snapped, but then he consented and hopped over to Crow. "All right, why do you need me so urgently?"

"Well, yes," Crow replied, "I would like to have you as a friend. I never get to talk to anybody, but as friends we could always visit each other."

Hawk readily agreed. So they talked to each other for a while until Crow remarked that he had to leave. He said, "Why don't you come eat at my place tomorrow? I'll have some real delicacies for you."

"All right," Hawk replied, accepting the invitation. "You can count on my being there."

With that, Hawk flew off and hunted on his way home. Crow, who was also homeward bound, spotted a bullsnake along the way and killed it. He decided to carry it home and save it for his new friend. After all, he had invited him for a feast. He wanted to serve Hawk a great dish, and the bullsnake was huge.

Early the next morning Crow was already busy cutting the snake into pieces. He used some sort of cooking pot into which he cut the snake. He was still engaged in this task when Hawk arrived. "Haw!" he announced his arrival.

"Come in," Crow shouted back from down below. Hawk did as

bidden and entered. Sure enough, Crow was still busy cooking. Hawk was really looking forward to the meal his friend was planning to treat him to. He had promised him delicacies, so he was expecting a meal rich in meat. Before long, Crow was finished and set out the food. "All right," he said, "move up. We're going to eat."

Hawk sat down. He had not seen yet what Crow had fixed for him, but it certainly was something greasy, as a bullsnake has a lot of fat. Hawks, of course, don't care for that sort of food. If something does not have a meat flavor, they can't eat it. Actually, the snake that Crow had discovered had been a dead one. It was already rotten, and since Crow had roasted it in this condition it made an awful stink. Hawk only took one bite and found that the food tasted awful. After all, it was rotten and greasy. Hawk only pretended to eat. He acted as if he were taking a piece of meat and putting it in his mouth and chewing it. In reality, however, he did not eat at all, but kept humoring Crow by saying, "How delicious! This really tastes great!" He complimented Crow more than once for the excellent food. Crow in turn felt proud. After keeping up this pretense for quite a while Hawk admitted that he was full. "I've eaten my fill," he exclaimed. "Thanks for inviting me to this feast. I really enjoyed the food. It was exquisite."

"It was indeed," Crow agreed. "I killed the snake only yesterday for you," he lied. "So I prepared it for you today."

Hawk thanked Crow and said how happy he was that he had done this for him and given him the opportunity to gorge himself. The two continued talking for a while. Meanwhile, Crow's house began to smell worse and worse. In fact, the stench was filling the air to a point where Hawk did not enjoy his visit any longer. So it was not long before he indicated that he was ready to leave. "I'll be on my way now," he said. "I have to go because I still need to do some hunting on the way home."

"All right," Crow replied. With that, Hawk left, but not without first inviting Crow also. "Come and eat at my place tomorrow," he said.

"Rest assured, I'll be there," Crow promised.

And so Hawk departed. On the way home he did indeed do some hunting. Hawk is an excellent hunter, of course, so he quickly dispatched two cottontails. One of them he wolfed down for supper after arriving back home, for he had not really eaten anything at Crow's place and was starved. After the meal he went to bed.

The following day Hawk rose early and skinned the second cottontail he had killed the day before. After removing its innards he carefully stored them away and then ate the meat. He had decided to cook the innards for Crow. That's the reason he had saved them. Soon he was busy cooking. He wanted to fix everything ahead of Crow's coming.

Crow had not forgotten about the invitation and was also up early. Without bothering about breakfast he set out for Hawk's place. In his mind he was already seeing all kinds of exquisite foods because he was convinced that Hawk too would fix something delicious for him. That's why he left with an empty stomach. Meanwhile, Hawk was cooking up a meal consisting of the innards and the skin of the rabbit. He had been disgusted with the supposed delicacies that Crow had offered him, so he was bent on getting his revenge by preparing this meal of rabbit skin and rabbit guts. These even still contained turds.

When Crow arrived he too announced his arrival by calling down from the rooftop, "Haw! Isn't anybody home?"

"Sure, I'm home. Come on in!" Hawk replied. "Have you come then?" he asked.

"Yes, I have," Crow answered.

"All right, come on down." Crow climbed down the ladder. "Have a seat there for the time being," Hawk said, "I'm not done cooking yet."

Crow did as bidden, sat down and waited. Meanwhile, Hawk was frying the turd-filled innards together with the skin. As the food got hot it gave off a terrible smell. Crow, taking in the smell, was already full of anticipation. "How delicious! What a pleasant smell!" he kept thinking.

Hawk could hardly stand his own food anymore because of its stench. But since it was his desire to get even with Crow and prepare a nauseating meal for him he said, "I'm fixing a real delicacy for you here." Crow was looking forward to the meal. According to him the fragrance from the cooking was most pleasant. Hawk himself could hardly bear it, and the poor thing felt nauseated just from the cooking. Finally, when he was finished and the food was all done, he set the dish out on the floor. Then he turned to Crow and said, "Well, I'm finished, sit down by the food."

Crow settled down by the food, which looked delicious and inviting to eat. As the two began to eat Hawk kept passing the dish to Crow saying, "Help yourself. I fixed this especially for you. Don't leave anything over for me. You can have it all."

Crow was devouring the food with great gusto. "How appetizing this is!" he exclaimed. "What did you cook that it tastes so good?"

Hawk was staring at Crow in disgust. He had hoped that Crow would not care for the dish he had served him. Instead, he had no complaints and ate with abandon. Truly, crows will gobble up just about anything.

In this manner Hawk fed his guest until he was stuffed. Crow had eaten up everything. "Thanks for inviting me to share this meal. I really ate my fill," he kept repeating. He was most grateful to Hawk.

With that, the two started a conversation. They were telling each other what animals they usually liked to hunt. When Crow showed no intention of leaving, Hawk began to resent his being there. He couldn't stand him anymore. He constantly recalled how he had not enjoyed his meal at Crow's house. Crow now told him what animals he really savored, such as stinkbugs, lizards, grasshoppers, and especially creatures that gave off a terrible stench. No wonder his place had smelled so dreadful, Hawk thought as he listened to him almost overcome with nausea.

Then it was Crow's turn to inquire about Hawk's preferences. "What animals do you like best?" Hawk mentioned those that have a lot of meat, such as cottontails, jackrabbits, chipmunks, and rock squirrels. After discussing all these matters Crow departed for home.

Hawk continued to ponder the whole thing. He just couldn't stand Crow and decided to end his friendship with him. He wasn't going to visit him anymore. It did not please him that Crow had eaten with such relish. It had been his intention to seek revenge on Crow and feed him something revolting. Instead, he had gobbled up all the food and eaten his heart out. Hawk no longer enjoyed himself, for he had failed to get even with Crow. His mind was made up now, he would no longer be friends with him. He knew that if he went to eat with Crow again, he would probably have to eat the same terrible stuff. He preferred never having to face Crow again. And so the two no longer visited each other. Hawk was so sick of Crow that he did not even think of seeking him out again. So he simply forgot him. I guess Crow still lives somewhere and Hawk too.

And here the story ends.

Coyote and the Ducks

Aliksa'i. They were living at Ismo'wala. Coyote had made his home there. Whenever he was pressed by hunger, he would go anywhere to hunt for something edible. Occasionally he headed southwest, and then again northwest. He never went northeast much, however. Only once in a great while would he start into that direction. For on his way northeast he had to pass close by the village of Oraibi, and for that reason he avoided that direction. Of course, people were living at Oraibi, among them a man and his wife who had made their home at the edge of the village. This couple had ducks as pets, a great many of them. Coyote had seen them there, but he couldn't get to them. Their owner was always doing something near them, and this had kept him so far from getting at the ducks.

Coyote's desire for the ducks was great, however, for they looked nice and fat. All the time he was mulling over in his head how he could possibly get through to them. He thought of nothing else. He really wrestled with the problem. One day when he couldn't resist any longer he said, "I guess I should go there one night when the people are sound asleep and try my luck. I might get one." This is what he thought.

One evening Coyote's mind was finally made up. "Today is the day; I really have to go there now," he thought. He had not had any supper that evening because he didn't have any food. No wonder he was all anxious with anticipation!

At dusk he set forth from his home and trotted toward Oraibi. When he reached the village, he peeked over the edge of the mesa and waited. No human soul appeared to be in sight. Repeatedly he tried to go ahead, but again and again he shied back. He would climb up from where he was, run forward a few strides, and then turn back again. Once more he hesitated. And with good reason, for some of the people had dogs as pets, and Coyote was very much afraid of them.

At last, however, he mustered up enough courage to go through with his plan. "It simply has to be done," he thought, and off he ran. He reached the place of the ducks. They were asleep in a little house, so he moved with the utmost caution. He stayed hidden wherever he could even though no one was in sight. There Coyote was now. He felt a strong urge to enter the pen through the vent hole in the wall, but then he lost his courage again. He made several attempts, but finally he said to himself, "Well, this is why I came!" With this thought he squeezed his way through the opening.

Indeed, all the ducks had been asleep, but at once they were aware that he had come in to get them. Coyote looked around among the ducks to see which one he should choose. It would have to be a fat one. He was still undecided when one of the ducks suddenly addressed him and said, "No doubt you came in here to eat one of us."

"Yes," Coyote answered, "that is indeed the reason I came in here. But I haven't chosen which one yet."

"Well, yes," the duck replied, "obviously you came with that in mind. But why don't you wait a moment before you grab one of us?

At least we would like to say a prayer once, and then you can choose whoever you see fit."

"That's fine with me," Coyote was happy to comply.

All the ducks now gathered in one spot after they had descended from their perches. Then the duck who was apparently the leader of the flock said to the others, "We'll say a prayer first. Then Coyote here can have his pick and help himself to one of us for a meal."

They were all assembled now in one place, and suddenly they started quacking. This is what their cries sounded like: "Quack, quack, quack, quack." It was really loud and crazy. The ducks were shouting at the top of their lungs.

The owner of the animals must have heard the din, for he said, "Apparently someone is molesting our pets. Let me go check," grabbing a big stick on his way out. Coyote was waiting patiently, but still the ducks were not through praying. And they were still at it when the owner entered the pen and found Coyote squatting there. He just dealt him a blow on the head as he sat there and killed him on the spot. Coyote had not selected one of the ducks, let alone grabbed one, and already he was killed by the owner of the ducks. So once again his plans were foiled, and he died for nothing.

And here the story ends.

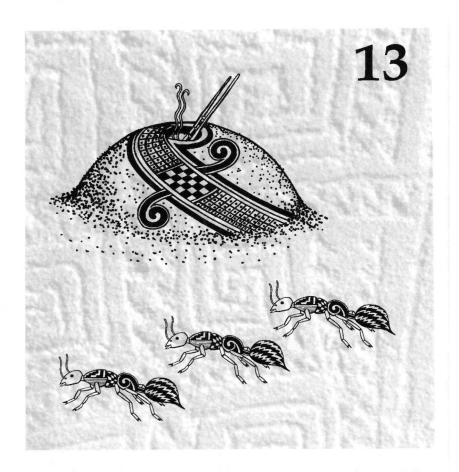

How the Ants Initiated Their Children into the Kachina Society

Aliksa'i. People were living in Oraibi. At a place northwest of this village was a reservoir. On the northeast side of this tank a large colony of ants had built their homes. Because they were so close to Oraibi these ants were quite familiar with how the villagers lived.

Among other things, the ants knew full well that the Oraibis held kachina initiations and performed the Bean dance ritual. And since they had many children, they wanted to initiate their young ones into the kachina cult just like the Oraibis. Having set their minds on looking into this matter, one of the ants volunteered to act as the leader of the Kachina society. It was he who had been thinking about having the children learn the kachina cult, so it was quite natural that he would also be the headman. He immediately appointed someone to impersonate the mother Angwushahay'i. In addition, he selected the two Hu' kachinas who would come to flog the youngsters. This was an important part of the initiation. Next, he sought out a place where they could prepare themselves for the event. He finally found a kiva for them at a site named Koritvi. He also entrusted the position of a guard to someone. After handing out all these responsibilities, he also assigned somebody the task of Bean dance Leader.

When everything was carefully planned, a date was set for the event. As the ants had decided to hold the ritual as soon as possible, they set a day four days away. At that time they would be initiating their ant children into the kachina cult. After fixing the date, the ants went through the days in anticipation of the event.

On the morning of the fourth day, the parents of the young ants chose for them those who would be acting as their godfathers and godmothers. The children, in turn, brought sacred cornmeal to their godfathers and godmothers and were busily scurrying about carrying out this task. On the eve of the fourth day all these matters had been taken care of.

Since the ants wanted this to be a brief ceremony, they did not bother with all the aspects of the Bean dance. Thus, on that same morning no kachina went around delivering bean sprouts or presents for the young children. They would not go through the complete ritual like the Oraibis. But they did wash the hair of the children who were going to be initiated. At the same time the two Hu' kachinas that typically are in charge of the whipping went to Koritvi to prepare themselves. The ant who was to impersonate their mother, Angwu-shahay'i, went along with them. So they all put on their costumes here. The leader of the Bean dance society who usually comes to narrate the legend also dressed for his role.

Adjacent to the ants' home stood another tiny anthill which, two days before this event, had been turned into a kiva. Now that the time had arrived for things to start the town crier made the customary announcement. "I guess you ant people have completed your preparations by now. Proceed to the small ant kiva with your children. Go with happy hearts!" This is what he announced. So they all brought their children to this location.

The ant people now went about gathering their new godchildren and delivered them to the kiva where the initiation was going to take place. Upon their arrival, the children entered, one after the other, accompanied by their godparents. Standing atop a mound above the kiva was the person who would signal to those at Koritvi when everything was ready. Wrapped in a blanket, he stood there waiting to give the signal. When everybody was inside the kiva, little Kooyemsis went around blessing the children with a mother corn, a perfect ear of white corn. They carried out everything the way it is done in the kiva of the Kachina society. So they also sprinkled the children with medicine water while they blessed them with the mother corn ears.

Meanwhile, the storyteller had finished costuming himself and was on his way to the kiva to narrate the legend. After entering he told the initiates where the kachinas would be arriving from. Apparently, they lived at various places and were known by their own individual names. After revealing to them where each kachina lived, he ended his tale and made his exit from the kiva.

No sooner was the storyteller gone than the ant on the lookout, who was supposed to signal to those who would come to do the flogging, stood up and shook his blanket as if he was airing it out. Immediately, Angwushahay'i, along with the two Hu' kachinas, her assistants, came out from Koritvi. They sped to the kiva. Upon reaching the kiva, they circled it four times and then entered.

Inside the kiva, at two locations, dry sand was spread out. On this sand were depicted in strict detail images of the two Hu' kachinas together with their mother Angwushahay'i. The two floggers now placed themselves on each side of the sand painting. The time had come for them to begin whipping the children. The first little ant was taken to the flogger on the southwest side of the sand painting. So hard did he strike the little fellow with his yucca whip that after only two hits he had nearly cut him in half at the waist. At this point, his godfather snatched him away. And then another ant child was brought to the flogger on the northeast side. He too received his beating. After only one strike his body was almost cut apart at the waist. His godfather also quickly pulled him away. This is how the two Hu' kachinas dealt with all the children down there. They whipped them so hard, they nearly tore them in two at the waist.

When they were done with all the young ants, the two floggers in turn struck each other and just about whacked their each other's legs off. Next, they both struck their mother and again almost cut her apart at the waist. With that, they emerged from the kiva. Once more

the three circled the kiva four times, this time in the opposite direction, and then they returned to Koritvi.

In this fashion the ants initiated their children into the kachina
cult. When the ceremony was over, the people began taking their
children out of the kiva. Having discovered the ill side effects of this
ceremony, however, they never again held initiations into the kachina
cult. And as a result of the flogging, ants are joined together today at
the waist by this kind of a small connection. The Hu' kachinas had
whipped them too severely.

And here the story ends.

How the Hopis Got Fire

Aliksa'i. Long ago when the Hopis first arrived in this area, it used to get very cold at night and they were freezing and miserable. In the mornings, as they looked east, they would see smoke rising in the air. There had to be fire somewhere, so they sent a strong boy to explore. He set out as bidden and journeyed east. He would travel by day and sleep at night, for it was bitter cold. Finally, he reached an area that was bright from the light of fires. Many people were at home there, and they all possessed fire and were able to warm themselves by them. This the young man reported back. After mulling this news over the Hopis said, "Let's tell someone to steal fire for us."

The men thought and thought who they might send there. The

young boy who had been there explained that no human being would be capable of stealing a firebrand or some of the hot coals. For the people living there were numerous, and it was their habit to spend the nights dancing by the edge of the fire. Also, there were guards stationed around their village, so a mortal could never succeed. Once again the men deliberated about whom they could possibly assign this task.

Finally, they decided to command Owl to go and get the fire for them. Owl was willing to give it a try. However, when it reached its destination, the fire did something to its eyes. As a result, Owl became blind. Still it tried. It was daylight now, but since it could not see, it was unable to make out where it was going. Flying back it eventually reached darkness again, and only then did it gain its eyesight back. This is how Owl fared and this is what it reported after its return.

The Hopis were anxious to have the fire in order to warm themselves. Wondering who among the animals might qualify to carry out the task, they agreed on Gopher. After all, he was accustomed to operate underground and would probably manage to steal the fire. The men carefully planned the route he would have to travel and at what point exactly he would have to pierce the ground.

Gopher did as bidden and was burrowing his way along. Upon reaching his goal he surfaced. Indeed, it was only a short distance to the fire. And so Gopher stole the fire. Holding the firebrand in his mouth he reentered the tunnel and hurried away. But since he was moving along underground, the smoke could not escape and began to fill the tunnel. By now the smoke was so thick that the poor thing could not see properly anymore. At one point everything became black. Not knowing what to do, Gopher kept stumbling along bumping into all sorts of things. When he finally arrived, the firebrand was gone.

The leader of the Hopis inquired why he had come empty-handed. "Yes," answered Gopher, "your planning was all fine. But on the way back the firebrand began to smoke. Instead of burning well it started smoldering. The big tunnel I had dug turned completely black. I was coughing and tears were running from my eyes. There was nothing I could do. I'm afraid you'll have to find someone else." With this Gopher walked up to the men and showed them his tail. Only the tiny tip of it was left. Nearly all of it had been burned off.

This is the reason gophers have such a short tail.

Once more the people were racking their brains about whom they should ask for help. So since Gopher had failed they agreed to call upon Coyote. Coyote believes everything and is constantly on the prowl. He's bound to be a good thief. Wherever he goes to pilfer a something, people don't notice him. His skills in this respect are extraordinary. For this reason the Hopis decided to employ him. Being the sucker that he is he would probably consent to taking on the task, and so they asked him to go.

Coyote did as told and made it to the fire. There he quickly grabbed a firebrand and dashed off. He still had not got all the way back when his pelt got singed and the fire began to flame up, and his entire skin got burned. For this reason coyotes are sort of yellowish-brown now. The moment the flames lit up, however, Coyote got so scared he cast away the firestick and ran home. In this way he, too, returned empty-handed.

By now the people were pondering for the fourth time whom to ask for help. Someone suggested getting a big bird. He could snatch up the firebrand, fly up and return it to them. If he got singed, he could throw the fire down to them, they thought. Thus they decided on Vulture. "He's always circling the sky and therefore mighty and strong. He can probably do the feat," said the leader of the Hopis. So they bade Vulture to come.

Vulture replied, "All right, I'll try for you. If the fire people don't harm me or kill me, I may be able to bring you the desired thing."

"Well, yes, go in strength," the leader wished him. With that the big bird winged away eastward.

By the time Vulture arrived at his destination, night had begun to fall. Sure enough, people were still lighting the fires. One of the fires was not quite ablaze yet. This Vulture somehow managed to approach. And no sooner had he snatched up a burning stick than he took to the air and with the firebrand in his beak made his getaway.

As Vulture flew along, a strong breeze set in, which really fanned the flames. As they licked higher and higher, they burned the bird's head. There was nothing the poor thing could do. In the end, as Vulture was nearing Hopiland, all the plumes on his head had caught fire. At this point the bird began to fall. He let the firebrand go and crashed with it to the ground.

The Hopis who had witnessed his fall ran to the bird. With words of pity they kept rubbing his head. All of its feathers were singed. By rubbing his head they put out the flames. But because they rubbed so hard, they removed all of the bird's feathers. For this reason vultures are bald-headed now.

The bird, of course, had dropped the firebrand. The Hopi leader was elated and after gathering his people they all got fire from it. They carried it back to their houses and after spreading the word to wherever the people were living, everybody came to borrow fire. So now the Hopis possessed the fire, too. Thanks to Vulture they were warm and were able to cook their meals.

This done, they turned to Vulture and said, "We're glad you accomplished this feat for us. We're overjoyed. We cannot feed you our Hopi food, however. Instead, you can clean up our leftovers. Then it won't be as smelly around here anymore."

This is the reason Vulture is accustomed to gobbling down rotten things only. He is constantly flying around feeding on what has been discarded. And so this way he cleans the earth. This is how the Hopis instructed the bird, and in this manner they acquired the fire to stay comfortable and warm and cook their food.

And here the story ends.

15

How Coyote Became Infatuated with Girls

Aliksa'i. People were living at Oraibi. At Ismo'wala Coyote had made his home. His grandmother was his only relative. In Oraibi lived a couple with three children, all of them girls. They had their fields at Hovaqaptsomo. Because they had only daughters and no son, the girls tended their plants there. It was their father who had established the field for them, but since they had planted them, they were the ones who took care of the crops.

Coyote is constantly on the move and hunting about. At harvest time people would not always pick all the corn ears from the stalks, especially the short ones. Those they overlooked once in a while. For this reason Coyote from Ismo'wala roamed the fields and when he came across any leftover corn ears, he would bring those home to his grandmother. In this way the two got their corn. Among the many things that were ripe and ready for picking, the girls also had water- melon growing there. So Coyote, upon leaving his home in the evening and reaching the field by nightfall, always gobbled up some watermelons that the girls had saved there to let them ripen. He did this in a rather wasteful way. Since the girls' father was usually busy with things at home, his daughters generally went to the field. They often reported that a coyote was eating holes in their watermelons. One day when their father came to the field, he traced the animal's tracks and set up a deadfall stone trap. While it stood there, loaded, the girls would arrive to inspect the plants and hoe weeds. Before returning home they always checked their father's trap. This is how they spent their days.

Of course, Coyote kept seeing the girls who had their crops there. Once in a while he would even go early to the field and simply watch them. As he did, he felt a strange longing for them, poor thing, but he did not know how to approach them. So one night when he and his grandmother had eaten supper and were just sitting there relaxing, he turned to the old woman and said, "Grandmother!"

"What is it?" she asked.

Coyote explained that he was toying with the idea of paying those girls a visit. His grandmother replied, "Oh my, you poor fellow. None of them will take a fancy to you. Their father also won't want anyone as homely as you for a son-in-law. However, you can always give it a try. Go and look them up. Perhaps one of them will give in to you." Then his grandmother added, "But before you do that, let me first give you some instructions. Once you have carried these out you may go visit the girls." So she said, "The next time you head over to the village of Oraibi, creep among the houses. When you spot one with a vent hole, crawl through it to the inside and search for a bow.

Normally people have bows hanging from a peg in the wall. The same is true for quivers. Those too usually hang somewhere. These are the things you must enter a house for. Once you have gotten hold of a bow and quiver, look for buckskin leggings. Some people have those, and if you are lucky you will find them in the same house where you find the other things. Next, search for yarn, including some that is red. Also, look for the dark woven shirt that is embroidered with blue yarn and tied at the sides. All people own shirts like these. Then bring everything here. After leaving the village, however, go over to the mesa edge and look for red ocher. Usually there should also be that reddish-brown rock, iron ore. That is similar to red ocher and will also do. Just search around and you'll find it. Then bring all those things back to me."

Coyote was happy with this favorable response. His grandmother had said the right thing and consented to his wish to visit the girls. He went to bed with great anticipation. The following day he spent mulling the matter over until the end of the day approached. He had been hunting far and wide during the day. Now, as evening fell, he returned to his grandmother. Immediately upon his arrival the two had supper. Since his grandmother had told him what to do, she had cooked early so that they could eat without delay. "We'll eat early. Perhaps you want to go to Oraibi right away and look for those things I told you about."

"Yes," Coyote replied, "I was thinking of doing that soon."

No sooner had the two eaten than Coyote left. Without wasting any time he headed straight for Oraibi. He climbed up to the village on top of the mesa and then made his way among the houses. He was searching for one with a vent hole. Finally, he found one and entered it. Looking around inside, he found exactly what he was looking for. First a bow, which he removed from the wall. Then, searching some more, he also spotted a quiver. That too he helped himself to. Both items he carefully stashed someplace and then continued his search

for a dark shirt. He discovered one draped over a storage beam attached to the ceiling. Buckskin leggings were also hanging there. He
grabbed both things and then looked around for yarn. He found that
too, even though it was dark night, for Coyote has excellent eyesight.
The yarn had the very color he needed, red and blue-green. With all
these items over his arms he emerged from the vent hole.

Having made his exit, Coyote ran to the mesa edge where he
searched for the reddish-brown rock. Soon he saw some. He grabbed
a small lump and then returned home with all his treasures to his
grandmother at Ismo'wala. It was deep in the night by the time he
arrived and his grandmother was already asleep. Without saying
anything to her he laid down his things. Then he too bedded down
and soon was sound asleep.

The next day both coyotes woke up in the morning. As they were
eating breakfast Coyote said, "Grandmother!"

"What is it?" she asked.

"Well, everything you instructed me to get last night I brought
home."

"I'm glad to hear that," she replied. "I'll dress you up this evening and then you may go visit the girls. I suggest you go when it's
close to sundown. At that time the girls normally finish their work. If
they are still home, you're bound to chance upon one of them. And if
your luck really holds, one of them will talk to you." This is what the
old woman said to him.

Coyote felt proud. After all, he had gathered all sorts of clothing.
After breakfast he took off hunting as he was accustomed to do. As
usual, he went to eat from the girls' crops. Every so often an ear of
fresh corn got ripe there that he would then bring home to his grandmother. It was still early in the day when he reached the field, and
since the girls had not yet arrived, he broke off a few ears from the
stalks and carried them home. When it became evening and the sun
set, his grandmother started dressing her grandson. The first thing
she did was rub the iron ore stone to break it up. She then pulverized
the pieces. When there was enough to paint his face she stopped.

Then she said to Coyote, "All right, come here. I'll get you ready now."

Coyote did as told, and his grandmother first put the dark shirt on him. Next she wrapped the leggings around his legs. Then she tied his hair in a knot using red string. How well dressed he already looked! The blue-green yarn she now wound around his wrists and around his legs just below the knees. Finally, she applied a coat of iron ore to his face. As a result, Coyote Boy really looked dapper.

By the time Coyote walked out of the house it was not yet fully evening. He turned in a northeasterly direction, for there in the northeast was Hovaqaptsomo, and southwest of it was Ismo'wala. Between these two locations the deadfall trap had been set. As Coyote strolled by the trap he merely glanced at it, but, much to his surprise, spotted a cottontail caught in it there.

As he stood there eyeing the dead rabbit, he became tempted by it and stepped up to the deadfall. He carried a bow of course and had his quiver on his shoulder. There was no doubt in his mind that he had to have that meat. He understood that the deadfall had been baited with the animal, so he was quite apprehensive as he tried to get at it. Deciding to snatch it away with his snout, he carefully stuck his head inside the trap. But, as he sank his jaws into the meat and pulled, he dislodged the prop stick under the flat rock. Coyote was not able to pull out his head before the heavy stone fell and buried him. He tried to extricate himself, but the miserable thing merely kept pulling himself this way and that. The deadfall stone had also caught his hands and arms, and since it was extremely heavy, he could not get out from underneath it. He kept struggling and kicking his legs, but in vain. By now quite a bit of time had passed and he had failed to free himself. Eventually, he just lay still and died. What a shame! Here he was, all dressed up and dying there in that trap and never making it to the girls.

Some time the following day the girls headed out to the field to tend their crops again. When they checked on them, they saw that they had to hoe weeds. They worked almost till sundown, then went home. On the way they decided to check their father's trap. As they came in sight of it, much to their amazement, they spotted someone caught in it. Leaving the trap undisturbed, the girls simply took a quick glance at it and then ran home. After they got there, during supper, they turned to their father. "Father!" one of the girls exclaimed.

"What is it?" he asked.

"I don't quite understand this, but someone is trapped in your deadfall. You've definitely caught something. We left the thing alone and came right home."

Since it was already pitch black outside as they were eating, the father did not feel like heading right out to the trap. "I'll go check it out tomorrow," he said. "Let that creature stay there. He's weighed down by the stone and can't escape."

When they girls had glanced at the trap, they had only seen legs sticking out from it. However, they had buckskin leggings on, so one of the girls thought she needed to tell her father about that. "But the thing in it looked like a human being," she protested. "Please, go and check it out right now."

"I won't go there this late at night," he insisted. "If it is a human, I can't do anything for him anymore. I'll go and check out the trap tomorrow and lift up the stone. If it turns out that a person was caught, I will have to tell the other people," he said. "If he is from this village, we'll tell the village crier to make a public announcement. If someone can't find their child, they will realize that something happened to him and for that reason he failed to return home. Anyway, tomorrow I'll go take a look, not sooner." When their father showed no desire to go, the girls, poor things, were sad. After all, someone from another village could have been coming through the area by the trap, and if he was the one lying there, how could they notify his parents? The girls were very unhappy about all this, but their father had no intention of going to the trap during the night.

The next day the family had an early breakfast. The sun was just a little way over the horizon, and already they had eaten. After dressing the father said, "Let me go take a look at the trap now. You came home with a strange story last night. I want to see what's going on. Who knows what I'll find?" With that he descended the mesa. He climbed down on the southwestern side and then continued in a southwesterly direction. Soon he reached the crops and headed for the place where he had set up the deadfall. As he came closer he didn't see anything in it. There was no doubt, however, that it had fallen. Not before he stood in front of it did he see someone's legs sticking out. Whoever he was, he wore buckskin leggings. Something was bothering the man however. Somehow the tracks were all wrong and confusing. "I wonder what being this is," he pondered as he inspected the site. He was dumbfounded. The thing really had strange tracks.

Finally, he stepped up to the fallen slab and lifted it up. Much to his surprise a body lay there, clad in a dark shirt. And, what was even more puzzling, a tail extended from the body. "What creature has a tail like that and is dressed so elegantly?" he mused. As he pulled the body aside he realized that it belonged to a coyote. A coyote dressed in shirt and leggings and with leg bands tied around his knees—who would have expected that? And it also had blue-green yarn wrapped around its wrists and its hair bound into a knot with a red string!

The man now pulled the animal completely out. Its appearance was fanciful indeed. The face was decorated with red stripes extending from the bridge of the nose to either cheek. This really amused the man. He just stood there cracking up. He was all by himself, but he was shaking with laughter. As he wondered what to do with the creature, it occurred to him that he could haul it to the field, skin it, and use the pelt as a scarecrow. So he removed the animal and fixed the trap again. Having set it up properly he slung Coyote over his shoulder. He couldn't help but laugh as he walked along with such a strange load on his back.

And so, after hauling Coyote to his field, the man set about skinning it. First, he took off the clothes and then pulled off the skin. Having done that, he drove a long pole into the ground in the middle of the field and hung the pelt from it. He now had a nice dark shirt, buckskin leggings, a quiver, and a bow, all nice things that he decided to take home and replace with some ugly rags. With those he would return and dress the skin.

The man also decided to wait until later to tell his daughters. Upon his return with all those nice clothes he did not say a word to his daughters. He simply gathered up a tattered shirt and some shabby leggings. These he took back to the field and dressed up Coyote once more. Then he went home.

The man now bade his daughters go see for themselves what he had caught in the trap and hung on a pole. This thing, he said, would now stand watch over their crops. It had been an evil creature, so it served it right to hang there like that. It was definitely this thing that had gobbled up their corn and cut holes in their watermelons. To punish it for that he had strung it up on the pole. "Go and see for yourselves," the father kept urging the girls.

No sooner had the family finished lunch than the girls headed out to their plants. Indeed, upon arriving at the field, they saw something attached to the top of a pole. As they got close to it they realized that it was a coyote. It really looked odd in its outfit. The girls were greatly amused by the sight and laughed and laughed. They were at a loss as to why the animal was all dressed up like that. It really was funny. In this manner, however, they had gotten even with Coyote, and it was for this reason that their father had set up its skin there as a scarecrow.

Meanwhile, Coyote's grandmother was waiting for the return of her grandson. Maybe he had lucked out and gone home with one of the girls. That's what she was thinking. But if he had done that, he surely would have let her know. So the old woman kept waiting, poor thing.

By now two days had passed, and Coyote still had failed to return. So the granny went in search of him. As she searched here and there she eventually also reached the deadfall trap. However, it was empty. So the old woman trudged on toward the field. "That's where he had seen those girls," she thought. "He probably went there."

As she reached her destination and scanned the area, she at first did not see anybody walking about. But there, in the middle of the field, stood a figure. She started off in its direction and was nearing it from the edge of the field when, much to her surprise, she found her grandchild standing there. "I must go to him and talk to him," she decided. "He can't hear me from here." So she walked over to him and could not believe her eyes. There the poor thing hung on a pole, completely skinned. There was nothing but his pelt left. How she cried over him, dressed up so fancifully. The poor granny was heartbroken. "How terrible to find you in this state," she lamented. "Why on earth did you have to lust after those girls like the humans? Now you've ended up like this." The poor woman was crying in anguish. Devastated and without searching further, she trotted on home. There would be no daughter-in-law for her. And all that was left of her grandson was stuck on a pole. This is how the old granny lost her grandchild. She was all alone now.

And here the story ends.

16

The Cicadas and the Serpents

Aliksa'i. Many people were living at Oraibi and there were settlements all across the land. At a place called Tsu'akpi all kinds of
serpents, including rattlesnakes, had made their home. When it got to
be summer and the weather turned warm, they would roam the land
as serpents are accustomed to do. But in wintertime they were all
underground, where they would transform themselves into human
shape. To do so they simply shed their skins and hung them from a
peg on the wall of their house.

At Tuuwanasavi the cicadas were at home. Some of them were
the colorful kind, others were white as clay. Just like the serpents at
Tsu'akpi, they all lived together in one place.

One day long ago, a blizzard had been blowing, and now the ground was covered with a great deal of snow. It had never snowed this much before at the beginning of the cold season. Everything was buried in snow, and the land was white as far as the eye could reach. Since the sun was barely shining, it was bitterly cold.

Already the wood supplies of the people were giving out, and still the weather was not getting any warmer. The snow, which simply would not melt, also prevented the people from going after wood. More than one tried, but they did not get far before they became exhausted from plodding through the deep snow. The freezing weather also continued. From one point on they hardly had any wood left. Finally, some people actually froze to death.

By contrast, the area where the cicadas lived was free of snow. They possessed the knowledge of warm weather and heat and for this reason were always comfortably warm in their homes.

The serpents were not accustomed to the cold either and began freezing to death. So their headman assembled his strongmen and said to them, "How terrible! We can't go on like this. It just doesn't get warm, and because we can't get out and hunt around, we've used up all our food. We're starving to death and dying from the cold. Therefore I suggest that one of us who still has some strength left seek out the cicadas. When he gets there, he can plead with them to have mercy on us and let the weather get warm. But we're not only asking for ourselves. There must be others out there praying for warmth." This is what he said, whereupon one serpent expressed his willingness to take on this task.

It was Sandsnake that had volunteered. "I can give it a try at least," he said. With that he slipped into his skin, thereby transforming himself into a sandsnake again. He did not intend to make the journey in his human shape. And so he left the house and started forth. However, he had not yet reached his destination when he became tired and so cold that he was forced to turn around. By the time he returned home he was completely exhausted.

The headman bade someone else try, for they couldn't go on living under these conditions. Only if it got warm could they recover. This time a big bullsnake volunteered. "I can give it a try at least," he said.

"Yes, indeed, try your luck," said the headman. "You're very strong and might get there. I'm afraid it's been cold so long now that it doesn't seem that it will ever warm up again," he said, encouraging Bullsnake to be strong on his journey.

Bullsnake also dressed in his skin, leaving the house and heading out in the direction of Tuuwanasavi. True enough, it was biting cold. No wonder the first one, poor thing, almost froze to death before it returned. Bullsnake had barely left his home when he met the fierce north wind. But he mustered up his courage and moved along. He knew that under the present conditions they would die soon, so he kept striving on through the deep snow. At least he made it somewhat farther than Sandsnake, but in the end he also got exhausted before he could reach his goal. He too, poor wretch, was forced to cut short his journey and return home.

The older serpents were unhappy when they heard that he had not succeeded, but they did not reprimand him for his failure. After all, it was extremely cold outside. Someone else would have to venture forth, though.

Before anybody said anything, Whipsnake spoke up. "I'll go. I alone will be able to get through the snow. You two are heavier than I. That's why you sank in. If I move along on the surface of the snow, I might make it there." He was already dressing as he spoke.

As soon as Whipsnake had his skin on he departed. The temperature was as cold as before, and there seemed to be no sign of the sun. Thick clouds engulfed the entire sky, rolling in big waves toward the northeast. The ice-cold northwest wind was also not letting up. It occurred to Whipsnake that he might not reach Tuuwanasavi, but he was not willing to turn around. He might not succeed in locating the cicadas, but he was going to continue on braving the north wind. He grew a little angry with himself for volunteering, but it just wouldn't do to head back. It was his own fault that he had volunteered. He didn't want to embarrass himself, so he struggled on.

Whipsnake climbed on top of the snow, and since he was very light, slithered along quite nicely. In addition, he was an excellent runner, which allowed him to move along quite forcefully. He knew he was nearing his destination when the air began to get warmer. No longer freezing and somewhat strengthened by the warmth, he now moved along at a rapid pace.

Eventually Whipsnake reached the home of the cicadas, where there was a large area completely free of snow. Right in the center of this clearing stood a ladder protruding from under the ground. He headed toward it, for this had been the idea of coming here. By the time he arrived at his destination the air was gently warm. The ground was covered with green plants and flowers. He had just come through the severest winter and now here he was in the middle of summer. No wonder Whipsnake stared in amazement. How glad he was to have gotten here without falling victim to the cold. "Thanks, I arrived without harm," he said to himself.

He stood there listening. No doubt, the cicadas lived there. He climbed on the roof and called inside, "Hey! Isn't anybody home?"

True enough, they were there, for he heard a voice, "Sure, we're home. Come on in, stranger." Whipsnake entered and the cicadas welcomed him. Just as outside, the temperature was nice and warm inside their house, and they were living very comfortably there.

An old man, not wasting his time, bade Whipsnake to come over to the firepit and smoke with him. Just as their smoking ritual was coming to an end, a few of the women were setting out some food for him. When they finished their smoke, the old man said to him, "All right, eat first. When you're full, you can share with us the reason for your visit." Whipsnake ate. All kinds of delicacies had been served. He ate watermelon, muskmelon, roasted corn, all the crops that normally grow only in the warm season. He was starved, so he really gorged himself.

When Whipsnake was full, he explained to everybody why he was about. He told the cicadas how they were suffering from the cold at home. "Two of us attempted to come here, but failed. The poor wretches were so frozen that they had to turn around. However, because I'm so light, I did not sink in the snow and that's how I managed to get here. Not many of us are alive any more, so I came to implore your help. We all know that you command the warm weather. Have mercy with us and let it get warmer earlier in the year again. Then we can leave our homes and set out in search of food."

The old cicada replied, "Is that so? I'm sorry, indeed. This must have happened because we've been so tardy. Go back and tell your people not to worry anymore. We'll set things right for you again. All this must have come to pass due to our tardiness. Go deliver this message now." And then he added, "As soon as you get home, tell them to wait for us in four days."

Upon receiving these instructions Whipsnake said, "Very well. I'll go back and deliver your words." As he was leaving, someone else spoke to him. "Wait a moment. I'll come with you. Then things will be different." Whipsnake stopped to wait.

The cicada that had spoken to him picked up a flute somewhere and said, "All right, let's go out together now."

With that the two climbed out on the roof. The cicada walked away from the kiva in a westerly direction and then stopped. He held out his flute in the direction of the serpent's home and started to play. As he did so, a narrow lane, clear of snow, was forming all the way to his home. Apparently, the cicada was blazing a trail for him. Before long, there was a clear road all the way.

When the cicada was finished, he said, "All right, now you're bound to get to your house quickly. Go happily." Whipsnake set forth. Indeed, not much time passed and he was back. The other serpents were elated. They were convinced that he had been to the home of the cicadas. No sooner was he back than he related the cicadas' words. The serpents were glad to receive such good tidings.

Happy in their hearts, the serpents now waited for the coming of the cicadas on the fourth day. As best as they could, they cleaned up their house. When the appointed day arrived, they were full of expectations. They could not sit still any longer and were filled with joyful apprehension.

The sun had just started its slide down the horizon when the cicadas started out at Tuuwanasavi. One behind the other, they formed a long line on the way to the serpents. But they did not go as cicadas; rather, they came transformed as human beings, just like us. Each one carried a flute, had a bell tied around his hand, and was clad in a rabbitskin blanket.

The serpents could clearly hear the visitors as they were arriving. Upon reaching the serpents' home, the cicadas shook their rattles, and then the serpents invited them in. So many entered that they filled the entire kiva standing along the walls. Then they started dancing. And this is how their song went:

Haw'o my mothers, haw'o my fathers.
Gray Flute members, Blue Flute members our fathers.
Beautiful life
We will awaken.
Aa'aa'aahaa, aa'aa'haa'aa, aayaa.
Sunny we will make it.
Through a bright and sunny day we will go along.
Aa'aahaa'aa ii'iihii'ii'ii
For sure
Colorful cicadas, clay-white cicadas.
Beautiful life
We will awaken.
Aa'aa'aahaa, aa'aa'haa'aa', aayaa.
Sunny we will make it.
Through a bright and sunny day we will go along.
Aa'aahaa'aa, ii'iihii'ii'ii.

This is how the cicadas sang. And while they danced the temperature rose inside the kiva. By the time they finished the dance, the serpents were completely covered with sweat. The cicadas only staged one dance, then they filed out of the kiva. The serpents were grateful for the entertainment. After exiting the cicadas returned home.

All the way home the cicadas played their flutes. As they were walking along, the snow began to thaw. And not only along their trail. All across the land the snow was disappearing and the weather was warming up.

From that day on, everything on the land began to grow again and things started to bloom. Only after the cicadas had danced, and once more all life on earth was warm.

And here the story ends.

17

The House Mice and the Boy from Huk'ovi

Aliksa'i. People were living at Huk'ovi. And all across the land people were settled in other villages. Northwest of Oraibi there used to stand a lofty stone pillar, but it had collapsed at one point, and now the house mice had made their home there.

Once a young man from Huk'ovi was hunting along the southwest side of this pillar. However, his luck had failed, and already it was nearing early evening. Feeling he could not return home empty-handed, he continued his hunt, but he did not make a single kill. By now, night had fallen, so he set out for home.

As it was now totally dark, the boy had no idea which way to go. Having lost any sense of his whereabouts, he simply headed in a random direction. As he walked along, he suddenly spotted a glow of light and decided to head toward it. He thought the light might be coming from a village, so he went that way.

He had not yet arrived at his destination when he grew so tired that he paused to take a rest. While he was sitting there, much to his surprise a voice spoke to him. "What are you doing here at this time of the night?" No one seemed to be there, so while scanning the area, the boy thought to himself, "I wonder who just spoke to me." But even though he did not see anybody he replied, "Yes, I'm on my way home. Who are you?" he asked.

"I'm sitting right here next to you," came the reply. Once more the boy looked about. This time, as he glanced down, he spotted a house mouse sitting right nearby, looking up at him. "Are you the one who spoke to me?" the boy asked.

"Yes, it was I," he answered.

"I see," the boy acknowledged, and then he told the house mouse what had happened to him. When he had ended the house mouse said, "Is that right? So that's the reason you're sitting here at this un-godly hour. When I saw you, I came right over. It looks like you're quite a distance from your home. You won't be able to find your trail home in this darkness. You must have seen our place. Sure enough, there is light coming from there." With that, the house mouse invited the Huk'ovi boy to accompany him home. He urged him not to go roaming about at this unusual time of the night.

Since the boy was weary and exhausted, he readily agreed. Both now headed for this place. It was not very far to go. The home of the house mice was just northwest of Oraibi, but the youth was unfamil-iar with the location.

The house mouse and the boy quickly reached their destination. No doubt, there was a kiva there. The two ascended to the rooftop of the kiva where the house mouse announced, "How about some words of welcome? I'm not alone." Several voices welcomed them and bade them enter. Evidently, a large number of house mice were living there. No sooner had the boy been ushered in than they started darting back and forth trying to make him feel at home. What a friendly group of little people they were! The house mouse who had brought the boy instructed the women to prepare a meal. "Go ahead and get a large meal ready. I'm glad I brought home a visitor. If he joins us for supper, we'll enjoy it all the more," he said. Busily the women fell to fixing supper.

When they were done, they set out the food. Now they all sat down to supper and ate with great gusto. When they had eaten their fill, they gathered around the boy and he talked with them about many things. All the while the young house mice posed many questions to him.

As time passed, it became so late that the house mouse who had brought the boy to their home ordered the kids to go to bed. With the children off to bed this particular house mouse inquired of the lad, "Won't you come with us? We should go and shell corn for ourselves. Whenever we do that and bag it to bring it home, we're barely able to carry the load. We've tried this in the past. When we bring the corn home bit by bit, it takes us quite a long time before we get it all here," he told him. "Since you're much stronger than we, we were hoping that you would haul that bag of kernels here for us. That would really last us quite a while," the house mouse pleaded.

The boy from Huk'ovi took pity on them and, without reluctance, agreed to the request. After all, he felt grateful to them for the way they had welcomed him. It was because of them that he was not out there in the night lost and suffering. Hence he said that he would be more than willing to do this for them. "All right, then where is the building where you make your piki, which would also be your store-house?" he inquired.

"We'll take you there," the house mice replied, whereupon they filed out one by one, taking him along. They all proceeded to the foot of a mesa and then ascended to the top. The youth followed them, thinking, "I wonder where they have their piki house. We still haven't come to it." This is what went through his mind, but he kept silent.

Soon they approached a place from where the glow of a light could be seen. From all appearances the place was a large settlement.

They were actually nearing Oraibi from the northwest. The lad, however, was not aware of this. He simply came ambling along behind the house mice. Upon their arrival there, they stopped at the northwestern outskirts of the village, at someone's storehouse. Every one of them quickly entered. When the youth remained behind, the house mice told him to follow them inside, which he did, entering through a doorway. All the house mice now began to shell kernels off the corncobs.

Some time later when they had accumulated enough, they stuffed the kernels into a sack and told the boy that they would now go. And so, returning to the home of the house mice, the boy this time followed along with a bag of corn on his back. Back home the house mice thanked the boy for his help.

Already, before their return some of the children had awakened from their sleep. They were cranky now and were crying for watermelon. The elders wanted to fulfill their wishes, so they agreed right away and said, "Let's hurry back and when we return, we'll have a melon snack before going to sleep." Everybody was of one mind, so once more they pleaded with the Huk'ovi boy to accompany them. He really couldn't refuse them, so he said yes.

Again they left their abode and proceeded towards Oraibi. This time, however, they went to a different place, entering a house and scourging around inside for melon. The piki house was located directly below the people's living quarters, and so there was no entrance from ground level. The youth was hesitant to enter the home. The residents were bound to hear him if he entered through the hatch in the roof. So he wanted to wait outside, but the house mice prompted him to follow them in.

They urged him to enter through the vent hole in the wall. Again he readily agreed, and then he began to make his way in through this small opening. He first stuck his head in and then inserted himself through. The poor lad was grunting all the while as he was squeezing in. At long last, and after much effort, he was inside.

By the time he got inside, some of the house mice had already gnawed through a melon on their own and were feasting on it while waiting for him. There was a lot of hustle and bustle, and they were making the strangest noises as they were eating.

The house mice now told the boy to eat a melon before their return home. Again he consented without hesitation and broke one of the melons open. Everybody was thoroughly enjoying their feast.

Next the house mice asked, "Why are you eating so quietly? It's so much more delicious when you eat smacking your lips," they said to him. To this, however, the boy did not agree.

But the house mice did not stop prodding. Eventually, he gave in and began yelling at the top of his lungs. The house mice chided him, "No, not like that. Someone's bound to hear you and come running."

The boy retorted, "I have to yell like this. This is the only way I know how to make a noise," he said to them.

The boy was still carrying on in this manner when the woman of the house said to her husband, "Old man! Go downstairs. Someone's screaming down there. Perhaps something bad has happened to the poor thing." So the man climbed downstairs.

The minute he entered the piki room the house mice heard him and scattered in every direction. In no time all of them had left this place and were scurrying home.

The young boy was still yelling at the top of his lungs when the old man stepped up to him and asked, "Who are you carrying on like this here in the dark?"

With that, the man took the boy along with him and returned to his wife upstairs. There the boy gave the elderly couple a complete account of his adventures with the house mice.

Having heard the full story, they laughed at the youth. They explained to him that he was in the village of Oraibi. Also, they did not let him go home. Instead, they urged him to spend the night at their place. During daylight he would certainly be able to get home without a problem. So they gave him some bedding. As a result, he spent the night there and the next morning returned home without any trouble.

This is what the boy from Huk'ovi experienced after encountering these house mice. And because of the events that night the house mice children never got to eat any watermelon.

And here the story ends.

Coyote and the Lice

Aliksa'i. People were living in many settlements across the land, but Coyote lived all by himself at Ismo'wala. To be sure, he had relatives, but he did not live with any one of them. They lived elsewhere.

Coyote of Ismo'wala was a lazy creature. All the time he was planning how to come by something without having to exert himself. So he did not mind devouring carrion whenever he came across some. However, if he failed to find any he was forced to hunt for his food. He had also made it his habit to steal things. The poor devil was a habitual thief. For this reason the other coyotes did not care for him.

In the beginning he lived in the vicinity of his relatives and went about freeloading meals off them. As a result, they did not want him about anymore. One day one of his relatives told him right to his face that he thought he was a moocher. For this Coyote pouted and decided to leave the place. That's why he now lived alone at Ismo'wala.

Southwest of him apparently some lice had taken up residence. Among them were a man, his wife, and their children. In the morning the young ones would go off and play. When evening began to fall, they would return to their home. They never went about during the night. So their parents, never worried about their safety, usually expected them home by evening.

One day an eagle had killed a jackrabbit near his place. After consuming only half of it, he took off, leaving the rest behind. On that same day the young lice happened to be coming through that area and discovered the rabbit carcass. After climbing up on it, they began playing in it. Some of them were clambering in and out of the jackrabbit's head, others were swinging on his whiskers. They were having such great fun that they were totally unaware that Coyote also had arrived on the scene.

Stumbling upon the dead animal made Coyote feel elated. He immediately pounced on the leftovers and began devouring them. As he had not eaten a meal yet that day, he ate with great zest. And so he failed to notice that he gulped down the young lice along with the meat.

Apparently, Coyote had swallowed a large number of the young lice. But since there were so many, he did not eat all of them. Some of them tumbled out of his mouth and others were not inside the hare, so they did not meet with the same fate. This was the misfortune that befell those youngsters.

The few louse children who had been spared returned home crying. Their parents asked them Why the tears? and Why hadn't all of them come home? Usually, they roamed about together in a single group and never split up. Finally, one of them calmed down a bit and, still sobbing, told his parents what had happened.

Father and mother louse in turn now burst into tears. The whole family was lamenting and wailing. It took them quite a long while to regain their composure again.

Coyote had devoured the rabbit with such fervor that he apparently had gulped down some of the meat without chewing it. He therefore did not squash any of the louse children, who were now stranded unharmed in his stomach. However, they were crying because they did not know how to get out.

Coyote did not know this, so it did not bother him. Someone, however, had heard the sobbing of the louse kids. This creature happened to be a parasite. Both animals and humans are often infested with these creatures. The jackrabbit had them, and Coyote had swallowed the parasite without knowing it along with his meal. Because of this the parasite too was imprisoned in Coyote's stomach together with the louse children.

When the parasite heard their crying he approached them. It was completely dark in there, but he headed directly toward the place where the crying came from. Upon finding them he walked up to them and asked, "Why are you poor things crying? Be glad nothing happened to you. So don't carry on like this," he said to them.

One from the louse group replied, "True, we're unharmed, but we have no idea how to get out of here. Also, some of these younger ones are still nursing, so now they are craving their milk and won't stop crying. We don't know what to do with them," he explained.

The parasite said to the lice, "Don't cry. There's bound to be a way out for us. I too have children and am anxious to get out of here. But since I'm alone, I have no means of escaping. I need someone else's help. But if we stick together I'm sure we'll be able to make it." The parasite's reassuring words made the louse kids sob a little less.

The parasite now revealed to them what they were to do. He simply instructed them to follow him. Thus he led them forward in an unknown direction. They had no idea where they were going. After all, it was totally dark inside Coyote's stomach.

Trekking along, they all held each other firmly by the hand, as the parasite, their leader, had directed them to do. For this reason, the very young ones were in between the older ones. From one point on in their journey, the group was going along with their feet sinking into something that stank dreadfully. Along this place the ground was very soggy. They were still sloshing along when the parasite said to them, "We're about to reach our destination. So you back there at the rear gather here up front." Obeying his instructions, they all moved to the front.

When everybody had gathered there, the parasite added, "Just about here there should be an opening to the outside. But it does not open itself just at any time. So all of you climb up on this wall and walk back and forth along it. Sometime later there will be an enormous quake. But don't stop what you're doing. I'll let you know when we'll be going out." Obediently, the lice scrambled up along the wall and did as the parasite had directed.

Evidently the group had reached the rectum of Coyote and was trekking to and fro along his anus. They were approaching the rear end of Coyote, which was the reason they were going along sinking into his turds. This constant stomping all over Coyote's anus caused it to itch. So he scratched his behind, but the itching did not abate. The next time Coyote scratched somewhat harder, but his rear continued to itch. The poor thing sat there scratching and scratching himself. When no change occurred, he began to scrape his butt along the ground. Again there was no improvement. Each time he scratched himself he tried a different method. Meanwhile, quite a bit of time had gone by, yet his behind had not stopped itching.

By now Coyote was nearly going berserk. He was now scratching himself so hard that he had started to bleed. He stopped scratching and now simply dragged his hind end along the ground. Eventually, he did not know how to cope with the itch any longer, so he ran around in circles howling at the top of his lungs. In the process he collided with many objects, as a result of which his body shook fiercely.

When again he bumped headlong into an obstacle, he let out a great fart. As he farted, he blew out all the little lice along with the gust of gas that escaped. They were just blown out of his behind, one after the other. It was like a great windstorm that blew them off a great distance beyond Coyote. And out with them came the parasite. This was how they escaped from Coyote's stomach.

When all the lice had gathered themselves together, they set out for home. It was still daylight outdoors when they arrived. The other family members were overwhelmed with joy to have them back.

This was what happened to the lice that day. For this reason, people say one should not eat only meat. Because that causes one's behind to itch.

And here the story ends.

The Deer Mice

Aliksa'i. People were living in Oraibi and in other settlements all across the land.

Here at Oraibi lived a couple with three children—a teenaged boy and his two younger sisters.

In those days the only source of meat was game animals. So whenever it was time for a ceremony or some other festivity and people wanted to fix some meat for the occasion, they set out hunting, and whatever prey a hunter hauled home on his back was cooked. Of course, not all the hunters were equally skilled, which meant that a poor hunter might return empty-handed. Then again, once in a while, a hunter would arrive home with several kills. He then shared the meat with a relative, especially with a paternal aunt. Others, poor things, were not skilled at all and only once in a great while were fortunate enough to bag an animal.

The teenaged son of the Oraibi couple, as it turned out, was not a good hunter at all. The poor lad had never succeeded in killing any prey. He would roam the land, but he never made a kill. Every time there was a hunt, he participated. But he always failed to return with something for his mother and sisters. Small wonder, then, that they were envious of those who were successful. They used to say, "If only our older brother were lucky just once, we could have a dish of meat. If only he came home with a cottontail or a jackrabbit or two so that for a change we could have a feast." Each time the boy went hunting they talked like this. But it was to no avail. The poor boy probably never would kill anything.

One day, as morning came again, there was snow on the ground. The people were eating breakfast in their homes when the boy's father said to his son, "Why don't you try just one more time? Today snow is blanketing the land, so jackrabbits and cottontails will leave clear tracks behind. When it is like that you can easily follow an animal and catch up with it. Go down the mesa early, when you're done eating. Who knows, you might be lucky and get a couple."

The son agreed. No sooner had he finished breakfast than he began gathering his gear. His younger sisters also did their share by preparing some journey food. The moment he was about to leave the house they handed him the provisions.

The boy set forth in a direction southwest of the village. After descending the southwest side of the mesa and reaching the plain below, he started searching for rabbit tracks. However, not once did he come across a single spoor.

In this fashion the boy slowly moved in a southwesterly direction. He had already put quite a distance between himself and the village when he reached the corner of a mesa. This corner he followed along in northwesterly direction, always looking for prey. Eventually, he came to the end of the corner, but instead of branching off from there, he continued stalking toward the northwest.

Near noon, he passed Apoonivi on its southwest side. He now decided to proceed a little bit further northwest and then turn around again. If he did that, he thought he would make it back to the village by nightfall.

As he continued on, he came upon a man's field and headed through it in a northeasterly direction. He had barely crossed the field when suddenly he heard voices. He had heard them quite clearly. They seemed to be coming from somewhere in the northwest, so he looked in that direction and, much to his surprise, noticed the glow of a fire.

The boy had passed through this area on many previous occasions but had no recollection of anyone living there. Curious to find out who it was, he headed in the direction of the glow. Lo and behold, he soon saw a kiva hatch from which the voices were coming. So he got down on his stomach and looked inside from the edge of the kiva opening.

Down below he saw a large crowd of beings who were engaged in some activity. As he stared at them he realized that all of them were deer mice. They were tiny creatures, amusing in appearance. He had no idea what they were up to. Whatever it was, it was really funny and made him laugh. So he stayed where he was even though it was bitter cold outside. Northwest of the firepit sand had been spread out, and on it a deer mouse lay stretched out. The poor thing was crying out in pain. Again and again he seemed to be trying to get up, but without success. In the end someone came up to him, trying to help him to his feet, but the poor thing could not get up.

He was still trying to help him up when the other deer mice came rushing towards him from all sides, crowding around him. Then they did something to him. Before long someone shouted, "So!" and all of them scattered in every direction. Now the deer mouse who had been lying down managed to stand up, and then he too ran around the kiva. Everyone else then burst into shouting and laughter.

When all the shouting had died down, another deer mouse lay down on the sand. Once again, the rest scurried up to him and did something to him. After they were done and left him, the deer mouse in question, poor thing, was somehow disabled. He tried to get on his feet, but screamed in pain just like the fellow before him. A second time the other deer mice dashed up to him and, scurrying around him, did something to him. Then they ran off again, and the deer mouse in question stood up without any problem.

This routine the deer mice kept up while the boy was lying there by the kiva hatch, watching with fascination. "I wonder what those things are up to down there," he thought. "Well, if I just go in, I should somehow be able to find out." Deciding on this course of action, the boy quickly descended the ladder without announcing his entry. In case the deer mice should ask him why, he would simply reply that he was cold. He would use this lie as a reason to enter.

By now the boy was inside, but none of the deer mice had noticed him. They were wholeheartedly concentrating on what they were doing. When they were finally finished, however, one of them spotted the visitor and alerted the others. The leader of the deer mice came up to him and greeted him. "Are you about, stranger?" he said.

"Yes," the boy replied. "I guess it was not proper of me to simply enter your kiva without first notifying you."

"No harm done. We were so involved in what we were doing that we wouldn't have heard you even if you had called in," the chief replied, and he bade the boy have a seat. The other deer mice were also generously uttering words of welcome. No one complained that he had stepped in unannounced.

The deer mouse chief now took the boy to a place next to the firepit. There both of them squatted down side by side, and the chief told the married and unmarried womenfolk to serve the stranger some food. The women started cooking and while they were engaged in this task, the deer mouse chief shared a pipe with the boy. When this formal smoke was over, he asked the boy why he was around at such a late time of day. The latter explained that he had set out hunting and was on his way home when darkness caught up with him just as he arrived at this place where, much to his surprise, he had discovered the deer mice. He had grown curious as to what they were doing. That was the reason he had entered their home.

"And you didn't kill a single prey, for I see you are empty-handed," the chief continued.

"That's right, not once did I come across a single animal. That's why I carry no load on my back."

"Well, that's really too bad. Come on, eat. I'm glad these women are done cooking. You must be starving. You poor thing, you've been on your feet all day suffering for nothing." With that, the boy settled down to the food that was set out on the floor and ate. When he was stuffed, he said to the deer mice, "Thanks for the meal. I was really starved." He was happy to have eaten. With that he said he would now be moving on home and rose to his feet.

But the deer mouse who had smoked with him would not hear of it. "Stay a little while. It's dark out there. If you walk around in this darkness, you might fall down a cliff somewhere and no one will find you. Also, there's snow on the ground and it's bound to be cold outside." He refused to let the boy leave. The boy briefly thought about it and then agreed to stay.

The deer mice now declared that they were going to resume what they were doing and invited the boy to accompany them. The boy inquired as to exactly what it was they were doing, but they did not reveal anything. Instead, they crowded all around him and pulled him over to the area where the sand was spread out. Having maneuvered him there, they bade him lie down. The boy complied without any objections.

No sooner had he laid down than all the deer mice rushed up to him and touched his body in various ways. Before long they dashed off again and told him to rise to his feet. He was under the impression that they had not really done anything serious to him, but as he placed his hands on the ground and tried to get on his feet, a severe pain shot through his hands. The boy, poor thing, kept massaging them, but the pain did not go away. So badly did his hands hurt that he screamed at the top of his voice. Finally he said to the deer mice, "Ouch, why did you hurt me this way? Help me, please," he pleaded with them.

A second time the deer mice now ran up to him and, having

placed him on the sand again, started touching him. When they were finished, they scattered in all directions and once more bade him rise. This time, as he tried, his hands did not hurt, and so he quickly jumped to his feet. When the deer mice saw that, they all teemed around him again.

Then they dragged him a second time to the sand area. After stretching him out on his back, they went through the same motions as before, only this time they broke his legs. When he tried to get up, he cried out in pain. Before long the deer mice came running back, and when he stood on his feet again without the slightest pain, they crowded around him as before.

This time the deer mice did not continue. Instead, they settled down in various places and just sat there. The boy stared at them in wonderment, impressed by what they were capable of doing. "You really know how to heal," he said to them.

"Yes indeed, we truly have this knowledge. So whenever something happens to one of us, we examine him ourselves by laying hands on him and then we cure him. We do this here each night so we don't forget this skill."

"So that's how you manage to do that. I can't believe how quickly you can heal someone," the boy exclaimed.

The deer mouse leader now said, "If you want to learn this healing skill, we'd be happy to teach you."

The boy, however, showed no interest. "I guess I don't really wish to learn that. It might be a lot of work to practice this skill."

The deer mouse chief replied, "You should really learn this. For no one there at Oraibi is familiar with the healing art. Each time a person falls ill, the poor thing has to go all the way to Walpi to consult a medicine man for treatment. Someone should really take care of people at your village. That's the reason we staged this demonstration for you. We were not just showing off."

The boy thought about it and then agreed. Yes, he really did want to learn the art of healing. He thanked them that they were not holding back their special knowledge. The deer mice, in turn, assured him that he had made the right decision.

Once more now they led the boy to the spread-out sand and placed him on his back. This time, however, they did nothing to him. Instead, they all circled around him chanting a song. As he lay there, he soon fell asleep. Some time later, when the deer mice were done, they woke him up again. He woke up as a medicine man. The deer mice exclaimed, "Thanks! That's the way it's going to be. Now that you are a medicine man you will treat your people. You cannot exclude anyone. You are obliged to help everybody." In this fashion they initiated the boy in the art of healing.

Meanwhile, it was dark night, so the deer mouse leader asked everybody to go to sleep. All of them bedded down, and the boy, too, passed the night there with the deer mice.

The following day, when the boy still had not returned home, his relatives became worried. They checked where he usually slept, but he was not there. That morning when they sat down to breakfast they did not really feel like eating. All sorts of bad thoughts were crossing their minds. Maybe someone or something had attacked him. Maybe he had fallen into a crack and could not get out. It even occurred to them that he could have frozen to death. These were some of the terrible things they were picturing in their minds. Finally the father said, "I'll go search for him. I should at least do that much. Unfortunately, he didn't tell us where he was headed. But I will first set out in a southwesterly direction. I might come across his footprints somewhere and be able to track him down. There hasn't been any wind, so his tracks must still be visible." With that, he grabbed his blanket and announced that the would go after his son. He took some journey food along for the boy because the two girls and her mother had prepared some for both of them. And so he started out from the village in a southwesterly direction.

Meanwhile, the deer mice too were waking up at their home. After all of them had breakfasted the boy announced that he would have to leave shortly. "I had no luck hunting yesterday, so I must return home and hunt on the way. If I don't get home soon, people will worry about me." With that, he thanked the deer mice. He told them how glad he was that they were living there and that he did not have to sleep out in the cold. Also, he assured them that with what they had taught him he would try to benefit his people.

"You just go along without worrying about hunting. We also put that ability in you last night, so from now on you'll be a skilled hunter. On your way home you're bound to kill at least one prey."

"Is that a fact? Thanks, indeed. I owe it to you if I succeed. May you live here without sickness and with happiness in your hearts. I'll go now, but I won't forget you." With these words he departed.

Instead of heading toward the base of the mesa, the boy now moved along stalking game in a southeasterly direction. He still had not made it very far when he bagged his first cottontail. He did so without great effort. He continued on and quickly dispatched another one. He noticed that the cottontails and jackrabbits seemed to be showing themselves to him, offering themselves so to speak. Wherever one of them ran into a hole, his tracks were clearly visible. And even when one was hiding inside a bush, he would see him clearly, much to his amazement. He had not covered a great distance yet and already he had seven big kills. Since his load had gotten quite heavy, he decided that seven was enough. So he quit hunting and steadily hiked homeward with the rabbits slung over his shoulders. First, however, he headed to Leenangw Spring to quench his thirst. Then he headed straight for the village.

Just as he was approaching Oraibi from the southwest, his father was descending the mesa on the southwest side too. The boy's father was still too far away to recognize him. He only thought, "I won't pursue my son's tracks for the time being; instead I'll walk up to that stranger and ask if maybe he's seen him." With this thought on his mind he hurried to meet that person.

Eventually, when the two were getting closer to each other, the father did recognize his son, and the minute he came up to him he embraced him. With a lump in his throat he said, "Thanks that you are unhurt and on your way home. When you did not return, we got worried, so I started out to search for you. I see you killed a lot of rabbits. What a surprise! Well, let's go home. Everybody is bound to be waiting for you." With these words he relieved his son of a few of his rabbits and then they went home together.

Sure enough, when the father arrived with his son, the boy's mother and his younger sisters were overjoyed to have him back. Also, they were elated about all the prey he had brought. In happy spirits they set to skinning the rabbits. When they were done with this chore, they lit their pit oven and in it roasted the boy's prey, together with sowitangu'viki. Soon everything was cooked, and the whole family ate with great gusto.

From that day on all of them lived again happy in their hearts. Each time the boy went hunting now, he killed game without fail. So the family now also ate meat for meals just like the other people. Whenever there was a special festivity at the village, they too had a big stew with meat like the rest of the people.

As time passed the days got warmer again. Now the men and boys went down to the plain below to tend their fields. The women and girls, in turn, had their many kinds of responsibilities in the village that they were busy carrying out. The boy's younger sisters, meanwhile, had reached an age where they could also help, so their mother fashioned a water canteen for each of them with which they could haul water.

Long ago, when a woman decided to plaster her house, she would tell someone to fetch water. So the younger of the two girls volunteered to carry water for her mother. Since she had just received her canteen, she was looking forward to this task and showed no signs of laziness. Later she asked her mother if she could plaster the house wall with the help of her older sister, and her mother said yes.

So the girl went to haul water. She had made two trips, and before long she returned a third time to the spring. This time, as she descended the trail, she failed to see a little rock right on the path and slipped on it. She struck the ground hard and hurt herself badly. Her new water canteen, poor thing, was shattered to smithereens. The girl tried to get back on her feet, but could not do so, for the pain was too great. She had no choice but to lie where she was and wait for someone to come along and help her.

Quite a bit of time had already passed, and still no one came. The girl shouted, "If anyone hears me, please come help me. It looks like I hurt myself pretty bad." In this way the poor girl kept yelling there, but nobody was nearby and came down the trail.

Meanwhile, when the youngest girl failed to return to her mother and sister at the village, the two began to wonder why. After all, it was not very far down to the spring. So the woman sent her daughter after her. In this way the girl came across her younger sister lying on the trail. She tried to load her onto her back but could not lift her. So she went to fetch her mother in the village, and then the two together brought her back to the house.

This had just happened when the girl's father and her brother were returning from the field. When they saw the condition the girl was in, they were very unhappy. The father declared he would go to Walpi the following day and take her to a medicine man for treatment.

The boy objected, "Don't take her to Walpi. That's too far. If you carry her all the way, she'll be in great pain. Why don't I examine her after we have eaten? Maybe I can help her."

The father would not hear of that and replied, "Don't try anything on her, because you might do something wrong. You don't know anything about healing and might seriously injure her if you do that yourself." The boy said nothing in return.

After the meal, however, the boy secretly examined his older sister. The girl was still in great pain, but as he was checking her out he recognized what the problem was. The girl's hip had been dislocated. That's the reason she was in such pain and was unable to walk. As soon as her brother laid hands on her, the pain subsided. He asked his sister, however, not to tell anyone for the time being. As a result of her brother's treatment the girl slept comfortably that night, without feeling any pain.

The following morning, after breakfast, the girl would not let her father take her to Walpi. "I think I'm healed. It doesn't hurt any more. Put me on my feet and I'll try to walk around." At first her father refused, but the girl would not relent. Finally, her father helped her stand up. True enough, she had no trouble whatsoever walking about. The father was curious as to how she had been healed so suddenly. The girl now revealed that her brother had laid hands on her the night before. As a result she had awakened completely healed. Everyone looked at the boy in great amazement, wondering how on earth he had cured the girl.

From that day on the boy would heal anyone who sought him out. As soon as the word spread among the people, they started flocking to him. When they learned about him, even people from other villages came to the boy for treatment. Because of what had happened to him at the deer mouse kiva, he now was able to take care of the people. He became really famous.

The boy did not forget the deer mice and every so often visited them at their home. Each time he paid them a visit he brought them a gift. Also, each time when he was there, he worked with them on a medical problem so he would not forget his healing art. He always stayed until the next day and then returned home. I guess he's still going there.

And here the story ends.

20

How Mockingbird Took a Wife

Aliksa'i. People were living at Oraibi. Among them was a girl who did not love anyone, even though boys constantly flocked to her house. They kept bringing her all sorts of presents, but she steadfastly refused to marry any one of them.

Pavayoykyasi evidently had also heard of the girl, so he said, "Let me give it a try too." He therefore fashioned all the things required by a bride, the two wedding robes, one large and one small, the large sash, the wedding boots, and the reed container. Then he went over to Oraibi and headed straight to the girl's house. The girl was grinding corn when he arrived. Pavayoykyasi set down his bundle outside the house and entered.

Without ceasing her grinding, the girl inquired as to the purpose for his coming. The young man replied, "I came because of you. I left my bundle of gifts outside. Go get it and take a look at the things inside. They are yours if you want to live with me. That's the reason I am about."

The girl brought in the young man's bundle and inspected everything. The wedding things it contained were truly beautiful. All of them had a yellowish hue. However, the girl said to Pavayoykyasi that she was not interested and did not want them.

"Very well," the young man replied resignedly and returned back home. His attempt at winning the girl had failed.

Rooster also made his home at Oraibi. He had learned of Pavayoykyasi's unsuccessful visit to the girl's home. Therefore he too decided to seek her out. And so he did. The girl was roasting her coarsely ground cornmeal when he arrived. Without delay he entered the girl's house and was looking at her belongings when she came in behind him. Rooster, of course, was dressed magnificently. Not only did he wear a beautiful red shirt, but he had tied a red feather to his head also. From his ears dangled long turquoise earrings. Rooster's entire appearance was that of a gentleman. The girl asked, "What brings you here?"

"Well, yes, I came because of you, of course. I would like to get married to you and so I came to fetch you."

Rooster was friendly and courteous, so the girl readily accepted his proposal. "All right," she said, "let's indeed get married."

Rooster was elated and replied, "Four days from now I will come for you and take you with me." With that he left for home.

The four days were not up yet, but already Rooster was on his way to the girl again. It so happened that at a place southeast of Oraibi Mockingbird had made his home. He saw Rooster arriving at the girl's house and said to himself, "I have to go to her too. Then I'll settle down with her." As he said this he headed over to the girl's home.

Rooster was still at the girl's house when suddenly Mockingbird arrived and declared, "I am going to marry this girl."

The two now became really possessive of the girl. Rooster cried, "No way, I won't have that. After all, I'm chief here at Oraibi. It is I who, at the crack of dawn, first breaks the silence with my crowing. All the villagers then rouse from sleep."

"Me too," Mockingbird shot back. "I also utter my calls early in the morning, and it gets daylight. I suggest we test each other's powers. Let's see whose call really makes it get light. We'll compete four days from now to determine which of us is more powerful."

Rooster agreed. Then both he and Mockingbird returned home. No sooner had Rooster arrived than he began to ponder his situation. "I wonder whom I might ask for help." This is what he kept mulling over in his mind. Early the following day he set out in a northwesterly direction. He ran as fast as his legs would carry him, always straight northwest. Eventually he came to a place called Awat'ovi. Since he had been running extremely fast, he was completely exhausted when he reached the top of the bluff. He had to take a rest, and as he sat there catching his breath he heard a voice. "Come over here," it said. Much to his surprise the voice belonged to a girl. She now approached Rooster. "Come on in," she urged him. Rooster obeyed and entered.

As it turned out, a great many girls were living there. They welcomed Rooster politely and made him feel at ease. One of the girls disappeared into a back room, and when she came out she had some corn kernels on a tray. These she placed in front of Rooster and bade him eat. "Here, have some food and then you can travel on again. Once you've eaten something your strength is bound to return."

Rooster devoured the meal. When he was finished he expressed his gratitude to the girls. "Thanks for feeding me. I'll be on my way now." So saying, he got up and continued on his journey.

Once more Rooster headed in a northwesterly direction. Sure enough, he really felt revived by the meal. And so he finally reached Moencopi. Without halting he bore straight ahead. In a while he came to a canyon. He descended into its depths, followed it for a while, and in due time emerged on the other side of the gorge. From there he continued in a southeasterly direction.

At long last he reached his destination at the base of a cliff. He immediately began to crow, and after calling out four times at the top of his lungs, the cliff opened up. Rooster entered. Lo and behold, there was a multitude of chicken fowl there: men, women, boys, and girls. They greeted him happily. "Have a seat, you who are about. It's been a long time since you were here last." With words like these the chickens welcomed him. They too served him corn kernels for a meal.

When he had finished eating they inquired of him, "Well, you must have come for a purpose."

"Indeed, I have. I'm in a contest with Mockingbird over a girl at Oraibi. In four days we intend to test our strength. That's what we decided. For this reason I came. Maybe you can help me win that girl."

"Of course we can. Rest assured, we'll help you in this test."

Mockingbird, meanwhile, after arriving back home, called the giant bird Kwaatoko to his side. "Four days from now Rooster and I will compete for a girl at Oraibi. I want you to come too and be there on that day," Mockingbird requested.

Kwaatoko agreed and promised to be there on the appointed day.

In turn the chicken folk beyond Moencopi now began their magic work. They chanted four long songs. Upon finishing they all crowed in unison at the top of their lungs. Once more they sang four long songs, and again they crowed loudly when they were done. They repeated the singing a third time and ended it as before. As they were chanting for the fourth time, they completed only two songs before they crowed as loud as they could. Then their leader said, "We did everything correctly. It will now get daylight." Sure enough, they sang the two remaining songs, and it became light.

When the whole undertaking was successfully completed, the leader of the chickens was elated. "Things are bound to work out for you now," he assured Rooster. "You can go home now without worrying about your challenge anymore. Have something to eat first, though, and then you can leave."

Once again Rooster was given a big meal and then set out for home, following the same route back that he had taken on his way there. After a while he began to feel really tired and by the time he neared Awat'ovi he was staggering along. As before, he encountered the girls, who were glad about his coming. "I'm exhausted," Rooster cried. "I can't make it back to Oraibi."

"Once you've eaten you'll gain your strength back," the girl assured him.

They served him another meal, but when Rooster was finished he said, "I won't make it back to Oraibi. I'm just too tired."

"Don't worry, we'll fix that. We know a trick that will make you run. That way you're bound to reach Oraibi." With that they fastened a few cornhusks to his tail.

Now Rooster started forth once again. He went a little distance in a southeasterly direction and then fell into a run. No sooner had he started to run than the cornhusks made sounds behind him. This so frightened Rooster that he dashed off with great vigor and reached Oraibi in no time. Only when he arrived at his home did he remove the husks from his tail. That done, he felt greatly relieved. No doubt, the girls had managed to help him.

Before long it was time for the contest. On the night of the fourth day Mockingbird headed over to Rooster's house. Upon his arrival he exclaimed, "All right, let's find out about each other now and see who is stronger. You go first," he said to Rooster.

"Very well, I'm going to beat you."

With that Rooster began to sing. He sang four long songs, where-upon it started to dawn. He sang twice more and was about to end when Kwaatoko spread his wings out to the full size of the sun. Rooster kept chanting and chanting, but daylight would not come. Kwaatoko's wings blocked all of the sun's light. That is what Mock-ingbird had told the giant bird to do. Finally, Mockingbird said to Rooster, "I'm afraid you did not succeed. It did not get daylight. Let me have a go at it now."

Both of them headed over to Mockingbird's house. Upon arriving there Mockingbird said, "All right, now it's going to be my turn." With that he started to utter his calls. No sooner did he make his first call than it became daylight, for Kwaatoko moved aside at that very same moment. "You beat me," Rooster admitted. "Your powers are greater than mine. So you can marry the girl." With that he departed for home.

Mockingbird immediately rushed to the girl's house. Upon his arrival he said, "I beat Rooster at his game. So I am going to live with you."

And so the two got married. As time went by Mockingbird's wife gave birth. She delivered twins, a baby boy and a baby girl. Life went on after that for the people of Oraibi. As it turned out, however, one of the twins, the little boy, was Rooster's child. The little girl, on the other hand, was Mockingbird's child. As the years passed, several people in Oraibi in turn became the offspring of these twins. It so happened that those who were descended from Mockingbird, like a girl, never quit talking. And those who were descended from the little boy were all gentle and never ill-tempered.

   This is how the Oraibis were created as offspring of those two. Evidently for this reason, those who trace back their ancestry to Mockingbird are all chatterboxes, while those descended from Rooster are nice to other people.

   And here the story ends.

21

The Owl That Made Off with a Little Child

Aliksa'i. They were living in Oraibi. Long ago, a great number of people used to live at that village. Among them was a couple who had a child. The child was never satisfied and always wanted this and that. Generally in the evening, during suppertime, was when it displayed this poor behavior. It kept asking for things and constantly was in a bad mood. When the parents scolded the child, it would burst into tears and simply did not stop crying. Telling it to quit was of no use, so the parents usually went along with its wishes. But even then it kept wailing. Once in a while, the parents got so weary of the child's behavior that they took it outside and left it there.

One evening at the supper hour, the child started to act up once more. Again it wanted things done its way. The woman's husband had gone to the kiva and the mother and child were alone. The child wanted something special and began to howl. The mother grew angry and said, "Stop crying, will you? If you don't quit, I'll throw you out to the owls!" The child, however, was not about to heed this warning. So the mother, tired of the child's obnoxious behavior, grabbed it, opened the door and cast it outside. There the little thing continued its wailing until, some time later, it fell asleep, all huddled up in a corner.

Owls make a habit of being out and about at night when it's dark. As a rule, they perch on the rooftops, and this was the case when the woman cast the little child outside. Immediately, an owl leaped from its perch and winged down to the child. "You poor thing," it said, "did your mother throw you out?" The child remained silent. "You poor babe, I'll take you along," said the owl, and it loaded the child on its back and flew off. The owl carried the child all the way to Mongwupsö, where it had a nest. The owl had children of its own, and when it got there, it placed the little child next to them in the nest. It did not devour it.

When the child's father came home from the kiva, he asked his wife, "Where is our child?" The woman, who suddenly remembered what she had done, replied, "It wanted this and that again, so when it started crying, I set it outside. I'm sure it's still out there somewhere."

The two went out to search, but the child was nowhere in sight. They went around from house to house asking for their child, but were not able to find it. Having failed to locate their child, the couple finally went to bed. But sleep would not come. The woman was sorry now that she had thrown the child out. The next day the husband and wife searched again. They looked all over the village, but to no avail. They questioned all the people, but no one could help them. No one had any idea where the child had disappeared to. Not knowing what to do, the couple became quite despondent. They were sure that the child had been taken by some creature.

And so time passed. One day a young man from Oraibi went hunting near Hotevilla Spring. As he was stalking the area, he became thirsty and decided to go down to the spring for a drink. After quenching his thirst, he climbed back up to the mesa and followed its edge in an northeasterly direction. There to the northeast of Hotevilla is a large point, which he crossed at the top. As he did he thought he heard a voice. Listening carefully, he determined that the noise was coming from the northwest side of the point. When he headed to that side and peeked over he discovered, much to his surprise, a nest with young owls in it, and in their midst a little child. The child was beginning to grow feathers like an owl. Its eyes, too, were starting to turn yellow like an owl's. The young man could hardly believe what he saw and thought, "I wonder whose child this is." With that he stopped hunting and immediately returned home.

As soon as the hunter reached Oraibi, he spread the word that he had come across an owl's nest with a human child in it. Someone with him at the time suggested, "That may well be the child of that couple. Remember, some time back they were searching for their child. They said it had disappeared. So it's quite possible it is theirs. I'll go over to them and tell them about it." With that he left and headed over to the couple's house.

There the man related what the young hunter had said. He told them that the lad had been hunting at Hotevilla when he discovered an owl's nest with a little child in it. According to the hunter the child's body was already beginning to grow feathers just like an owl. The couple replied, "Ask the young man who saw all of this to come here. We want him to take us there."

Upon his return to the young hunter, the man related to him what the couple wanted and the lad went over to them. Both husband and wife urged him to take them to the spot where he found the child, and he agreed. A few other people also volunteered to come along. The man's wife, however, did not join the group.

The hunter led the men to the place. When they arrived, what the hunter had said turned out to be true. When they peeked down the cliff they found the child sitting in the nest. It was the lost child. One man was lowered down to the nest. He took the child out, enfolded it in his arms, and then the two were pulled up again. They were just to the top of the cliff when the owl that had taken the child in the first place flew up to the men and said, "This child was clearly cast out. That's whey I brought it here." Addressing the child's father in particular, the owl continued, "When you reach home with your child, you and your wife must seal it up in a room. There you must keep it for four days. You cannot look in on it during this time. Not until the fourth day, after sunrise, may you look in. If you fail to do this, you will lose your child forever."

And so the men returned home with the child. And it was really true, it had feathers just like an owl, and its eyes were yellow. Upon handing it over to his wife, the husband said, "We're supposed to put our child into a room and then seal the door."

This the couple did, following the owl's instructions exactly. After putting the child in an inner room, they plastered the entrance shut. They then simply waited while the little child was in there. The first day passed, and then the second. The parents heard their child doing things in there and saying all sorts of things. The mother, meanwhile, could hardly sit still. The way she behaved in the house clearly indicated that she strongly wanted to look in. On the third day she came all the way to the door, but did not open it. She had a powerful desire to peek in, but then she put her desire aside again and did not. On the morning of the fourth day she got up at the crack of dawn. Turning to her husband, she said again and again, "Its the fourth day now. Let's open the door!"

Her husband, however, refused. "Remember, the owl bade us not to open the door until after sunrise." But his wife could not hold back any longer. "After all, this is the fourth day," she kept insisting. "Everything will be fine. Let's just open up," she said again and again.

The husband did not agree with his wife. Nevertheless, the sun had still not risen when the woman could not hold back any longer and went over to the door. It so happened that there was a small crack in the door, and when she saw this she peeked in. No sooner had she done so than the doorway burst open. The plaster that had covered it flew in every direction and an owl emerged. It quickly flew outside and then towards Hotevilla.

When the man realized what had happened, he grew angry. "I had a feeling that his would happen, for you simply would not listen. The owl definitely told us not to open the door before sunrise. But you would not listen and had to peek in. Now we've lost our child for good," he reproached his wife. "We'll never get it back again. This means we'll have to be without a child." He was very angry with his wife, so much so that his wife began to cry. But, of course, all of her crying was in vain.

This is how the couple lost its child. It was all the woman's fault. One should not cast out one's child at night if it cries, for an owl may take it and not give it back.

And here the story ends.

22

How Coyote and Hummingbird Satirized Bat in a Song

Aliksa'i. People were living in Oraibi. All across the land they were settled in villages. At Ismo'wala Coyote had made his home. Northwest of Oraibi, up the slope from the water cisterns in a northeasterly direction, lies a promontory by the name of Kosantuyqa. Here Hummingbird had his home. Northeast from there extends a cliff wall on the southeast side of which is tucked away a rock shelter called Nawayvösö. There Bat had made his home. All three of them were friends and regularly visited each other.

Coyote had never paid a visit to the home of Hummingbird or Bat. Instead, he would ask them to come to his place. There, all together, they had a great time talking about all sorts of things that came to mind. At times they laughed their heads off. Occasionally, they planned something special, which they then did. For example, they would gamble. Way back in the past the ancient ones had a custom of playing totolospi and sosotukwpi. The former was a board game, the latter a game involving sleight of hand. Whenever they played these gambling games they stayed awake deep into the night before they returned home. But since Hummingbird and Bat could fly they were home in no time. Bat lived in a recess under the rock over-hang and simply hung from the ceiling when he slept.

Coyote, of course, is a varmint that is always roaming about hunting. Upon killing his prey he was accustomed to set it aside for later use, and because he killed all sorts of animals, he always had a big supply of meat. From time to time Coyote would then invite his friends to come and feast with him. Accepting his invitation, they ate all kinds of meat dishes. Usually, they ate with great gusto.

One day it occurred to Bat that he should be entertaining his friends. He thought of asking them over for a meal. However, he had nothing to offer, for he had never killed a prey in his life. The poor thing had nothing and had no idea what to feed to his friends. He pondered and pondered the matter. Then he thought of the people of Oraibi. Long ago the ancient ones would kill a pronghorn and cut its meat into flat thin slices. These they would then drape over storage beams that were attached to the ceiling and leave them there to dry until winter. When the jerky was dry they used it in different ways. They roasted it on embers, crushed it in a mortar, or cooked gravy from it. The pulverized jerky they ate together with parched corn by pinching bits of it with the fingers. Bat now remembered all these various recipes for eating pronghorn. He therefore decided to head over to Oraibi and go from house to house, hoping to luck out some-where and bring some jerky home. He was set on stealing it. He would then have something to serve to his friends.

Bat had to wait for a while yet. He knew that he would not be able to go until it became dusk. Finally, when it was dark outside, he headed over to Oraibi. Upon getting there he flew around in the village. However, he failed to find anything and had to return home empty-handed. He was not happy about this, poor thing, because he had nothing to feed his friends. He did not sleep well that night worrying about the matter.

In this fashion Bat made it to the following morning. As a rule, bats spend the daylight hours asleep, so he could not hunt around for any creatures. So he sat up all day long and kept racking his brains about what to do. Finally he thought it would be best to return to the village and search for a vent hole in a house. If he spotted one he could get inside through it and search in the back room. In this way he might find what he was looking for.

Once more Bat waited until evening fell and nighttime came. It still was not totally dark when he left his place and headed over to Oraibi. As he flew about he would seek out some people's home and look for a vent hole. By now, all the lights were out and the people were in bed. Eventually, he entered through one vent hole and flew around inside. As he did this he found what he wanted—jerked meat that was hung out to dry. He helped himself to one slice by peeling it off the storage beam to which it was clinging. Having done that he came out through the vent hole again and carried the jerky back to Nawayvösö. Upon leaving it there in a safe place, he returned to the house. To be sure, the piece of meat he had stolen was big, but it was not enough to fill all of their stomachs. This was the reason he had to go back. So once again he grabbed a slice and carried it home. Three times he repeated this process until he had stored away three slices of jerky.

It now occurred to Bat that they would need something else to go with the meat, so he headed back to Oraibi and searched around until he spotted a container with piki. This time he had a cloth wrap with him into which he put several pieces of the wafer bread and then hauled them back to Nawayvösö. No sooner had he stashed away his booty than he remembered something else. They would need some salt. So Bat flew back once more and searched until he found some. He packed a small quantity into a bag and carried it home. Only now was he satisfied and felt that he could settle down. He was happy for he now had stored away plenty for his friends to eat. In this happy frame of mind he slept.

The next morning Bat visited his friends Coyote and Hummingbird and invited them to come and have lunch with him. As it was getting noontime he already had a fire going in his firepit. He knew he would have to roast something if his friends came, so he had the fire going ahead of time. Apparently, he also had a kiva there in the rock shelter where he lived.

A thump on the roof of Bat's underground home announced Coyote's arrival. Bat bade his visitor enter. Coyote stepped in and was surprised to see the huge fire. That very moment Bat placed the meat into the pit. Pushing the embers apart he buried the stolen meat slices deep inside to cook them.

Before long, Hummingbird too showed up. Bat asked him in with welcoming words. "Have a seat," he urged him, "you couldn't have come at a better time. I'm just getting my roast going. As soon as it is done, we can eat," he kept saying.

Waiting for the roast to get done the three friends talked to each other. When the meat was cooked, Bat did not take it out right away. Instead, he laid the piki onto a platter and set it out on the floor. Next, he poured water into a bowl and dumped the salt in. This he kept stirring, for it was rock salt that he had used. Coyote and Hummingbird watched in amazement and were wondering where on earth Bat had gotten these things. They were surprised that he owned piki and rock salt in the first place. Every so often the two glanced at each other in disbelief. Bat now dug the meat out of the embers and served it. From all appearances it was meat with lots of fat. All three now fell to eating. Since Bat had also provided salt water, they dunked their piki into it as they munched away. They ate abundantly. Coyote and Hummingbird thanked Bat for the feast. When all of them were full they moved away from where the food was set out and began to talk. Bat had an inkling that his friends would ask him where he had gotten the food he was dishing out to them, so he wondered how to come up with a story and whom to attribute his lies to. Coyote and Hummingbird knew full well Bat would never be able to make a kill. If he told them that, they would never believe him. Now, over there at Honansikya, Badger had his home, so Bat decided to name him as the one responsible.

After a length of time Coyote said, "What a delicious meal we had!"

"I couldn't agree more," Bat replied.

"Where did you get all these delicacies you fed us?" Coyote continued.

Bat said, "Badger gave them to me. It's thanks to him that I was able to serve you this food." Both of Bat's friends nodded, but they did not believe a word. Finally, the two indicated that they were ready to go home. "Thanks for the lunch. We'll be on our way now," Coyote and Hummingbird said and departed at the same time from Bat's place at Nawayvösö.

The two climbed up through a box canyon somewhere and then continued on from there, talking about Bat as they went. They were convinced that they had been lied to. "No way Badger could have given him all of that," they kept saying. They simply would not believe it. As they passed Kosantuyqa to the southeast, Hummingbird turned off into a different direction. "All right, from here I'll go alone," he said to Coyote, whereupon he headed toward Kosantuyqa. Coyote in turn ran along the southeast side of Taalawtuyqa, descended Oraibi mesa on its southwest side, and from there continued to his home at Ismo'wala.

When he got home Coyote still was thinking, "I wonder where Bat got all the meat he fed us." The question really intrigued him. Before long, Hummingbird showed up at Coyote's place, only to talk about Bat again. Coyote, who could not get the matter out of his mind, finally said, "I suggest we satirize Bat in a song. Let's compose something along those lines."

The two were of one mind. It was obvious to them that Bat had stolen the meat. Somehow they had figured out that they had been lied to and were now wondering how best to put this into a song. Racking their brains over how to put the song together they tried and tried but did not succeed. "Let's leave it be for the time being," Hummingbird finally said. "We'll get it done somehow. I want to return home and go to bed."

So the two went home. Then both of them worked by themselves on the problem of how to phrase the song. By the following day Coyote had finished his version and immediately headed over to

Hummingbird at Kosantuyqa. "Come to my place," he said, "I've finished the song, so now we can learn it by heart."

"All right," Hummingbird replied, "I'll see you later."

When sundown was near, Hummingbird had an early supper. As soon as he was done he set out for Ismo'wala, for he had not forgotten Coyote. He went to Coyote's place to learn the song. Upon his arrival he climbed to the rooftop of Coyote's underground place. He perched on the ladder that stuck out from the hatch and called down, "Haw!"

"Come on in!" Coyote replied. "Have you come?"

"Yes," Hummingbird replied and entered.

"There, have a seat," Coyote said. Offering Hummingbird a comfortable place to sit, he made him feel at home. When Hummingbird was settled down Coyote said, "Let's not mess around now. We should get right to it and learn this song. I'll sing it to you first and when you learn it, we can sing it together."

With that, Coyote began to sing and teach Hummingbird the song. Each time they stopped, the two had to laugh. They were laughing at the expense of Bat, who was unaware of this, of course. He probably thought they would not figure this out. So he had no idea that they were composing a song about him. Coyote and Hummingbird were really upset that Bat had fed them stolen food. As Coyote was singing his voice sounded like thunder. As Hummingbird joined in, he did so with his tiny voice. Thus, when they chanted together, one did so in a booming voice and the other sang in an extremely high voice.

Hummingbird said, "That's enough for the time being. Let's continue tomorrow. By tomorrow I should have memorized the song. As soon as I know it really well, we can get up and dance with it. When we are done practicing we'll ask Bat over here. We can all come here then and dance together." This is how the two laid out their plan.

With that, Hummingbird left to go to bed. Upon arriving home, he was all alone, yet still he could not help but laugh out loud at Bat when he reflected about the matter. Finally, he fell asleep.

The next morning, as Hummingbird woke up, he still remembered everything. When evening came, he headed over to Coyote

again. Reaching Ismo'wala, he entered Coyote's place. "Have you
come?" Coyote said.

"Yes," replied Hummingbird.

"All right, let's start again. I already had my supper a while ago."

Once more the two friends sang together. Each time they ended
the song they had to laugh. It was just too funny. Finally, they had the
song memorized, so they stood up to practice the dance steps. Coyote
said to Hummingbird, "All right, you must start the song."

Hummingbird, however, did not want the role of the song starter.
"No, you start," he countered.

Coyote objected. "I'd like you to do the starting. I'll pick up the
tune after you. For if I begin, Bat will realize that I was the one who
composed the song. So you be the starter."

Hummingbird kept saying, "It should not be that way."

Coyote, however, persisted until Hummingbird had to consent.
As both got into standing position, Coyote had the rattle. So he gave
it to Hummingbird. And so, standing there in front of the niche at the
far end of the kiva under the stone bench, Hummingbird shook the
rattle. Then he began to sing and Coyote joined in with his booming
voice. Poor Hummingbird, in turn, could only sing in a high pitch. In
this manner they kept practicing there. By the time they were finished
they were really enjoying themselves.

After two repetitions of the song Coyote said, "All right, that will
do for now. Tomorrow I will go and tell Bat. So let's go visit him
tomorrow. We'll talk first as usual and then, at a later time, we will
urge him to dance with us. Since we three haven't learned a song
together, we'll simply rehearse with ours." This is how the two con-
spired. After that Hummingbird left for home to go to bed.

The next day the two were going to carry out their plan. Coyote
started out by going hunting first. Giving the village of Oraibi a wide
birth along its southeastern side, he slowly headed in the direction of
Bat's home at Nawayvösö. Upon reaching Bat's place Coyote asked
him to come along. He told him that he had been hunting, that he had

bagged a prey, and that he was inviting him to a meal. Bat gladly accepted the invitation. "All right, I'll be there," he assured Coyote.

"By all means," Coyote replied. "I'll have a roast, so come for supper. Let our friend Hummingbird also know on your way. I suggest you two come together." In this manner Coyote instructed Bat. Then he ran straight home. He did not bother to stop at Hummingbird's because Hummingbird already knew what was going on.

As soon as Coyote got home he skinned his prey and roasted it. Just in time for evening, his jackrabbit was nicely cooked and juicy, so he dug it out of the embers and waited for his guests. Before long he heard them coming. No doubt, it was Hummingbird and Bat. "Hey! How about some words of welcome?" he heard them calling in.

"Come on down, strangers," Coyote shouted back.

Sure enough, the two that entered were his friends. Coyote was being exceedingly hospitable to them. "All right, you two, make yourselves comfortable. You came just in time. I dug up the roast a while ago, so we are ready to eat."

With that, Coyote set his jackrabbit roast out in front of them. He also had salt, so they dipped their food into salt water while they ate it. In this manner the three friends feasted and devoured everything with great gusto. When they were finished, Coyote cleared the dishes away and then they sat there passing the time. As always they were talking about all sorts of things and kept laughing. After a while Coyote remarked, "I've been thinking about something."

"Let's hear it. What is it?" Hummingbird and Bat asked.

"We really should entertain each other for once."

"All right, what shall we do?"

"Let's have a dance. I think we really should stage a dance."

Bat inquired, "What will we use for a song?"

"Well, as long as we just rehearse we can use any old song," Coyote replied.

Hummingbird and Bat had no objections and readily agreed. Bat added, "Yes, indeed, let's dance."

All three of them rose from their seats and lined up, one after the other, in the area in front of the niche at the far end of the kiva under the stone bench. When everybody was in position Coyote said to Bat, "You go first," and placed him to the front of the line. Bat complied. Then he turned to Hummingbird and said, "And you be the song starter." As before, Hummingbird did not really want that role. Coyote himself was going to be the last in line.

Finally, they were ready, so the tiny Hummingbird began to sing. What a skinny thing he was there in the middle. And Coyote, the big guy, at the end of the line like a huge stopper. In this line all three began to stomp in tune to the following song:

> Bat, Bat
> Is hanging by his heels, is hanging by his heels.
> Shit is plastered all over his legs,
> Is plastered all over his legs.
> He's only got an empty house, only an empty house.
> Bat, Bat
> Has no fat.
> And keeps no meat.
> To his buddies stolen meat
> He serves as stew, he serves as stew.
> He's only got an empty house, only an empty house.

This is how their song went. This was only the upward verse, so they were going to start the downward portion. Bat so far had not noticed a thing and was stomping with great enthusiasm.

So they began the downward verse, and it was not until they were about to get to the upward part again when Bat finally caught on. He jerked to a stop and exclaimed, "You are making fun of me in that song. Someone must have told you what I did." He was furious. "This is the last time I'll come here. We're not going to be friends any longer." Bat said this and was quickly gone from Coyote's house.

Coyote and Hummingbird now too stopped dancing and just stood there. Finally they said, "Too bad he noticed what we were up to. He shouldn't have served us that meat. He who can't kill on his own just went somewhere and stole it," they kept reproaching him. They were slightly upset. But then they too had eaten the stolen meat, so they thought they might get the holes in their stomachs everyone said you would get for eating stolen meat. After all, they had shared the stolen food with Bat. They were not at all happy about the effect of their song. "We won't have him as our friend anymore. Let him alone suffer from kleptomania." That's what Coyote and Hummingbird said to each other. But they felt sorry that they had satirized him, and so for a while they said nothing to each other. Then Hummingbird left. After that the three never again went to visit one another. They simply forgot each other and disappeared. Since they broke up their friendship, none of them was interested in the others anymore. I guess those three still live somewhere.

And here the story ends.

23

How Weasel Befriended the Moon

Aliksa'i. People were living at Oraibi. Somewhere northeast of Pivan-honkyapi Weasel had made his home. Because the poor thing lived all by himself, he was thinking of finding a friend. For this reason he roamed the area far and wide, but usually without success. He even ventured into the village of Oraibi, for he had seen dogs and cats there among the houses. He would not refuse them if they wanted to be friends so he went among them. The dogs, however, always chased him and barked at him. So he failed to make friends with any of them. And since the poor thing lived all alone, no one ever sought him out. Nobody ever came to visit him.

Once in a while Weasel left at night to search for someone to be his friend. On one such night as he was roaming the area again, he was passing alongside a big gorge, and since he was a little tired, he sat down somewhere to rest. Sitting there right by the edge of the gorge he looked about. It so happened that at that very moment the moon appeared in view. After a while it had traveled way up in the sky. At first, Weasel did not give this any more thought, and when the moon had gone up as high as it could go, he headed back home. It took him a fairly long time to return, and when he finally reached his house he immediately went to bed.

The following night Weasel once more left his house and sauntered forth. He returned to the very spot where he had rested the night before and settled down. Sitting there he waited for the moon. And, indeed, he was still sitting there when the moon rose again. Weasel sat there for a long while, and by the time the moon had gone up as high as it could go he had grown tired. He was sleepy, so he decided to go back home. As soon as he was back he slept again. The following morning, after eating breakfast, he remained at home. As he sat there his thoughts went out to the moon. Each time it had risen all by itself and then traveled on all by itself. At no point did it meet anybody before it eventually went down and disappeared under the horizon. Weasel had seen all of this, so he decided to speak to it the next chance he got.

No sooner had Weasel finished his supper than he left again to wait once more at the gorge. After he was sitting there for a while the moon came out as before, and when it was a little ways up in the sky, Weasel called out to it. "Hey, moon!" He waited for an answer, but the moon did not reply. Once more Weasel called out. "Moon, I want to talk to you! Won't you say something back to me?"

The moon, however, remained silent. When he heard that the moon made no reply, Weasel stopped trying to talk to it. After entering his house he thought the matter over. "I really wonder why it didn't answer me. It was way up in the sky, so it surely must have seen me." Then he thought, "Maybe I spoke to it from too far away and it just couldn't hear me."

The next night, Weasel left his house once more and watched until the moon was way up. This time he went quite a bit farther from his home, for he was looking for a tree. When he found the tallest one around, he climbed up and began calling the moon again. "Hey, moon, I would like to talk to you." But, as before, there was no answer, so Weasel climbed back down. He did not say anything to the moon, for he was sure he would not receive a reply. Instead, he decided to try again from somewhere else.

Meanwhile, the moon was traveling in a southwesterly direction and was pretty far away when Weasel reached a butte. It was a big butte, so Weasel climbed all the way to the top. Standing at the top of it Weasel called out, "Hey, moon, I would like to speak to you." However, there was no reply. So Weasel asked, "Why on earth don't you answer a poor guy like me? Don't you realize that I want to talk to you?" But the moon didn't say a thing.

Without uttering another plea Weasel climbed down from the butte and scampered on home. There was nothing else he could do. By the time he got to his house he was exhausted, so he decided to go to bed. After all, he had walked a long way. Once more he didn't get a any response. Soon he was sound asleep.

The next morning, after waking up, Weasel could not think of anything else, so wrought up was he over this matter. He did not feel like doing anything and kept racking his brain about how to talk to the moon. There was no doubt, it was traveling along there high in the sky without anybody's company. Nor did it ever halt in its tracks until it had disappeared below the horizon. Weasel had seen this with his own eyes and was determined to give it another try.

All day long until evening he whiled away the time sitting around at home. When it seemed time to go he went out, but this time he headed in a northeasterly direction. His destination was a deep canyon. He squatted down at its edge and waited for the moon to rise. Finally, when it appeared and was slightly up, he called out to it again. "Hey, I'd like to talk to you." No sooner had he uttered these words than an answer came back. It too said, "Hey, I'd like to talk to you."

"Is that a fact?" Weasel exclaimed. "I've been trying to talk to you for days, but you never answered me. Maybe you are hard of hearing," he added. The moon spoke the same words back to him.

Weasel asked, "What is it you are interested in?"

The moon responded in the same fashion. "What is it you are interested in?"

Weasel replied, "I'd like to have you for a friend."

Again the moon agreed. "I'd like to have you for a friend."

Weasel was delighted. "Agreed, we'll be friends."

The moon followed suit with the same reply. "Agreed, we'll be friends."

Weasel was beside himself with joy. For whatever feelings he expressed the moon answered with the same words. Soon he had made known to the moon everything he had wanted to say. So finally he said, "The Hopis have a custom of always giving food to the sun. On many an occasion I've heard a Hopi say when he is about to have a meal, 'All right, here, Sun, eat.' Never have I heard one say though, 'Moon, eat.' I've thought about this, so I'm going to ask you what food you relish. I'll try to find it for you and bring it here so you can eat it." With that, Weasel asked the moon directly, "What is it you really enjoy eating?"

The moon replied, "What is it you really enjoy eating?"

Weasel replied first, "I really relish meat."

The moon's answer was no different. "I really relish meat."

Weasel was surprised. "Is that so? I'll make sure I get some for you. Then you can make a meal of it." With this promise he went back home. He headed straight for his home and after arriving there quickly gobbled down his breakfast and then set out hunting. Since Weasel typically kills kangaroo rats and little critters like that, he hunted around until he had bagged about six. With these he returned home. Keeping them stored in a safe place Weasel waited until evening fell again. When the night was back, he shouldered his prey and once more ran out to the canyon to the very same place where he had spent the night before. After squatting down it occurred to him, "Moon certainly won't be able to pick up what I have here. After all, he can't come near me." Again and again he pondered how he could possibly hand the meat over to him.

It so happened that a pine tree stood over on the other side of the canyon. Upon spotting the tree Weasel ran over to it and climbed all the way to its top. Then he draped his prey over one of the highest branches. Having done this he climbed down and headed back to the place where he always waited for the moon. There he sat waiting without paying the least attention to his prey.

Before long, the moon was rising again. As it traveled along in the sky it reached a point about the same height as the pine tree, and when Weasel looked at it he noticed that the prey was gone. Evidently, moon had helped himself to it. Weasel was far away from it, so when he couldn't see the meat, he was sure the moon had picked it up. Weasel was elated. "Thanks for taking the meat," he said in a voice that was not very loud. He really was happy about this turn of events.

With that, Weasel returned back home. The following day he headed back to the area with the pine tree. It was still daylight, so he explored the area by the tree. Apparently, the wind had been blowing the night before. It caused Weasel's prey to fall down and lay there under the tree. When Weasel chanced upon the meat he looked it over carefully. Then he thought, "The moon must have killed these animals for me. After all, he knows what I like, for I told him so." This is how Weasel reasoned. Happy about the gift of meat, he picked it up and carried it home. There he devoured everything with great gusto.

From that time on Weasel felt sure he had made friends with the moon, so now he headed out to the canyon to talk with it regularly. He had noticed that it was only here that the moon would answer him, so he visited his friend only there. It never occurred to Weasel that it was his own voice that made an echo there, which he had mistaken for the voice of the moon. Since the moon was the only one to talk to him, Weasel always returned to this particular spot. In this way he thought he had befriended the moon. I guess he is still visiting it there.

And here the story ends.

24

Sand Cricket

Aliksa'i. They say people were living at Mishongnovi and in other villages all across the land. All the many different tribes were settled there.

On the southeast side of Mishongnovi and northeast of Qa'ötu-kwi at Taawa Spring, Sand Cricket had made his home with his grandmother. The two lived there all alone, as Sand Cricket was still unmarried.

At Mishongnovi lived a girl who was so beautiful that all of the young men wanted her. For this reason they would flock to her home. Each night they came to court her. And not only just the youths who resided at that village. The young men of the distant villages too had heard of her. So they also raced to Mishongnovi in the evening. I guess there was not a soul who did not try his luck. Thus, every night the girl had a suitor. How they yearned for her love! Their only desire was to go there and see her.

But the girl did not love any one of them. She knew the characters of her suitors quite well. Some were very industrious. A few were good hunters, while yet others had wealthy fathers. But despite their qualifications she had yet to say a welcoming word to one of them. Eventually, some of the youths became disenchanted and did not bother to go there anymore. From then on, it was only those who were not discouraged and who were determined in their hearts who continued to seek her out.

Even from the faraway place called Kiisiwu a stranger had come several times to Mishongnovi in pursuit of the girl, but he did not fare any better. He was a very handsome youth whose good looks surpassed his rivals. Still, the girl did not want him and also rejected his advances. What sort of a man she was looking for no one knew, for she had not taken a liking to anyone.

One day Sand Cricket was about in that village and discovered the young men as they were waiting for their turn to approach the girl's home. Curious as to why they were there in such a great number, he decided to find out for himself. In order to do so he climbed on the roof and headed over to the upper story of the house. As he was quite tiny, no one knew he was there. Upon nearing his destination, he went to the vent hole in the wall. He found yet another wooer sitting there. The poor fellow was trying hard to engage the girl in a conversation, but she did not utter a reply. Instead, she busily continued grinding her corn, not even bothering to look up. Finally, when he received not a single response, he gave up and got down from the roof.

Now Sand Cricket quickly scurried up to the vent and peeked in. As he looked in he discovered a beautiful girl grinding within. She had a lovely face and her skin was light in complexion. Since she had no shawl draped about her, the lightness of her shoulders was clearly visible. She had powdered her face with the flour she had ground, but its white color was hardly noticeable, so light was her skin. And she wore her hair in large butterfly whorls on the side of her head, which was just the hairdo you'd expect on an unmarried Hopi girl.

Sand Cricket only cast a glance inside and then climbed down from the roof. But he had seen enough. He instantly became infatuated with the girl. Now he too had to have her. After this experience he returned home. So taken was he by the girl that all the way home he kept thinking of her and picturing her in his mind. That evening when he went to bed, he again was picturing her. The poor thing was distraught. He did not know what to do because he was quite homely. He yearned for the girl, but he did not have the courage to speak to her. He knew there was no reason that she should fall for him, so he let it go at that. After that night he visited the girl's place several times, but never tried to talk with her.

However, the girl was constantly on his mind. As a result, Sand Cricket was not at ease. One day when he could not keep his thoughts to himself any longer, he revealed them to his grandmother. In the end he said to her, "Grandmother, isn't there anything you can do to help me so that I might marry her? I want her just as much as the others. She also seems to be a hard worker because when she is grinding corn, she has more than one bowlful of cornmeal sitting beside her. I'm also thinking of you when I think about this. If I marry her, you won't have to worry anymore about cooking, for she will most likely take over that chore," he explained to her.

His grandmother replied, "Oh my poor dear grandson. I've truly been hoping that this would happen to you, that you would find a girl and marry her. You'll have to have someone you can rely on as you live. I will not be around forever. But that girl will never marry anyone as homely as you. She hasn't even responded to those who are well off and good looking. I don't mean to dishearten you by saying this, and I'm not really telling you that you should not seek out the girl, but when you go there again, at least try to start a conversation with her. If she doesn't respond, you needn't feel too bad about it. After all, she also paid no attention to the others," his grandmother advised him.

Sand Cricket replied, "All right, but I'm sure I'll be unhappy if she doesn't speak to me. But tonight I'm going there to find out what is going on," he informed her.

Sand Cricket was anxiously awaiting now for night to fall, but somehow it was taking forever to get dark. At some time he became so frustrated with the sun he exclaimed, "Why are you so slow in going over the horizon? Look, I'm eager to see a girl. Whenever one needs to finish a task during daylight, you go down right away," he yelled angrily. His grandmother kept silent. She understood that he was restless.

At long last it became evening. The grandmother prepared supper, but when she invited her grandson to eat, he refused. Sand Cricket was set on going at that very moment, but his grandmother stopped him and said, "Hold it. You can't go so early. Someone is bound to be at the girl's place this very moment. Just wait a little while before you go."

Shortly thereafter the boy once again begged to go. This time his grandmother did not object but asked him not to leave just yet. With that, she disappeared into the back room of their home, returning with a most beautiful blanket. Handing it to her grandchild she remarked, "Now, at least conceal yourself in this when you go to find out how she's going to react to you. Since it can't be helped that you're so homely, she won't want you when she looks at you," she warned him.

Sand Cricket accepted the blanket from his grandmother. "Thank you very much," he exclaimed. "I guess I'll be going wrapped in an extremely nice blanket." He took great pleasure in this fine gift.

Wrapped in the blanket, he then departed to see the girl. Heading towards the village he arrived when it was still not totally dark. Upon his arrival at the girl's home he discovered another suitor sitting by the small vent hole. He was clearing his throat to attract the girl's attention, but she never bothered to look up. Next, he spoke to her, but she made no effort to respond. Discouraged, the lad did not linger any longer and went on his way.

Sand Cricket now climbed up on the roof and, tightly wrapped in his blanket, settled down by the vent hole. Having accomplished this he said to the girl, "Girl, I also have come to see you." But, alas, the girl showed no inclination to see who he was and made no effort to cease her grinding. Once more he addressed her. Still, the girl did not react.

Sand Cricket now began to ponder how he could get the girl to talk with him. So he said to her, "Don't stop your grinding, because I'm going to sing a song for you. Once you've learned my song, you too can sing it while you do your grinding." With that, he started singing. This is what he sang to her:

Sand Cricket, Sand Cricket
Is asking for a hairbrush.
Sand Cricket, Sand Cricket
Is asking for a hairbrush.
Why is it that while you have no hair
You're asking for a hairbrush?
He'ee'ew, he'ew, he'ew, he'ew,
Already I have ground my corn.

In this manner Sand Cricket sang for the girl. The little ditty was so humorous that the girl smiled. The moment she smiled she stopped her grinding and said to him, "How cute, what a funny song you have." Sand Cricket had managed to get the girl to speak. The song he had sung described himself of course, but the girl was unaware of this. She actually looked up at him but failed to catch a glimpse of his face. This was because he was sitting there with only his eyes peeping out from behind his blanket. The two now started talking and enjoyed each other's company so much that they did not realize how late it had become.

Soon the girl's mother came up to the second story and told her daughter to get ready for bed. "It's late. You'll have to come down and sleep," she ordered her daughter.

"All right, I'll come down after you. Just let me put what I've ground here in a container first," she replied. While she was heaping the cornmeal into a bowl, she said to her visitor, "You can come again tomorrow. I'll be expecting you at about the same time." With this invitation and after storing all of her cornmeal she went downstairs. Sand Cricket, glad in his heart, went on his way home.

As it turned out, one of the boys interested in the girl had spied on Sand Cricket as he was talking with the girl. He grew jealous that someone as unattractive as Sand Cricket had attracted the girl's attention. Apparently this was the youth from Kiisiwu. He had recognized the suitor as being Sand Cricket. Upon discovering this, he went home burning with anger.

As soon as Sand Cricket got home he told his grandmother that he had gotten the girl to smile and also that the girl had been very friendly towards him. His grandmother, however, did not believe him. Since Sand Cricket did not want to argue with her, he went to bed.

Meanwhile, he visited the girl a couple more times, and on the last occasion when he was about to go home, she said to him, "Wait a moment, I'm going to give you something before you leave. I want you to take it along with you." Emerging from behind her grinding bin, she went into an inner room and before long came back out. Walking up to him, she presented something to him in a bundle. Sand Cricket took it from her but did not check its contents. He only replied, "Thank you very much for what you've wrapped up for me." Then he climbed down with the bundle.

The minute Sand Cricket reached his home he unwrapped the girl's gift. Much to his surprise, he found some of her rolled piki. Immediately he roused his grandmother to tell her about this, but once again she did not believe that the girl had personally given it to him.

From that time on he went to see the girl several more times. Each time as he was about to leave, she would bundle some of her piki for him to take along. Finally, after Sand Cricket had come home a number of times with this gift, his grandmother accepted the fact that he had found himself a girlfriend.

Several visits later Sand Cricket got the notion to stay over at the girl's home and sleep with her. This intention he shared with his grandmother. "Grandma," he said, "tonight when I go see the girl, I've decided not to come home to sleep. So don't bother waiting up for me."

His grandmother replied, "O dear me, is that what you intend to do? If you stay there, you'll have to reveal yourself to the girl. When you do this and she sees who you are, she'll take a dislike to you. Because you're bald, you poor thing," she warned him.

Mulling his grandmother's words over carefully, Sand Cricket realized that she had spoken the truth. He now felt quite dejected. A good amount of time passed before he spoke to his grandmother again. "Grandma, can't you come up with an idea how I might get some hair so that my dream could become true?" he inquired.

Apparently his grandmother had been giving this matter some thought already, for she said to him, "Yes, of course I'll help you. That means, however, that for once tonight you can't go see the girl. Instead, I want you to gather some things for me so I can prepare you so you won't be bald when you reveal yourself to her." The lad was overjoyed when he heard this from his grandmother. The old woman now carefully instructed him what things he was to get and where he was to go for them.

Sand Cricket left immediately and made his way towards Mishongnovi. He did not enter the village, however. Instead, he headed toward the trash heaps on its outskirts, where he went about in search of a hairbrush. Each time he came across one, he removed whatever amount of hair was still clinging to the brush and carefully placed it in a container. This hair had obviously once belonged to the villagers of Mishongnovi. Whenever one of them brushed his hair, some of it would come loose and stick to the brush. When the person felt like throwing the brush away, he would do so with the hair strands still attached. Evidently it was these hairs Sand Cricket was after. Finally, when he figured that he had enough, he made his way back home.

Upon his arrival his grandmother cried out with delight, "Thanks, this should be enough. But for now let's go to bed. In the morning you'll have to go get me some other things at a place a little further away. After you return I'll fix you up for your appearance before the girl." With this, the two went to bed for the night.

The following day Sand Cricket rose early and headed to the woods northwest of Mishongnovi. What he was after was juniper pitch. Although he had set out without having breakfasted, he did take along some journey food. Upon reaching his destination, he went about seeking the pitch. Before long, he collected the amount his grandmother had requested. So then he halted his search. He now unwrapped his food bundle and ate it where he was. Having satisfied his hunger he returned home. Once again his grandmother was pleased to see him bring back what she needed.

Together the two now ate their lunch. Then Sand Cricket's grand-mother began to heat the pitch to liquify it. When she was done she bade her grandson come to her and said to him, "All right, my grand-child, come over here so I can fix you up. When you go visit the girl tonight, you won't need to be ashamed to show yourself to her." Sand Cricket did as bidden. He went over to his grandmother and squatted down before her.

The old woman took the melted pitch and placed it by her side. Then she smeared it over the entire scalp of her grandson. Next, one by one she attached to the pitch all the hair strands that Sand Cricket had brought home. It took quite a while to complete this task. To Sand Cricket, who was anxious for her to finish, the job seemed to take forever.

When the old granny was done, she cut the hair bands in a straight line just above the forehead. The same she did with his side-burns, cutting them even with his earlobes. The last thing she did was tie the hair at the nape of his neck into an oblong knot. Now Sand Cricket looked very handsome. Having fixed her grandson's hair like this, the old woman said to him, "Make sure now that when you get there and plan to spend the night, you do not stay in a place where it's too warm. Your hair is sure to fall out from the heat. Also, you'll have to keep from lying down. If you should happen to lie down, the pitch will melt from the warmth that your head puts out." These were the instructions she gave him to follow. Sand Cricket most readily agreed. So this had been the old woman's intention when she bade her grandson collect hair and pitch.

The boy now looked forward to the coming evening. As before, he was restless. But first he ate supper and waited until it was dark before he headed for the girl's home.

When he arrived, he found the girl grinding corn as usual. At first he kept himself completely covered with his blanket, but later he shed it. The girl, upon seeing him fully for the first time, nearly swooned. No doubt, it was a very handsome youth who had been visiting all along, and she was overjoyed that she had spoken to him.

Again, the two were so enraptured with each other's company they did not realize how late it had gotten. This time the girl discour-aged the boy from returning home and asked him to stay and marry her. Elated, Sand Cricket quickly accepted the girl's proposal.

The two were now going to sleep together, so the girl laid out her bedroll. Then she invited Sand Cricket to bed down beside her. Sand Cricket, however, excused himself, saying that he needed to go move his bowels. "Go ahead and lie down," he said to her. "After I return, I'll also do the same." Thereupon he went out.

Upon his return he discovered that the girl had not yet fallen asleep. Once again she urged him to lie with her. Sand Cricket just sat there for a while, then, once more, he explained that he had to go to the bathroom again. "I have a slight stomach ache. Perhaps it was something I ate this evening that caused it," he lied. Then he went out and soon returned.

Sand Cricket could not think of another excuse now, so he lay next to the girl. However, he did not stay put very long before he got up again. He kept this up all night. He was still at it when daybreak began to approach. Sometime during the night the girl had fallen asleep and therefore did not notice his restlessness.

The gray of the dawn had just appeared when a noise caught the girl's attention. Sitting up, she listened attentively. Apparently, someone was singing just below them. Both of them were now listening to the singing. There could be no doubt. That was the voice of Hahay'i Woman who was singing there at this time. Dancing right outside the girl's house she continually cried out her particular call. This is how her song went:

At Taawa Spring
My boyfriend has long sideburns adorning his head.
Aayay, his sideburns are fake.
It is morning, hee, hee.
At Taawa Spring
My boyfriend has long sideburns adorning his head.
Aayay, his sideburns are fake.
It is morning, hee, hee.

Each time she concluded her song, she ended it with "Haahaay'i" in a long drawn-out cry. Apparently she was trying to tell the girl that she had spent the night in the company of Sand Cricket. It was Hahay'i's grandson who had been coming to see this girl from Kiisiwu, and since she had ignored him, Hahay'i became upset about his. For this reason, she was trying to get this point across to the girl through her song. However, the girl did not catch its meaning.

Sand Cricket, on the other hand, understood that Hahay'i Woman's song was about him. He felt that if the girl were to think about Hahay'i Woman's song, she was bound to grasp its meaning. He concluded that it would be impossible for him to settle down there with her permanently.

So, while the girl was still listening to Hahay'i Woman, Sand Cricket slipped out past her and went home for good. In this fashion it came to be that he found a beautiful sweetheart but did not get to marry her. Perhaps he still lives somewhere without a wife.

And here the story ends.

Why the Pocket Mice Staged a Dance

Aliksa'i. People were living in the areas around Tsimonvösö, Huk'o-vi, and Qa'ötaqtipu. They also had settled at Oraibi. All of them were Hopis. Southeast of Höwiipa, near a hill, Pocket Mouse had made his home all by himself. Southeast of his abode and slightly northwest of Tsa'aktuyqa is a ridge on whose northeast side a large group of pocket mice were living. Over at Mongwupsö an owl had his nest, and it was from here that he went hunting in all four directions, mostly for mice, lizards, and snakes. As a rule, he did his hunting during the night.

Pocket Mouse was no different. He too went forth to hunt in every direction. Once in a while he would head in a southwesterly direction and search for something to eat on the northeast side of Qöma'wa. There, a little distance beyond Tsimonvösö, the land was flat and people had fields there. Amidst these plants he frequently stalked all sorts of creatures. Then again, if he felt like venturing farther away, he went to a field belonging to the Sparrow Hawk clan and did his hunting there.

One day Pocket Mouse decided to go hunting to a place far away again, so he had an early supper. When darkness had fallen, he left his abode and headed in a northeasterly direction. After crossing the entire cliff wall on the northeast side he continued on in a southeasterly direction, on the way bypassing the homes of the other pocket mice settled along the northeast side. Eventually, he reached his destination, a place on the northeast side of Tsa'aktuyqa where he started to hunt.

Pocket Mouse was still engaged in this task when he sensed something coming his way, making a chopping motion at him. Instantly lifting his head, he saw that an owl had swooped down at him and tried to strike him with its wing. The poor guy scuttled under a bush to shield himself, tightly crouching under a branch. Once more the owl made a dive at him as he lay there flat on his stomach. "If I don't leave this place he'll kill me," he thought. With that, he quickly got on his feet and ran back in a northwesterly direction, ducking underneath all kinds of bushes as he hurried along. Whenever he spotted a big one, he ran to it as fast as his feet would carry him. As soon as he would reach it, he stopped momentarily and then pressed on again. Meanwhile, the owl kept pursuing him. Whenever it was right above him, it swooped down at him. Pocket Mouse, poor thing, was running along at full speed, protecting himself underneath all sorts of things. Soon he passed the pocket mice on their northeast side and continued on in a northwesterly direction. Then he changed course again and ran straight southwest. In this manner he reached his abode and quickly ducked inside, breathing hard. He was scared to death, for the owl had nearly done him in. So there he was back home again without having bagged any prey for himself.

After a while when Pocket Mouse had caught his breath again he peeked outside. It looked as if the owl was still flying around in the area. So he waited there at the top of his ladder looking at the sky to check if the owl had left. He still had a mind to go in search of some food, but the owl was flying right overhead. This made it impossible to leave. He therefore forgot about going to search for food and resigned himself to staying put. He needed to sleep anyway, so he spread out his bedroll and lay down. Having failed to kill anything, the poor guy slept on an empty stomach. Unfortunately, he had no food reserves stored away.

The following day, as it got daylight, Pocket Mouse mulled his situation over. "I'll try again tonight," he thought. That morning the first thing he remembered was what had happened to him the evening before, but as he started doing things he forgot the whole affair. When darkness came he departed again, totally unaware of his previous encounter with the owl. Once more he set out in a northeasterly direction. "I'll go into the area southeast of Bacavi and look around for some game," he decided and headed exactly in a northeasterly direction. When he reached Bacavi where the terraced gardens are, he hunted about the area southeast of them. Suddenly he remembered the owl. "Dear god," he thought, "last night it chased me around and here I have ventured this far from home. It might decide to come again and try to kill me."

No sooner had the thought crossed his mind than he turned back, but it was too late. The owl had already arrived and dove down at him. Again and again it struck at him with its wings and even succeeded in hitting him slightly. Pocket Mouse fell over on his nose but instantly got on his feet again and scrambled under the branches of a bush. While he was under the bush, the owl rose skyward once more. When Pocket Mouse saw this he ran on again. Meanwhile, the owl was coming at him a second time, so he quickly sought refuge under something. Not before the owl had completed its dive and flown back up again did Pocket Mouse continue his flight.

Doing this repeatedly, Pocket Mouse was finally getting closer to his house, so he doubled his efforts. As soon as the owl had risen skyward, he scrambled on and rushed inside the safety of his home. The poor thing was breathing hard and totally exhausted. As he sat there he thought, "I won't be able to kill anything today at any time. That devil won't quit chasing me."

Once more Pocket Mouse peeked out through the hatch in the roof. Scanning the area, he saw no sign of the owl. So he stepped outside and had ventured away from the house when the owl came flying by a third time. Frightened, Pocket Mouse jumped back into his house. Sitting around he nibbled on a few leftovers that he still had. When he was done with that he bedded down and soon was sound asleep.

The next morning Pocket Mouse thought his situation over. "Maybe he'll leave me alone tomorrow," he thought. This time he spent the entire day remembering the terrible experience with the owl. When evening came he ate a few leftovers and waited. "Maybe I should just sit tight and pay more attention to the owl. It is probably watching me to see if I leave my house so that it can come after me." So Pocket Mouse stayed put, sitting on top of his house and keeping a lookout. Before long, at about the same time as the night before, the owl was winging around again. Evidently it was observing him. So, without going anywhere Pocket Mouse went back in his house. "I won't be able to leave this place without the owl chasing after me," he thought. So he stayed at home and whiled away the time sitting around. Eventually, he rolled out his bedding and lay down. "Once more I have to sleep without having eaten a decent meal," he thought.

The following day Pocket Mouse spent sitting around until it was completely dark. Stepping outside again, as the night before, he thought, "I can't leave this place anymore to search for food." He had just thought of going back down the ladder when the owl showed up. Now Pocket Mouse had no choice but to seek refuge indoors. "I won't have a chance of finding any food for myself today," he thought. Once more he had to stay home with nothing to eat. Once more he slept on an empty stomach.

The next morning Pocket Mouse was mulling over his options. "Maybe I can do something to that owl, or perhaps even kill it." All day long he sat there racking his brain until finally he had an idea. "I might as well go look for something."

With that, Pocket Mouse left the house. He felt safe now, for it was daylight, and owls are never about during the daylight hours. He headed out to a place in the southeast where greasewood grows. Upon reaching the area, wherever he came across a tree with big branches, he broke some off. When he had accumulated quite a large stack, he began hauling them home, one branch at a time. It was incredible how hard he worked. Finally, all the branches were at his house, so he trimmed them neatly, removing all the little twigs that stuck out from the main trunks. When this chore was finished, he sharpened each branch and lugged them back out, again one at a time. This work completed, he rammed the sharpened poles in the roofing material along the edge of the kiva hatch. To achieve this he dug a hole first, inserted the branch and then packed the hole down with earth. Since Pocket Mouse was tiny, this was hard work for him. The sticks for him were like beams for humans. Finally, he was done. Contemplating the result he said, "That's the way it's going to be. Somehow or other I'll kill that owl."

With that, he climbed back down into his house and just sat there waiting. "Tonight I must go outside again. As soon as I do that, the owl will chase me," he thought. He decided to go in a southeasterly direction and roam the area there.

When it was about time for the owl to return, Pocket Mouse left the safety of his home and headed out to a mound in the southeast. Being mindful of everything around him he was on full alert. For he knew full well that the owl was after his skin. Sure enough, he was still looking about when suddenly it had arrived. It still had not swooped down at him and already Pocket Mouse was running toward a large clump of grass. The instant he reached it, the owl dove down at him. Completing its dive, it sailed skyward again. At this moment Pocket Mouse dashed off in the direction of his house, the owl in hot pursuit.

Again and again the owl came flying down, almost touching the ground, while Pocket Mouse, poor guy, kept running for dear life, using whatever cover he could find. Before long he reached his house and was climbing up to the rooftop when the owl rose into the air again to prepare for a new dive. Quite intentionally, Pocket Mouse took his time ascending to the rooftop. He had planned, at the owl's next dive, to jump down through the hatch, so he paused where he was. Sure enough, the owl came swooping down and was already quite close when, at the last moment, Pocket Mouse jumped aside into the covering of the hatchway. By this time the owl was almost upon him and as it struck after him with its wing it impaled itself on one of the pointed greasewood branches. With such great force had the owl arrived that it rammed the pointed stick right through its body. It flapped its wings helplessly.

Now Pocket Mouse had a chance to quickly duck into his house. Down below the owl could be heard slowly pounding the rooftop with its flapping wings. Finally, there was silence, so Pocket Mouse thought, "I really should take a peek at it. Maybe it managed to pull itself free and flew off."

However, as Pocket Mouse looked out he saw that the owl was dead. It had hit the pole straight on and impaled itself right through the heart. Pocket Mouse laughed. "I knew it, it wouldn't be so hard catching you when you pestered me," he cried. "It was your own fault that you died this way." Pocket Mouse stood there smiling. Then he wondered, "What shall I do with the corpse?" The thing was huge and he would not be able to haul it away. After standing there for a while he decided to go somewhere. "Now that I have got rid of this pest I can safely go and find myself something to eat."

Pocket Mouse returned to the area from which the owl had driven him away and, after looking around for a little while, lucked out and killed something. After hauling his prey home he ate. For two whole days he had not had a decent meal, so he was starved. At long last, he now had food, so he concentrated only on eating. He ate quite hurriedly, poor thing, and when he was full he went to bed.

After a good night's sleep Pocket Mouse woke up the next morning thinking about the owl. By now it was daylight, so he went out to the dead bird and inspected it. There it lay on the ground. Pocket Mouse stepped up to it and began to pluck out its downy body feathers. He spent all day doing this. He also pulled out all of its wing feathers, especially the slightly shorter ones. He did not bother with the really long ones. When he was done with this task he wrapped them up in a bundle and took them inside his house. Now that he had all these feathers he wondered, "Who can I possibly give these to? Maybe someone would want to wear them. What on earth will I do with them?"

Pocket Mouse kept pondering what to do with all the owl feathers he had stored away. Meanwhile, he had bedded down, and suddenly a thought struck him, "Hey, why don't I tell the other pocket mice about this? Maybe they would agree to stage a dance with me," he thought as he lay there. Finally, he made a decision. "Tomorrow I'll ask the other mice if they want to help me perform a dance."

With this plan on his mind Pocket Mouse eventually fell asleep. The next morning after getting up he thought about the matter some more. He spent the entire day at home. After supper he left home and headed over to the pocket mice settlement. He had no idea how they would react to his proposal. When he reached his destination, he shouted "Haw!" down through the hatch.

"Come on in, stranger!" someone answered from below.

Pocket Mouse did as bidden and entered. There they were, all of them welcoming him. "Have a seat!" someone said. "So you are going around?"

"Yes," Pocket Mouse replied.

"Well, then, what is the purpose of your coming?" they asked.

Pocket Mouse explained, "Well, you see, I killed something and plucked out all of its feathers. I have tons of downy feathers and wing feathers, so I've been thinking about this matter for a long time."

"Is that so? What was it that you killed?" the leader of the pocket mice asked.

"I killed a great horned owl," Pocket Mouse replied. "It was always chasing me in the dark of the night. Each time I went out hunting, it came after me. So I wondered what to do to it so that I could go on hunting without fearing for my life. I felled some greasewood stalks, sharpened them and planted them around the entrance to my house. The bird swooped down right onto one of the pointed poles and was killed. I plucked out all of its feathers. So here is a splendid opportunity," Pocket Mouse continued. "It occurred to me that perhaps we could perform a dance."

"Whom did you have in mind to impersonate?"

"Well, I thought kachinas."

"Is that a fact?"

"Yes," Pocket Mouse firmly replied. "Since I killed an owl, we could use its downy feathers and wing feathers for our costumes."

"Well, that's up to you. You probably have a song already. That has to be part of the dance, of course."

"I will certainly compose a song," Pocket Mouse explained. I once saw a kachina dance at Oraibi. That's how I learned a song."

"Not bad, indeed," the leader of the mice said.

Pocket Mouse continued, "So tomorrow night I would like for you to gather at my place. We can then think about the song some more. We may have to sing it through two or three times before we can rehearse our steps. Those who are not forgetful will have memorized it right away. So this is what I had in mind."

"Agreed, let's do it," all the mice shouted their consent.

After that, Pocket Mouse returned home, happy about the outcome of his mission. On the way he decided to do some hunting. How wonderful it was to hunt again without having to fear for his life! As it turned out, Pocket Mouse was in luck and bagged a prey. After that he went back home. Greatly relieved about the response from the other mice he went to bed.

The next day at daybreak Pocket Mouse was already thinking about the song that they would dance to. He was full of anticipation, so he decided to do a few things ahead of time. He took the feathers out and began tying them together. At first he tied the soft and downy ones together into larger bunches. To these in turn he attached two wing feathers each so that they stuck out from the bunches. He had no idea, of course, how many mice would come, but he figured that there would be enough for everybody. Soon a large pile of feathers was ready. As evening was drawing near, Pocket Mouse had an early supper. Then he climbed out on the rooftop and made a public announcement. "All you pocket mice that are living out there, listen to me! I'm sponsoring a dance. So whoever wants to help me should come to me here at the hill southeast of Höwiipa." This is how Pocket Mouse called out his message. He did not forget to tell them to come with happy hearts. With that, he went back inside and waited. Before long, there was a thump on the rooftop. Then someone slowly entered and made his way down the ladder. When he was down, Pocket Mouse said, "Sit down! Have you arrived?"

"Yes," came the reply.

One after another the mice were now entering. Evidently, they had heard his announcement, for a great many had showed up. Pocket Mouse was very proud about this fact. Assembled there, they were all chatting with each other. Finally, someone asked, "All right, then, what do you need us for?"

"Well, yes," Pocket Mouse replied, "I recently killed a great horned owl, and after I pulled out all its downy feathers and wing feathers, I thought there was a splendid opportunity for us to dress up with them. It occurred to me that we might dance kachina. That's why I had you gather here. Whenever the Hopis go on the warpath and kill an enemy, they stage a dance after their return. Since I killed this owl and plucked out its feathers, we can use them in our costumes. First we must learn a song, though, then we can rehearse our steps. I'm sure we need to practice no more than two or three times before we can start."

"Very well," the mice consented.

"That will be it for now," Pocket Mouse said. Tomorrow when we meet again, I will teach you the song. Let's go to bed now."

Everyone agreed to cooperate and were full of anticipation. They were looking forward to the event as they filed out of Pocket Mouse's house and returned home.

And, indeed, the following night the pocket mice showed up in great numbers. When all of them had arrived they said, "I guess these are all of us. No one else will come. So, sing to us what you have composed."

"Very well," Pocket Mouse replied, "listen carefully." With that, he started to sing. And this is how the song went:

Kooni, kooni, kooni, kooni.
Koonini'i, koonini'i.
Kooni, kooni, kooni, kooni.
Koonini'i, koonini'i.
Akwasa'a, siyala'a.
Koonini'i, koonini'i.
Akwasa'a, siyala'a.
Koonini'i, koonini'i.

Everyone complimented the song, which made Pocket Mouse feel very proud. Some of the mice had already picked up the song. Pocket Mouse said, "That'll be it for the time being. Let's go to bed now and come back tomorrow again." And so, the next morning, the Mice assembled again and practiced the song. On the fourth night they were ready to get into standing position and rehearse their steps. "All right," Pocket Mouse called, "let's practice and see how we step to this tune."

Pocket Mouse now chose one mouse to give the commands. He did not want to do this because he looked forward to doing some dancing himself. So, after selecting one who was to act as their father, he appointed another as their drummer and one as centerman. His task would be to start the dance by shaking his rattle. "That'll do," Pocket Mouse exclaimed. "Let's line up now one after the other, for that's the way it has to be."

The mice agreed and stood up. When they were all positioned properly, the centerman shook his rattle and they began to dance. One after the other they were jumping slowly, all these little mice, and then they hopped rapidly. The song fitted their steps, and they hopped exactly in tune with it. In this manner the pocket mice prac-ticed their dance. Then they finished and returned home.

After three more days of practice sessions Pocket Mouse de-clared, "All right, tomorrow we will hold totokya, ceremony eve. So tell your wives to make pik'ami, sweet feast pudding, and meat stew tomorrow, for other villagers might learn about our event and come to watch the dance."

With this news the mouse dancers returned home. Upon reaching their homes they said to their wives, "We'll have totokya tomorrow, so you must cook a stew and make pik'ami."

That same night the mouse women could be seen rushing about the fields competing for who could find the most corn kernels and things like that. Whenever one of them had collected a few, she would carry them home. A few of the kernels they ground up, and from others they were going to make hominy, so they boiled them together with the meat. The stew they had cooking was going to be their feast on dance day morning. This is how their husbands had instructed them.

On the night of totokya all participants in the dance came to Pocket Mouse's house, for he was the sponsor. All through the night they practiced, since it is customary not to sleep during ceremony eve. "This night we cannot sleep," Pocket Mouse explained. "We'll practice all night long and go out first thing in the morning. We'll dance one time only, and when the dance is over, your wives may fulfill their obligations by presenting the food to us."

With that, they filed out of Pocket Mouse's kiva, and their ceremonial father led them to the place where they planned to perform. That same evening Pocket Mouse had been planting pointed grease-wood trunks in an upright position. Along the edge of the place where they were going to dance he had inserted them in slightly bigger intervals, for at any moment an enemy might attack them. If they danced in the protection of these sharpened poles, they wouldn't be in danger. This was Pocket Mouse's reason for doing this, he explained to them. And so, the following morning, they marched out to the appointed place and began to dance in the midst of the sticks.

The pocket mice children and their mothers all had come to watch them. After dancing one entire sequence the kachinas stopped to return to their resting place. There the women mice then brought the food. And this is how their song went:

Kooni, kooni, kooni, kooni.
Koonini'i, koonini'i.
Kooni, kooni, kooni, kooni.
Koonini'i, koonini'i.
Akwasa'a, siyala'a.
Koonini'i, koonini'i.
Akwasa'a, siyala'a.
Koonini'i, koonini'i.

The dancers were hopping one behind the others. After breakfast they danced three more times. Then it was noon and the women once more dished out their food. As the leader of the dance, Pocket Mouse had made no stew of his own, but he ate well thanks to the women. He had to carry out the obligations of the chief.

After the feast at noon the mice continued their dance until early evening. All the pocket mouse children were by now familiar with the song and were jumping and hopping around in tune to it. The song had really affected them, and so the kachinas delighted every-body with it. After all, they were like kachinas, not social dancers. That was also the reason that they danced in a line.

Meanwhile, their ceremonial father had fashioned prayer plumes from the downy owl feathers. When evening came he bestowed these prayer feathers on all the participants. Then he bade everybody to return to his house. To this, Pocket Mouse, the sponsor of the event, added, "Take the prayer plume that you wear in your hair home with you. Guard it well, for one day if we want to dance kachina again you can dress up with it. Feathers like these are hard to come by."

After that the pocket mice returned home, everybody to his own house. In this manner they tried out a kachina dance and really liked it. Before they departed they decided that they would hold one again one day. Perhaps the pocket mice are still dancing kachina there.

And here the story ends.

Coyote and Badger as Food Robbers

Aliksa'i. People were living at Oraibi and in other settlements all
across the land. Over at Ismo'wala, Coyote had made his home, and
at Honansikya Badger had his den. There was also Gopher who lived
somewhere near Coyote. Coyote and Badger were good friends and
constantly visited each other. That's how they knew one another.

At Leenangwva, on the southwest side of the village, the Oraibis
had their water source. It was a running spring and next to it was fine
dune sand. Each time the wind blew, the water hole filled up with the
sand, and when this happened, the villagers had to clean it. In doing
this they opened it up a little, which caused the water to flow better
again. Now they were able to drink from it again and carry water

home.

Coyote is a varmint who is constantly roaming about and hunting in different places. One day his course took him through the area southwest of Leenangw Spring. He was thirsty, which was the reason he was headed for that place. He knew exactly where the water hole was, but as he got closer he noticed that a number of people were busy doing something there. He did not go near them. Instead, he stood there watching them from a hill. He was curious about what they were doing. Interestingly enough, men and girls were working together. Determined to find out what was going on, Coyote spied on the people from under a bush, lying flat on his belly. He was all eyes and paid close attention to their every move. From all appearances the Oraibis were cleaning out the spring. The men were inside loading sand on trays. These in turn they handed to the girls who passed them along from one to the other. These trays with the sand were passed successively from one to the next, then dumped out at the end of a long line. That's how it is still done today when the spring is being cleaned at Hotevilla. Usually kachinas bring the men down to the spring. Exactly in this fashion the Oraibis were doing it there at Leenangw Spring, with the exception, however, that no kachinas were present. In addition to all the sand, they removed trash and other debris such as dead tumbleweeds, for the wind blows all of these things into the spring. As a result, it gets covered and will no longer flow. Coyote carefully observed how all this stuff was being cleaned out.

When they were done with their work, the men all retired to a rocky mound in the southeast where the girls had deposited their food. This food they distributed among the workers and everybody ate. As he watched them eating Coyote became hungry for the food. But since he could not possibly walk up to them, he remained in his place. This is what he witnessed there at Leenangw Spring.

Coyote now returned home. From that day on he continually checked out that place. He thought that if one day the Oraibis should clean the spring again, he could help them and as a reward eat with them. That was the reason he kept visiting the spring. Nothing of the kind took place, however. People simply went there for water. Each time the women went there to haul water they had to stand in line for their turn. As not very much water was welling forth, the spring did not fill up quickly. And if many went after water in one single day, there was not always enough for everyone. After the first two or three had scooped out water, only a little was left, and the others behind them had to wait their turn. As a rule, they sat around for a while, and when the water level had risen again, they too drew their water. In this fashion the Oraibis obtained their drinking water there.

Once in a while when Coyote roamed about he headed over to Oraibi in search of something to eat in the dump and toilet area of the village. Occasionally, people threw away things like corn that they had allowed to spoil. Or they threw away uneaten watermelon that mice had eaten holes into. Coyote was looking for things like this along the refuse and toilet area.

One day as he came to Oraibi again, it was still early in the morning. This time he was rummaging around on top of the mesa close to the cliff where people also threw away trash when suddenly he heard a voice in the village. He stopped in his tracks to listen. He could clearly hear that the village crier was making a public announcement. The crier explained that they would be cleaning the spring at Leenangwva again and formally announced a date for the special event. The girls were expected to prepare food and take it down there. He let them know in how many days it would come to pass. On the appointed day the men were to descend to the spring and clean it of all debris. That was the content of the public announcement.

It occurred to Coyote that if he shared this information with his friend Badger, they could try to steal the food set aside for the workers. The minute he had found a few edible morsels at the dump he returned home. Immediately after arriving there he ate supper, and when he was finished, he went to visit Badger over at Honansikya to tell him that he had learned that the Oraibis were going to clean the spring. Upon reaching Badger's home, he discovered that Badger too had just eaten and therefore was at home. Coyote announced his arrival by shouting, "Haw!"

A voice from down below replied, "Come in!"

When Coyote entered, Badger said, "So you are about again. There, have a seat."

"Yes," replied Coyote, "I remembered you again. That's why I came to look in on you."

Badger made Coyote feel at home. Soon both of them were chatting away. In due course Coyote told Badger about the Oraibis' planned cleanup of the spring and told him the date that had been set for it. He also explained that during this event the girls typically go with the men and bring food to the spring. "It occurred to me that if the two of us team up, we could go there and steal their food."

Badger was all for it right away. In planning the undertaking, they decided that Badger would burrow a tunnel from Coyote's home exactly to the spot where the girls kept the food. Surfacing at that very place, they would then stash the food in the tunnel and carry it to Coyote's home. There they could share their spoils. Both animals were delighted with their scheme.

So Badger had agreed to carry out the tunneling. And since he knew in how many days the Oraibis would clean out the spring, he came early in the morning on that day to Coyote's den. Upon his arrival Coyote said, "All right, let's start our work without delay. You do the burrowing while I do the looking for you. You'll probably have to surface once in a while, and then continue on. I'll let you know exactly where to dig as you move along. In this way you will dig in the right direction." This is how Coyote instructed Badger.

Badger did as told and started tunneling. Coyote paid close attention to him, and each time Badger surfaced Coyote eyeballed his direction. Whenever Badger was right on course he continued digging again. Meanwhile it was getting close to noon, but the two were nowhere near Leenangw Spring, their destination. Obviously, Badger is not a creature capable of digging very fast. He digs a certain distance, then pushes the earth all the way to the starting point of his burrow and throws it out. Only then does he resume his digging.

This habit was hampering their progress. Noontime was close at hand, and Coyote was beginning to get impatient. They still had not reached their goal, and at noon the Oraibis were bound to eat their lunch. Coyote, poor guy, was anxious and excited. Badger was delaying things too much by running back and forth to push the loose earth out of the hole. Finally, Coyote said to him, "It's getting noon and you're not even close. Let me go look for someone who might be able to help us finish the tunnel quickly."

"All right," Badger replied. "I know I have to constantly push out the dirt. That's why I don't make much headway."

So, with Badger's permission, Coyote dashed off. The one he had in mind was Gopher. He knew that Gopher can dig extremely fast. That's why he ran to him. When he came to Gopher's place he was greatly relieved to find him at home. Coyote had lucked out in catching him there. Right away Coyote explained to him that he and Badger were trying to dig a tunnel to some food at Leenangw Spring, but that Badger was terribly slow and had to run back and forth, slowing them down. Maybe he would care to join them to finish the work more rapidly? This is what Badger related to Gopher.

Gopher was willing to go along. So Coyote brought him over to his den, where he followed Badger inside the tunnel. Upon reaching him he began to dig with great speed. Badger, in turn, pushed the loose dirt to the entrance. In this fashion Gopher was able to advance quite rapidly and before long the two broke through to the surface. It still was not noontime when they reached their destination. The Oraibis working at the spring were still busy. A few of them stood at the bottom of the water hole passing the sand from one to the other. They say there were once steps leading down to Leenangw Spring, so the debris was passed from down below up the stairs to the girls. They in turn dumped the loads out, one after the other, and paid no heed to their food. It never occurred to them that someone would dare bother it. They had left their food there many times before, and no one had ever disturbed it. For this reason they worked without watching it.

Meanwhile, the tunnel was completely dug out and Coyote was finally able to get his hands on the food. He handed it down to Badger and Gopher who were inside the tunnel, and they hauled it to Coyote's den. Finally, when Coyote had gotten everything, he reentered the tunnel, and then Gopher closed up the surface hole with earth. When all the food had been carried to Coyote's place, there was so much the three of them were practically buried in it. The first thing they did now was have a joint meal, long before the Oraibis had even finished cleaning the spring.

Eventually, the sponsor of the spring cleanup project announced to the workers that they had made it to noontime. He urged them to have lunch and then quit, in fact declaring that the work was completed. The girls then headed to the location where they had deposited the food. Upon arriving there, however, much to their dismay they discovered that it had vanished. Apparently, someone had made off with it. "Our lunch has been stolen!" they exclaimed.

The men who had followed them said, "That's impossible. There was nobody here at any time."

"But it is all gone," the girls protested.

The arriving men now began to search for tracks and follow them. It was evident that one single creature had been running back and forth there, a creature with tracks resembling those of a dog. But they could not recall seeing one all morning. The tracks ended at the very place where a gopher had thrown up his mound. So they thought, "The gopher must have loaded the food into his burrow. He pushed up a new mound here." With that, they began digging into the earth. "He can't have taken things very far away. The mound is still fresh," they remarked as they were digging after the animal. They soon had dug up the ground for quite a distance, but still they failed to catch up with the creature. It was nowhere in sight. Nor could the men tell in which direction the gopher had tunneled. He had closed up the hole with dirt, so it was impossible for them to see.

Since the gopher had disappeared the Oraibis were forced to quit their search. They knew that they would never catch up with the animal. "We must go to the village to eat," they said, and then all of them returned home. They had to go with empty stomachs, for all the food had been stolen. So they went to their homes in Oraibi to have lunch.

Badger, Coyote, and Gopher, on the other hand, who had pilfered all the food, were gorging themselves on it. In fact, there was so much that they were unable to devour it all, so they divided it up among the three of them. Badger and Gopher lugged their portions to their homes, and when all was stored away safely, continued eating from them. All three of them got to eat their fill thanks to the spring cleaners. I guess they're still eating from that food somewhere.

And here the story ends.

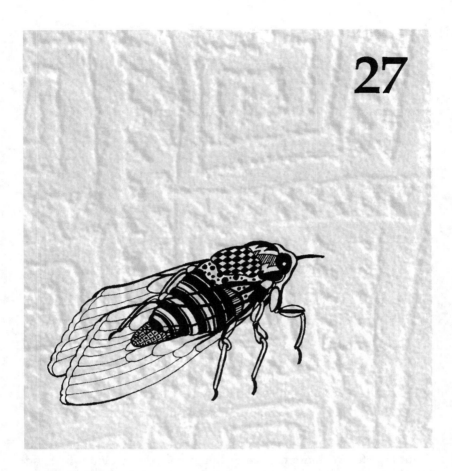

27

The Crying Cicada

Aliksa'i. People were living in Oraibi and in other settlements all across the land.

Long ago, the people of Oraibi used to eat all sorts of living things. For example, they made stew out of cottontails and jackrabbits. The same was true for antelopes that roamed the area in those days. To hunt bigger game such as deer, the Oraibis trekked all the way to Nuvatukya'ovi, the San Francisco Peaks. If they were lucky enough to bag a deer, they made a meal out of it too. Once in a while they even brought back a large elk. All these animals they used to cook and eat.

And cicadas were also part of their diet. In the olden days, it was usually very hot in the vicinity of the Hopi villages, so cicadas appeared in great abundance. Apparently, someone long ago had tried the taste of them and found it to his liking. As a result, people started eating cicadas regularly. And since the insects come out when it is hot, they used to be right out in the open there when the heat of summer was upon the land. Hence, someone who wanted cicadas would go hunt for them when the weather was hot. Upon bringing some home, a woman made fire under a cooking pot. The cicadas were then cast into the pot and roasted. In those days the cooking vessels were normally made out of clay.

There was also an old woman living in Oraibi. Once when she was at a loss as to what to cook for the family, she bade all her grandchildren go hunt cicadas. As soon as the sun was a little up in the sky, the children went down from the mesa to the plain and hunted around. Sure enough, as the air was getting warmer, the chirping of the cicadas could clearly be heard. Whenever one of the insects was singing somewhere, one of the children would try to sneak up to it, moving along, aiming for the spot where the chirping came from. If he succeeded in locating the exact spot, he would reach out for the insect and catch it if he was lucky. This is what the children were doing there now. One of them, who was not as old as the others, followed them around with a bag into which they put the cicadas.

In the village, meanwhile, the old woman got the cooking pot ready. After all, it was close to noontime. She already had a small fire going under the vessel ahead of the children's arrival. When it was about time for the hunters to come home, she added a lot of fuel and soon had a good fire going. Just when her pot got really warmed up, the children arrived and handed the cicadas over to their grandmother. They had caught a great many and the old woman was elated.

"Oh, thank you! Now we can have a feast. I'm so glad you're old enough to go get these critters," she exclaimed, thanking her grand-children. With that she carried the cicadas to the cooking pot and threw them in alive. For that is how one roasts them. After dumping them in the pot, she closed the pot with a sifter basket, stirring all the while.

The old woman was still busy doing that when one of the cicadas somehow managed to crawl out from under the sifter. It flew away from the woman and settled down not far from her. The poor thing had been burned on one side, so it squatted there crying.

Tsiiriiriirii,
Tsiiriiriirii.
Cottontails and jackrabbits
Used to be good meat for a stew.
But now we taste the best.
Tsiiriiriirii.

This is how the cicada wept.

The old woman heard something. Listening closely, she could barely make out a voice somewhere near her. Investigating the area next to her, she finally saw it. There beside her was a flat rock, and on it had landed the cicada she had heard talking. She paid close atten-tion to what it was saying. Finally she exclaimed, "Oh my, poor thing! Did you not get roasted with the others? Yes, you are very delicious. That's why we eat you. Sure, there are cottontails and jackrabbits out there, but they're very swift and good runners. That's why we don't get to eat too many of them. And because we enjoy how you taste, we're eating you, too," she said to the cicada.

Reproaching the old woman, the cicada replied, "You know very well that the weather gets warm because of us, and yet you eat us."

"Oh dear, that's right, we get warm weather because of you and here we are killing you," the woman admitted.

"Yes indeed," the cicada continued. "The minute I get home I'll tell the others, and then the weather won't warm up so early any more. Anyway, it's up to you. From this day on you can have winter when summer comes around. We're the only ones who know all about the heat, and look how you treat us."

"Oh dear, oh dear! I'll tell my people that we won't do that anymore," the old woman wailed.

"Well, since you are like this, we're thinking of moving somewhere else. All you do is kill us, which is wrong."

"I'm sorry, indeed. I assure you, we won't eat you any more. And we won't be killing you any longer. We need you to warm up the land for us early in the year so we can plant early and not have a hard time with our crops. When we have crops to eat, we don't need to hunt you any more."

The cicada, however, had grown so angry that it flew off without a response. It returned to the others, thinking that after telling them about its experience they would leave the area so the Hopis could not eat and kill them any longer. Upon reaching home it assembled the cicadas and spoke to them this way, "If we quit living here, they can't devour us any more."

The fall season was just about upon them as it spoke these words. And so the cicadas had departed when the weather turned cold. Since they normally leave around this time, none of the Hopis gave it much thought. All of the cicadas, however, had agreed to stop living there. They were unanimous in their decision and acted accordingly.

Thereafter, whenever summer rolled around, the weather simply would not get hot. The land did not warm up properly. Way back when lots of cicadas had made their home there, it always was hot during that season. There had usually been great numbers of them there, making their chirping sounds. But now after the cicada had told its people what it had learned and they had departed, the weather did not get as hot as before. It would still get comfortably warm, but by no means was the temperature as hot. And so the land failed to warm up early in the year, and the crops were late in maturing. When the people became aware of this, they did not eat as many cicadas as they used to, especially the old people who had some brains. They wanted the cicadas to return.

One man in particular, who was in charge of some ceremony, had been mulling this situation over. He thought that if he fashioned pahos with the cicadas and prayed to them, they might consider coming back. So he went out hunting for them and killed a few. He poked them on a stick, storing them for later. As he made his pahos then, he attached one of the dead insects on the prayer stick. Then he uttered the following prayer, "I wish you, cicadas, would have pity on us and return from where you went. Then it could get nice and warm again early in the season." Then he added, "And maybe it would be all right if we eat you. You see, we got to like the taste of you and now need you for our sustenance." This is the prayer he spoke, whereupon he deposited the paho with some cornmeal.

Evidently the cicadas consented, for they returned. Now the weather got hot early in the year once more. As before, the people ate them, but this time the insects did not leave. Thus, in spite of using them as food again, the Hopis harvested their crops early. From that day on they also made prayer sticks with cicadas. Whenever one does so, the weather quickly gets nice and warm. The cicadas, in turn, never returned to the place they had come back from. For this reason prayer sticks are still being fashioned during the Flute ceremony.

And here the story ends.

28

The Gambling Boy Who Married a Bear Girl

Aliksa'i. People were living at Wupatki. In addition, there were settlements all across the land. Long ago the Hopis used to migrate around
quite a bit, building their houses among the buttes and cliffs, which
accounts for all the ruins found there now. One such ruin exists at
Wupatki. Many people called this place their home once. In spite of
its small size, the place had enough inhabitants to permit gambling
with each other. Gambling has been part of Hopi life since way back
in time. Totolospi and Sosotukwpi were the two games with which
people gladdened their lives. Whenever they did engage in this form
of entertainment, they usually did so at night. The stakes involved no
valuables, as a rule only a straw from a hairbrush or broom. The play-

ers would tie a bundle of broom straws together and give these to each other. It was always the losers who had to hand over a straw to the winning side. When one group had lost all of their broom straws, they were beaten. The following day then, when it got light, the losers had to cook breakfast, which the winners came to eat. Customarily, they were served boiled beans with somiviki. In this fashion people used to gamble.

Slowly but surely the fervor displayed in this kind of entertainment got out of hand, though, when the players began gambling for real possessions. Eventually, they became so addicted that they did not even quit to go to bed. Among these gambling addicts was a young man who kept losing all sorts of things that belonged to his parents. This way, he gambled away his mother's woolen dress and shawl and his father's ceremonial kilt and embroidered sash. All these precious items he lost. When his parents noticed that these things were missing they kept asking each other who on earth could have taken their belongings. Assuming that it was their son—after all he had participated in the gambling—they put the blame on him. When they confronted him and asked whether he had gambled their things away, he had to admit that he was at fault. There was no denying the fact that he was part of the gambling crowd. When his parents heard him confess they grew angry, for those were the clothes they really treasured. Whatever people own in the way of clothing, they like to hand down to their children. Also, whenever a child desires to participate in a dance ceremony, it must have the proper costume. And because clothing of this kind is hard to come by, the parents were understandably upset. They felt that he should never have done this and they were anxious to learn from their son what had caused him to do it. Both husband and wife were of one mind about the seriousness of the transgression and in return they threw their son out of the house. "You can't live here with us anymore. Go somewhere else where you can live as it suits you," they said.

So the poor fellow had no choice but to leave. It so happened that he had a younger sister who was not at all happy about this turn of events. However, she didn't know what to say to her parents and therefore did not take up for her brother when he left. Upon taking his leave the boy descended to the southeast side of the mesa across a slope. There somewhere at a place to the southeast was a kiva, and crossing the area southwest of it he headed up the terrain in a southeasterly direction. He really had no idea where to go. Nor was he familiar with any other village. He had no real friend, so he was at a loss where to turn. As a result, he wandered around aimlessly. Out of frustration he finally set forth in a northwesterly direction. This route eventually led him to the large mountain range of the San Francisco Peaks. After skirting it on its northeastern side he continued on toward its northwest side. At long last he arrived in the midst of a forest. There were huge pine trees growing there and he pondered whether he should enter the place. Knowing that he couldn't return to his parents he decided to head straight through the forest.

The boy traveled northwest until he felt like resting. He had grown tired and it was getting to be evening. He had just settled down comfortably when suddenly he clearly heard the sounds of something moving along. As he looked up and scanned the area, a bear appeared before him. Rearing up on its hind legs, it was quite tall. The boy got frightened and jumped to his feet. Intending to run back from where he had come, he was about to make a dash for it when the bear addressed him. "Don't run away. I won't harm you," the bear said. "There's no need for you to flee."

The boy remained rooted to the ground and stared at the enormous beast. The bear stood with its talons spread out like a fan and the young man stood there with his eyes fixed on the bear for a long time. Finally, it was the bear who spoke again. "Don't run away. I won't harm you. I came just for you."

The boy continued to stand there without moving a limb. So the bear said, "You shouldn't be walking around here. Why are you?"

At long last the boy found his voice and replied, "I don't know where I'm going. I had no real destination in mind and was just wandering through here when I got tired. That's why I wound up here." The boy had no journey food on him, so he told the bear that he had nothing to eat. He explained that he was at a loss for what to do and that this was his reason for being there.

"Well, I suggest you come with me then," the bear said. "We live right here on the northwest side of the mountains, at a place slightly to the southwest. Let me take you there."

The boy now ventured near the bear, who fell back on all fours again and said, "All right, climb on top of me. Then grab hold of my fur."

The young man complied and mounted the beast. As soon as he was seated on top of the animal he grabbed its fur, and the bear lumbered downhill slightly to the northwest side and then headed in a southwesterly direction, bypassing the San Francisco Peaks on their northwestern flank. After a while the bear veered somewhat to the southwest and then arrived at the base of a cliff. Much to the boy's surprise there was a kiva there, which the two ascended. After getting up on the roof the bear had the boy dismount. "All right, this is my home," the bear said. "Follow me inside." With that, the bear disappeared into the kiva.

The young man entered behind the bear through the hatch. Sure enough, here was a place that looked inhabited, although nobody else was at home. After getting the boy inside the bear took him to the northeastern base of the abode and said, "Stay here for the time being."

As the young man glanced about he noticed some sort of altar that was set up just outside the niche that is commonly centered at the far end of the kiva at the base of the inside wall. Evidently, whoever lived here owned an altar. The boy had no notion who they might be, for with the exception of the bear no one was home.

The bear now disappeared into the back room in the northwest side of the kiva, where there was an opening. Upon entering, the animal transformed itself by removing its skin. Much to the boy's amazement, a young woman emerged from the back room. The girl, who was extremely beautiful, turned to him and said, "I'll fix you something to eat. You must be starved."

The boy stared in shock at the girl. It had evidently been she who had brought him here. Once more she entered the back room and when she reappeared she held a tray of piki in her hands. This she set out in front of the boy, together with water and kwiptosi, fine-ground corn. "Now, eat," she urged him.

The boy began to eat and was still helping himself when there was a loud thump on top of the roof. He had expected something like this all along. When people live in a kiva and someone comes, the visitors always call out or stomp their feet on top to announce their arrival. Someone had just stomped his foot, and the light quickly darkened in the entranceway. This typically happens as a person enters, grabbing hold of the ladder in order to descend. As he climbs down then it gets dark, for on his way down he appears to block off the entire entranceway. This is what happened in this case as somebody entered from above. As it turned out, it was another bear. The boy stopped eating and stared at the beast. The girl, however, remarked, "Don't worry, he won't harm you. We live here."

Upon stepping off the ladder the bear stood there facing the boy, looking through its paws the way these animals always do when they have a mind to attack a person. Whenever Bear kachinas enter a kiva during a night dance, they behave in the same fashion. This bear did the same as it moved toward the boy. But it left him in peace and passed him by to disappear into the back room. Upon coming back out it too had changed into a human being. The boy was amazed. Once again, it was no longer a beast that reemerged but an ordinary human. "I guess they live here," the boy thought, as he resumed eating his food.

It was getting evening, and the animals had probably been hunting to have returned this late. Before long, a third beast entered. This time it was a mountain lion. It did what this animal typically does, namely jumping down from on high. It still had not come all the way down the ladder when it jumped down to the floor. In a big leap it swung around the ladder pole, landing right next to the boy. The poor boy was frightened out of his wits. But the mountain lion simply strolled about and then it too disappeared into the back room. When it reentered, it too had been transformed into a human shape.

This process continued, and each time somebody came out of the back room he said to the boy by way of greeting, "So you also stay around here?" The boy answered as was proper. The last two animals to arrive were a badger and a gopher. Apparently, they also were sharing the living quarters there.

By now all the residents had returned from their outings. When the boy was finally full, he moved away from the food and settled down on one of the stone benches. There he sat now, listening to the others as they chatted in the comfort of their home. One of them asked the girl who the visitor was that was staying there with them and where she had picked him up.

She replied, "I came upon him not far from here on the northeast side. That's why I brought him here. He said he was wandering around in self-imposed exile and so was not on the way to a specific destination. For this reason I brought him here and told him he could remain with us for the time being."

The others indicated that if indeed he had no desire to go anywhere else, it would be all right for him to stay there with them. They all agreed on this point.

Meanwhile, night had fallen as the whole group sat there whiling away the time. Finally, the bear, who seemed to be the leader of the group, suggested they entertain their guest with dancing. As a result, they all exited the kiva, probably in order to go and put on their costumes. After a while the boy could hear the approach of some beings. Then there was the sound of someone shaking a rattle. Immediately, the person tending the fire shouted up to them, "Come on down!"

Kachinas filed into the kiva. They entertained the boy by staging a dance. When they were finished, they departed, whereupon a new group came down the ladder. Different kinds of kachinas, one group after another, kept entering just like during a night dance. It was well into the night when the dancing came to an end. The leader exclaimed, "This will do. Let's go to bed now. It is late."

So they all spread out their bedrolls there. The girl who had brought the boy now turned to him and said, "Come over to me. We'll go into the back room where we can sleep."

From all appearances the girl intended to sleep with the boy. It seemed that he was going to have her as his girlfriend. There was no question, she wanted to sleep with the boy and for this reason had made her bed in the back room. The boy did as bidden, entered the room and spent the night with the girl.

The next day, after it got light, all the animal people stayed home and did nothing.

And, as typically happens in stories, a year usually passes in no time. This was also true in this case. Meanwhile, the boy's parents and his younger sister were greatly troubled that he had not yet returned home. Sure enough, they had been very angry with him, and when he disappeared they had not really been waiting for him to come back. Nor did they have any idea where he had gone. But now, a year later, they were getting lonesome for him. The boy's parents were so distraught that they no longer even combed their hair. After all, he had been their only son. The animal people who kept the boy were certainly checking on his parents. And, as usually happens in a story, there is always someone who knows how a person's relatives are faring. So the animal people also were familiar with the state of mind of the boy's parents. They too were worried that the boy might get homesick and would show a desire to return home one day. He had never really become accustomed to their place and remembered his parents and relatives far away. One day he said to his wife—she was his wife now because he had been sleeping with her—"I wonder if I should not go back home."

His wife replied, "I think you should, for surely you must be lonesome for your parents and younger sister. Let me talk to my people here. Maybe they can advise us what is best to be done."

That same night the bear woman told her uncles that the man living there with them was toying with the idea of returning home and wondered if this would be all right.

One of her relatives replied, "Yes, it will be all right. After all, he did not grow up with us and will never get accustomed to living here in the forest. So let him return to his real home."

With that, the animal people went to bed. The following morning, as soon as it was day, they instructed the man at length in what they wanted from him after he left. As soon as they were done with breakfast they said to him, "Well, having lived here with us, you have certainly seen the condition of our altar. We always pray at this altar. Now, a game animal usually has a prayer feather tied around its wrist. One of them may even have a taqvaho, or male paho, attached to a crook staff. A bear has the taqvaho tied to his leg. For this reason we desire from you prayer feathers and taqvahos for ourselves. When you get home, make us some pahos once in while. No one is making any for us here these days. Just do that for us from time to time because it is these prayer items that help sustain our lives. If you do that we'll be grateful to you forever.

"And make every prayer stick just like a taqvaho," they continued. "Attach a little food bag to it and place in it a mixture of cornmeal and ground-up abalone shell. Be sure this little food bag is not missing," they impressed on the boy. "Carry these offerings to where you have your field and deposit them along its southwestern edge. We are then bound to notice them." This is how they talked to the man.

He replied, "Very well, I promise always to do this."

When the woman was ready to take her husband back, she changed into a bear again. Then they all dressed the man in beautiful clothes, for he had arrived rather shabbily dressed. Among other things, they had fashioned a buckskin shirt for him. The pants were also made of deerskin. In addition, he now wore leggings and red buckskin moccasins with rawhide soles, the traditional Hopi foot-wear. Thus, all his clothes were of leather. Dressed up like this, the bear woman loaded her husband on her back and carried him back along the same route as she had first brought him to her abode. Circling around the mountain range of the San Francisco Peaks she turned all the way to the northeast and there sat him down. From this point it was not far to his home at Wupatki.

Since the man's parents missed him so much, their daughter kept telling them that he would surely return one day. Her reassurances helped them to keep some of their strength, for they were sick from all the longing. So she was constantly saying that he would be back. That day the girl said it to them again, but her parents did not believe her anymore. "He won't be coming back as you keep telling us. He's taking forever. You're just telling us lies. He won't come as you keep insisting." That's how her parents responded to her. They simply would not take her word any longer.

Meanwhile, the man was heading home on foot from the place where his bear wife had dropped him off. Some time that evening he reached the house of his parents. Immediately, his younger sister announced his arrival to them. "Come on, get up. Your son is here!"

But the parents refused to believe her, and it was not until he actually entered that they were convinced of the truth. They had still just been lying there, for due to their grief, they no longer cared to get even out of bed. However now that he had finally returned they came to their senses again and rose at once with their hair still messy and unkempt. Since they had failed to get up they had neither washed it nor combed it. Now, however, the parents had no choice but to rise.

They were overjoyed to have their son back and quickly recovered from their ordeal. By evening they whole family was living at peace again.

The next day villagers everywhere learned of the boy's return, for they all knew of his disappearance. Everywhere people were talking about his return. His friends came to visit him and were happy to have him back. They still remembered him well.

Unfortunately the man had only been back a few days before he resumed his old gambling habit with all the other people. Once he started he became so absorbed in it that he completely forgot his wife in the forest. Neither were any of the instructions he had received from her uncles fulfilled by him. And since he had forgotten her, he also forgot to fashion the pahos for them. He would be busy at the place where he had his field, but never did he deposit any offerings there for them. Always at daybreak his bear wife and her uncles would head out to the field for the prayer items they had asked him to make for them, but never did they find anything. There was simply nothing there. The animal people, poor things, became quite unhappy about this. On many occasions they had checked the place at the field, but always in vain. The man had never left any prayer feathers for them. This made his wife furious, for she had given birth in the meantime. Maybe the man did not know this yet, or maybe he did know. The fact was that right after his return to his parents he never thought of his wife and her relatives anymore and totally forgot his ceremonial obligations. All of this went through his wife's mind. She began to seethe with anger.

One day, after having spent a long time gambling here and there, the man once again started thinking about doing some planting. He headed out to his field and hoed weeds. It was then that he suddenly remembered his wife. He must have had some knowledge of her pregnancy for, quite by intuition, he planted corn in three places. Evidently, he assumed that his wife had twins. For this reason he planted one lot for his wife and two for the children. After preparing these three lots he also planted corn in two additional locations for his parents.

When his bear wife noticed that her husband regularly went to check on his plants, she approached her uncles and said, "I want you to go to his field, pick half of all the fresh corn and bring it here."

The uncles obeyed and headed out to the field. It was dark night by the time they arrived there. As requested, they picked half of all the fresh corn and brought it home. Then they all feasted on it.

The following morning, as the man went to check on his plants, he noticed right away that some animals had eaten from them. He walked about trying to figure out the tracks, but he could not determine who the culprits had been. On the way back the animals had broken off parts of the corn plants and erased all traces of their tracks. They were therefore unrecognizable. The man was at a loss as to who it had been. He knew it hadn't been rabbits, so he kept wondering, "What on earth were those creatures that did this?" He was completely distraught, poor thing. Finally, he said to himself, "From now on I'll go there to spend the night. I swear, if I catch them in the act, I'll kill them." Upon his return home he therefore made arrows for himself. When he had fashioned a large pile, he said to his parents, "Tonight, after supper, I'll go out to my plants. Some animals ate from them and caused me great misery. They devoured almost all of them. If I go to guard the plants until they ripen, we can at least gather some corn at harvest time."

"All right," his parents replied. "But didn't you look for tracks to find out what animals were there?"

"Sure, I did. I walked all over, but couldn't tell what kind they were. They dragged leaves from the plants all over and erased all their tracks. Nothing is visible anymore. I have no idea who could have done the damage."

"All right, then," his parents replied, "go and sleep there. Maybe you can catch the ones responsible. They may come again during the night."

The bear woman and her relatives quickly became aware that the man slept at the field that night. So she advised her uncles, "Don't go to the field for the time being. My husband is sleeping there. I'll decide tomorrow what to do about this." The twins, her children, were quite grown by now.

When the man returned home the morning after his first night at the field he said, "Nothing happened. Maybe those animals intended to do it only once to cause me this terrible misery."

The following night he went out once more to sleep at the field. "They might come tonight if I'm not there," he thought. With that, he headed out to the field and when he arrived he collected wood along its edge and lit a fire. The purpose of the fire was to prevent any animals from coming too close. Then he moved to the middle of the field, covered himself in a blanket, and lay down. Soon he fell into a pleasant sleep guarding his plants.

When the bear woman's uncles went out to eat some of the corn again they spotted the fire. Because of this, they dared not approach and returned home.

The following morning when it got daylight again, the man walked about but found no trace of any animal that had come during the night. Once more he had failed to catch the culprits. In spite of this, however, he continued going to the field and sleeping there to guard his plants.

Only the portion that the man had planted for his parents was still left intact. So one night all the animals headed out to this lot and feasted on the corn once more. When an evil person intends to harm someone, he always aims at midnight. So all the animals set out in the middle of the night, the man's wife, her two children, and all their uncles. It was as if they were making a raid on the plants. Not only did they eat up all the corn, they also uprooted the stalks, just for spite. While some of them were engaged in this task, the gopher and badger were busy digging burrows and tunnels all over the place, for that is what these two are really good at. They made holes in the en-tire field. Finally, when they were satisfied with their destruction, they all headed home, with the exception of the bear woman and her twins. She had told them that they would stay a little longer. She now instructed her children to go to the place where their father was sleep-ing and chew on his bowstring. And so, when all their uncles had departed, the two approached their father while their mother waited for them at the edge of the field. He lay right next to them, pleasantly asleep, while they gnawed on his bowstring. This accomplished, the three bears went home too.

Some time later, when their father awoke, he went to inspect the plants. He had not heard a single sound of the terrible devastation, so when he saw that all his plants had been devoured and the ground churned up, he became extremely angry. This time, as he searched for tracks, he discovered some, and when he realized that they were the spoor of bears, he grew beside himself with rage. Full of anger, he returned home to inform his father that they would have to hunt down some bears who were the culprits. He explained that they had not only eaten up all of the crops but had also pulled out all the stalks and left the field in shambles.

Next the man sought out the village crier who was to broadcast the news of the bear hunt from the rooftop. The village crier did as bidden. The men who were going in pursuit of the bears, however, were somewhat reluctant because they felt inadequate for the task. A bear is an awesome creature and they, being only humans, did not think they would be able to overpower these beasts. At least some of them who were going to accompany the man voiced opinions along these lines.

The next day the group set out in pursuit of the bears. The man who was the sponsor of the hunt had eaten his breakfast quite early and had already gone ahead of the main party. Upon reaching his field he pressed on without waiting for the others. In the area where the animals had come through he followed their tracks and eventually caught up with them. This happened soon after he had entered a forest. He was still searching for the beasts when one of them emerged from the thicket. The man aimed his arrow to shoot it. When he pulled back, however, at that instant the bowstring broke where the two bear cubs had chewed on it. Since the string was partially unravelled, it was bound to snap in two. Having failed to kill the bear the man in turn was now attacked by the beast. Bears typically kill by ripping a person's chest apart and in this fashion the bear killed the man. Then it took off. The bear had been the man's wife. Her husband had probably recognized her in her bear's shape. She had been so filled with anger against him that she had killed him. Having accomplished her mission she lumbered on home.

Meanwhile, the other hunters were following the man, traversing the same area as he. Eventually they caught up with him; when they did they saw that he was dead. Now they really lost their nerve, for they knew full well that they had no chance against those beasts. So they picked up the man's corpse and carried it back to his home.

When his bear wife arrived back at her abode she told her uncles what she had done. They became very angry upon learning of her deed. "You should not have done that to him," they scolded her. She explained that she had committed this act out of anger. Her uncles, however, insisted that regardless of whether the man neglected to make pahos for them, she should never have killed him. All of them were quite unhappy about this turn of events.

Meanwhile, the hunters had delivered the dead body of the man. After preparing him ceremonially for his afterlife they buried him. Now that he had died, his parents and younger sister were sad and despondent.

That same evening the bear woman, the dead man's wife, all of a sudden announced to her uncles that her husband had not really died after all. She claimed that he could be brought back to life. So then the uncles ordered the two nephews to go and retrieve their father's body. The latter did as bidden. They headed out to the grave site, dug the body up, and carried it back to their home. The uncles were now going to try and bring him back to life. For this purpose they had already spread out a wedding robe next to their altar, before the nephews' arrival with the corpse. After bringing it inside, they laid it on top of the robe and then covered it up with something. Next, all of them sat down by the body on all sides and started chanting. They probably used a sacred ritual prayer song. This they sang until it got daylight. Early that morning they all went outside from their abode to pray.

Upon reentering, they saw that he had evidently come back to life, for he was sitting up. The animal people were elated and expressed their thanks that he had regained his senses again. Both the badger and the mountain lion are of course medicine men. They are the ones who remove objects with malignant powers that are implanted in their patients. They were also the ones who had planned the man's revival. So now they planned to instruct him in the art of curing.

For four full days they kept the man sequestered. On the first day they taught him the sacred ritual prayer song. It took him until night-time to learn it. The next day they showed him all the various medicines that are used to heal a sick person. On the third day they took him around to all the locations where the different medicinal plants grow. Some of them grow far away, but they went to all of them. Of course, they did not travel on foot. Since the man now had these beasts as his fathers, he did everything like them, in the form of a bear. By taking him around through all these areas, they not only taught him about these locations but also dug up the various medicines for him. Then they explained to him what a disease is. When they had initiated him like this into all the aspects of the art of healing, they reassembled back in their abode.

On the fourth day the man was supposed to return home again. His bear wife herself was going to take him back, so on the morning of the fourth day they washed his hair and ushered him outside to speak the morning prayer to the rising sun. When this ritual too was over, they dressed him in the same buckskin clothes that he had worn on his return home. As they dressed him, they also carefully bundled up all the different kinds of medicines that would be useful to him in his role as a healer. Prepared like this, his bear wife then set out to take him back. At some place she let him dismount, and from there he continued homeward on foot.

When the man arrived back home, his family could not believe their eyes. But he related to his parents how he had received a new life. People say of course that when someone becomes a medicine man, he has all of them as his children. He was now going to take care of them in that village there. He had been initiated into the art of healing, so in the role of the medicine man he would now help them.

And so, from that day on, the man took care of all the people there at Wupatki. As the word of his healing craft spread, everybody came seeking medical treatment from him, for he was extremely powerful and cured every person right away. In this fashion he worked for the people there. Soon the people from nearby villages also learned of him and came only to him for help. Once in a while Indians from far away came to fetch him, and he had to travel long distances and under great hardships. But he worked hard for every-body, no matter who it was. Since people kept coming from far away, he could not afford to be lazy. Also, he thought of it this way: He had died and had been brought back to life. He had been initiated into the art of healing and had returned to his village with this knowledge. It was as if through the art of healing he had become a member of his community again. For this reason he could not afford to be lazy. Rather, he kept urging himself on to treat his patients. It was as if he was living for this purpose only.

From that time on the man also fulfilled his ceremonial obliga-tions toward the animal people. Regularly he prepared pahos and prayer feathers for them and went to deposit them at the edge of his field. Each time he placed them there, the beasts noticed it and came to pick them up. In this fashion the man took care of them. In a way, he was paying them back. In this matter too he now never became negligent.

He also remembered his children and his wife far away. Once, his parents asked him if he would not consider bringing them to the village. Then they could all live together in one place while he con-tinued taking care of his patients. So he sought out his beast relatives, for he knew where they lived. He asked them if they would come with him, and his wife and two children said yes.

And so they accompanied him back to his village. They built their own house somewhere and then lived there. The father continued to treat people, and once in a while when a patient wanted to express his gratitude, he gave him a gift. Occasionally, a patient would even offer him one of his belongings. However, he never accepted any material things, except for food.

In this manner the man and his family lived there, and now that he had his wife there with him he was really happy. Evidently, she was a very beautiful woman. And so all four of them lived there from that time on, and I guess they still live there somewhere.

And here the story ends.

The Antelope Kids

Aliksa'i. People were living at Oraibi and all across the land people were settled in villages. Way back in those days they were enjoying a good life, and every summer they raised big crops. That's how people were living.

In the northwestern corner of Oraibi a couple had made their home. They were middle-aged but still going strong. However, though they had been married for a long time, they had not been blessed with children. Every morning as they stepped outside to say a morning prayer they asked for children. One day the man said to his wife, "I guess no one is going to have pity on us and grant us a child."

"Yes indeed," she replied, "but I won't give up hope."

"Neither will I," her husband said. And so the two continued to pray to the rising sun in the morning.

For some reason the village children were extremely fond of this couple. They arrived at their house as soon as the two had break-fasted and then just played there. When it got warm, the couple always went together to tend their plants. They would then simply hand their house over to the children. "You may play here for the time being," they would say said to them. "When you've had enough and get weary, just close the door." With that the couple would head out to the field. That's what the two used to do. On their way home they always came with a small load of wood. Since it was summer they would work till the very end of the day.

One morning as they were breakfasting the husband turned to his wife and said, "I've been thinking about something,"

"All right, what?" his wife asked.

"Well, I know you keep looking at those children. They are really accustomed to our place. I was wondering if we should not try to find a child somewhere. If we do, those kids could always be together with it here. From the first day we got married we've been wishing for a child, but nobody has taken pity on us. So I thought that maybe we should go to the children's shrine and pray there."

"That's fine by me," his wife replied. "If we really desire a child, we have to try everything."

Two days later the man said to his wife, "For once let's not go to the field tomorrow." So the following morning the two did not go to the field. Instead, the man bade his wife to take a bath. She was to thoroughly cleanse herself. His wife did as bidden and bathed for a long time. Her husband followed suit and then busied himself with various things. Apparently he was fashioning prayer feathers and prayer sticks. When they were properly finished, it was early eve-ning. Right after sunset the man said to his wife, "All right, you get ready now. Put on your nice woolen dress." That's what women in those days used to wear, black woolen dresses. "When you're done I'll have further instructions for you."

The woman combed her hair with great care and twisted it into side pigtails, the hairstyle of the married woman. Next, she put her dress on. By the time she was finished with everything it had gotten dark. The man now said, "Come here." He had laid something down on the northwest side of the firepit. They were his prayer feathers as it turned out. The woman went over to her husband, who now divided the heap of feathers. Handing her half he said, "Take these to the Buffalo shrine northwest of the village. I myself will go to the Antelope shrine southeast of here. If you are in luck you will see a figure walking about there. Keep an eye on him. As soon as he disappears sit down by the shrine and pray. Explain the reason why you want a child. Ask that we may finally be granted one. When you're through praying pull up your dress in front and spread your legs wide apart."

After these instructions the woman left, with her husband following on her heels. Walking in a northwesterly direction she crossed the edge of the village. There, at a place northwest of the earthen dam, is the Buffalo shrine. At a spot to the southeast is the Antelope shrine. While the man headed toward the Antelope shrine, the woman was on her way to the Buffalo shrine.

As she was nearing her destination, the reddish-yellow twilight was noticeable along the western horizon. A little daylight was still left. As she approached the shrine she could clearly make out a figure striding back and forth. Keeping the mysterious figure in view, the woman drew closer and closer, but the figure gradually became smaller, and when she finally reached the shrine, it had vanished. The woman squatted down now and fervently spoke her prayers. If only someone would have pity and bestow a child on them! Having completed this part she did as instructed by her husband and pulled up her dress in front. After a little while she covered her thighs with the dress again. Her husband, meanwhile, had carried out his own rites at the Antelope shrine in the southeast. He too had uttered a prayer for a child and then gone back again.

The man was the first to arrive back home. He entered the house and before long his wife came in. He asked her how she had fared, and she explained that someone had indeed been walking about by the shrine. "Very good, thanks!" her husband exclaimed.

That's what the couple did there that evening. From that day on life continued as before again. The two would go to their plants regularly, and the children kept playing at their house. But then one day the woman realized that she was pregnant. She was elated. Still, she continued going to the field with her husband to hoe weeds. Eventually, however, when her belly had swollen up quite large and she tired more and more easily, her husband said, "You keep getting tired. I don't want you to help me at the field any longer."

From that day on the woman remained at home. It seems that all the two were focusing on now was the day when she would give birth. Finally when her time came, she delivered without any complications. Much to their surprise she gave birth to twins, or "antelope kids," as the Hopis call them. A little girl was the first to come out, followed by a baby boy. The couple was overjoyed. This is what they had prayed for on so many occasions. After all these years someone had evidently taken pity on them and fulfilled their heart's desire. From that day on the couple lived in great contentment. The children who came to play were also pleased and spent all their time at the couple's house. The man was a skilled weaver, so as soon as the babies were born he wove a checkered boy's blanket for his son and a little girl's blanket for his daughter. The twins wore these blankets like shawls. They also wrapped themselves up in them as they slept.

Meanwhile, the twins were getting bigger, quite rapidly as a matter of fact, for they were not ordinary children. They had special powers. Their father labored hard in the field because now he had children whom he really wanted something for. Soon brother and sister were crawling around and, not long after, reached the point where they were walking about. They became strong. When a child reaches that age, it misbehaves and does all sorts of things. The twins were just like that. They got into all kinds of trouble. As a result, their mother got upset with them now and then.

One day as she scolded them, her husband overheard her outburst of anger. "Remember I've been warning you not to scold them," he rebuked her. "You're not supposed to get after them all the time. We suffered a lot when we had no children, and then it was as if they were given to us. So please don't scold them anymore."

From that time on the woman tried to restrain her scolding. The twins grew stronger and stronger. One morning when their father woke up, he heard someone making a noise. He strained his ears. Apparently, the kids had gotten up early and were in the back room doing something. Deciding to look in on them, he rose from his bed, stepped over to the back room door and peeked inside. What he saw caused him to stare in surprise. There was sunlight entering the room through an opening, and the twins were sliding down on this sunlight. They had spread out their little blankets on the rays of the sun and with great enjoyment were sliding down along them. The father could not believe his eyes. However, he went back to bed without saying anything to them and did not mention this to his wife. After all, he knew full well that the children were endowed with supernatural powers.

From that day on he caught them several times in the act of sliding on the sunshine. Occasionally, they would also dangle from the rays. Once when he was away in the field, the two did something that angered their mother so much that she whipped them. When their father returned home he found them sulking. He asked his wife, "Why are the children sulking?"

"Well, yes," she replied, "I remember you've warned me several times not to keep scolding them. But I got so upset that I beat them. That's why they're sitting there without saying a word."

The man became furious with his wife. "You simply can't obey. I can't constantly remind you not to chide them. I especially didn't want you to strike them."

Meanwhile, the twins had gotten quite big, the size children are when they are about two years old. At that age they can already run about. One day the twins' mother was grinding corn again. On this occasion the little girl got into the cornmeal in her mother's grinding box and messed it up, trying her hand at grinding motions. The parents therefore decided to get a metate for their daughter. They let all the people in the village know that in four days they would go quarry stone for a grinding slab. Over by Shungopavi there was a corner where people generally went to quarry this kind of stone. And so, four days later, the villagers headed out to this destination, among them also the twins' parents. They took their children along because they now were able to walk. Scrambling down the mesa to the plain behind their parents they kept running along.

Before long they crossed a wash, and by the time they entered an area covered with saltbush plants, the twins were exhausted and refused to go any further. They simply sat down and would not budge anymore. "Why don't we leave you here?" their father suggested. After all, they had brought along enough for the children to eat and drink. So the two sat down amidst the saltbushes and the parents left them food and water. "Just stay here for a while. We'll be back in the evening. Then you can come with us again."

The parents now followed the others and were the last to arrive at the quarry. All the people were already laboring away. They had to dig up the ground, for the rock was buried. Upon finding exactly what they were looking for, they would dress the rocks to the desirable size, load them on their backs, and set out for home. Again the twins' parents were the last to do so. Each of them dug up a slab. Since both were meant for the little girl, they selected small ones. By now some of the other people had already finished their work and were on their way home.

Before the parents had been gone for very long, over at a place southeast of the wash a big cloud of dust became visible to the children. In appearance it almost resembled a dust devil. The dust cloud was headed the twins' way. When it reached them it turned in front of them and from it emerged an antelope. It was a gigantic buck with huge horns. "So you are here?" he greeted them. The children merely stared at him. The little girl, who was a little older, finally uttered, "Yes."

"All right, I've come to fetch you. Climb on top of me," the antelope commanded.

Without demanding an explanation the two children complied. The little girl climbed up and grabbed the animal's horns. Her brother climbed up and sat down behind her. With the twins now on his back the antelope followed his tracks back along the southeastern side of the wash. After reaching a row of cottonwood trees, he crossed the wash to the northwest and then sped along in a southwesterly direction. There in the direction toward Oraibi the land is flat with only a few ridges. That area is known as Pangalanpi. That's where the buck was headed. Finally the animal ran up one of the ridges and, upon coming to a depression in the ground, stopped. "All right, go up there," the antelope bade the twins.

Much to their surprise they spotted a kiva with a ladder sticking out of it. The antelope ushered the children inside, whereupon watermelon and white piki were set out for them. The twins ate with great gusto. Then the antelope took them outside again and said, "Go to the northwest from here; there you can be happy with these." As the children looked in the direction pointed out to them, they noticed all sorts of animals. Deer and all the other game animals were teeming there. The twins played around with them until early evening, when the antelope buck called them again and said, "All right, come here to me, for we need to go back. Your parents are on their way."

Once more he loaded the children on his back and returned to exactly where he had picked them up.

True enough, it was not long before some of the people began returning from the quarry. When they met the children they asked them to come with them. "All right, why don't you come with us? Your parents are on their way." The twins, however, refused. They had their food, of course, which they had hidden somewhere together with the water. And, sure enough, their parents finally arrived. Their children joined them, as before, and ran along behind them. After all, they were not ordinary children. Finally, after sunset, the family arrived back at home. The little girl was full of anticipation. After supper all of them slept. The next day the mother of the little girl set up the metate for her. Within only a day or two she was able to grind by herself. Her mother also was engaged in the same chore. She had a storage shelf made from pegs in the wall. Each time she ground a lot of cornmeal she heaped the flour on a tray and then placed it on the pegs. The little girl imitated her mother and busily used her grinding stone.

One day her mother heard something as she was grinding in the back room. Her little daughter seemed to be singing. She listened carefully and could clearly hear a song, so she kept listening. By now the little girl had ground a large quantity of flour, so she heaped it on a tray and decided to store it next to her mother's. To reach the storage pegs she stacked a few things on top of each other and tried to set her tray next to her mother's. In attempting this, however, she bumped her mother's cornmeal causing it to crash down, landing right in the water vessel below. Frightened out of her wits, the poor thing tried to clean it out of the container. She was still engaged in this task when her mother entered. Angry at the child for causing this accident, the mother severely scolded her. So furious did she become that she whipped the child and threw her and her brother outside. There they were now, both the little sister and her brother, with tears streaming down their cheeks.

Meanwhile, it was getting early evening and the children's father arrived. The parents were not always together at home, but were usually out and about, so the father was not aware yet of his daughter's mishap. The woman set out supper, and the two started to eat.

At one point the man asked, "Where are the children? I don't see them here."

His wife simply sat there for a while. Finally she confessed, "They won't be coming. That little brat of a girl dropped my cornmeal into the water vessel. I chided her for that and beat her. Then I threw both her and her brother out of the house."

"Oh no, I'm sorry to hear that," her husband exclaimed. He did not enjoy his meal any longer. After only a few bites he left the house and went in search of his children. After going among the houses in the village, he finally discovered them. They had crawled under the cover of a pik'ami earth oven. That's where he spotted them. He asked them to come back to the house, but they refused. Again and again he begged them to come, until he had asked four times, but not before they made him cry did they relent and go with him. When they arrived back home he sat out some food for them, but they took only a few morsels. Then the family bedded down to sleep, for it was now nighttime. When the parents were fast asleep the little girl said to her brother, "Our parents never really wanted us. It's a shame they asked for us in the first place."

"That's for sure. So what are we going to do?" the little boy replied.

"Let's go look for our antelope father," the little girl suggested. "Our father and mother won't notice when we leave."

In this manner the twins plotted to go. And so they stole out of the house into the night. All the people were asleep and the moon was shining brightly. The two started out in a southeasterly direction, following a trail from the mesa top to a place below Oraibi and, upon reaching the plain, headed straight southwest toward Nuvatukya'ovi, the San Francisco Peaks. When they had covered a good distance, something approached them from the southwest. However, they were not frightened and continued on their way. Soon it was apparent that a huge antelope was headed their way. When he reached the children he spoke to them. "All right," he said, "I've come to fetch you. We noticed what happened to you, so they sent me out after you. Climb on top of me." With that the antelope lay down and the twins mounted him. The animal rose up and said, "Hold on tight. Grab my horns so you don't fall off." With these instructions the antelope dashed off. This animal, of course, is known for its speed, so he ran extremely fast. It seemed as if they hardly touched the ground, so fast did the antelope run.

Sure enough, it was not long before the three neared Nuvatu-kya'ovi. Eventually they reached the base of the mountains, and the antelope had to leap uphill. However, even though the terrain was rising, he kept his head up. They climbed all the way to the summit of Nuvatukya'ovi. As they arrived at their destination, firelight was visible from the opening of a kiva. The three climbed to the top of its roof, and the antelope jumped down into the underground chamber with the children still on his back. Everybody there greeted them happily. They were glad to see the little girl and her brother. "We are aware what your mother did to you," they said. "That's why we sent your real father after you. It was he who brought you here. Of course you'll have to go back home again, but we're keeping an eye on your parents now. There will be a time when you will hear from us again. This is not the last time your mother will punish you. Therefore we must take you back once more."

Then they all talked about more pleasant things. After a while the antelope chief said, "I suppose you should be heading back now."

"All right."

With that the antelope that had brought the children turned to them and said, "I guess it's time to leave." So the twins once more mounted their animal father and returned to Oraibi. They reached the base of the mesa before daybreak. There their father unloaded the children again and said, "All right, from here you can go on foot. I promise I'll be back again soon." With that he galloped off in a south-westerly direction.

The twins walked back home. Nobody heard them as they arrived. And so life went on again for all of them. One day the children felt like visiting their antelope parents at Nuvatukya'ovi again. They carefully planned when to go. Finally the day they had set arrived, and once more they departed when their father and mother were asleep. As before, they descended to the plain below Oraibi and had not traveled as far as the first time when they encountered their animal father, who loaded them on his back and carried them all the way to the San Francisco Peaks.

Again the joy was great when the three arrived, and all of them were happy together, but soon it was time for the children's departure again and their father took them back to Oraibi. Once more they reached their destination before daybreak. The antelope let them off right at the mesa base, from where the two walked up to Oraibi by themselves. Twice now they had escaped to Nuvatukya'ovi without their parents noticing anything.

Living their accustomed lives again, one day the twins did something to one of their mother's belongings. She became so irate about this that she whipped both of them. Therefore that night the two planned to seek out their real father again. As before they started out when their parents were sound asleep. Sure enough, their antelope father was there to pick them up. Upon their arrival at Nuvatukya'ovi everybody greeted them happily. Then they said to the children, "Your mother is not going to obey her husband. Even though he keeps warning her, she does not heed him. We will therefore teach you a song now. Let's do it without delay."

One of the antelopes then chanted a grinding song for the children. By the time he had finished the song four times, the children had memorized it. So the antelopes explained to them, "We want you to sing this song early tomorrow morning when you grind your corn. Your parents are bound to hear you. Then tomorrow night come back again and we'll have further instructions for you."

Following this, the twins' antelope father took them back to Oraibi again and dropped them off there. The children did exactly as told and began their grinding at the crack of dawn. Their parents still had not risen from bed, although the children were grinding away, singing the new song. When their father finally got up he heard a noise. Straining his ears, he realized that those were his children singing. He listened attentively, but when the twins had ended the song he felt great sorrow. Immediately, he told his wife. "I knew it," he exclaimed, "I just knew this was going to happen. You simply couldn't obey. It's quite obvious that we suffered at lot before these children were given to us. But you just could not heed my warning. Just listen to them for yourself and let me know what you think," he said to his wife.

No sooner had he said this than the children began to sing again. This time the couple listened together. The song was telling the truth. When the singing had ended, the man turned to his wife once more and said, "This is precisely what I wanted to avoid. That's why I kept warning you not to scold them. I had a feeling that they would do something like this. They are not just ordinary children. We must never chide them that harshly again. Maybe they will change their mind. This is how the song went:

> Remember, remember
> Over there in the northwest and southeast
> You two picked me like a flower.
> Watching your flower plants
> Your heart and your life is testing
> Gray-colored antelope, my father.
> Haya, haya, poor thing.
> My breath, I regret, must fade away,
> It is almost daylight. Hee.

With this song the children accompanied their grinding that morning.

The night of the same day, when their parents were asleep, the twins headed out to their father again. Sure enough, when they arrived again at Nuvatukya'ovi, they were greeted happily. Then the gathered antelopes said to the children, "You did just fine. Your parents heard you, so they are quite distraught right now. We first thought they would not mistreat you anymore, but in the end they did. Or rather, it was your mother who was the real culprit. She was the one who would not mind. Your father did not do anything. There- fore you may have little choice but to come home here to us. Never- theless, we'll try one last time. If your parents don't get it then, you will come home for good. Also, you are probably aware that in four days there will be night dances at Oraibi. On that occasion groups of kachinas will be going from kiva to kiva and dancing. Your parents will certainly want to go see them. So you will accompany them. Then, before it's over, let them know that you are weary of watching. Persuade them to let you go to bed. Your mother is bound to go and put you to sleep then. Once you are in bed she will probably tell your father to check in on you while the dance is going on. You must pretend to be sound asleep then. When your mother gets back to the kiva, your father will certainly come to check on you. One of us will also come to see you then. When the kachinas that own your father's kiva stage their last performance, we want you to join them. For the kachinas from your parents' kiva will impersonate us, dancing in the guise of antelopes. That's why one of us must come to your house at that time, to dress you up like those kachinas. When the Antelopes come to the kiva for the last time, you will join them. Nobody should be able to recognize you. However, if one of the spectators does, he will pull you aside when the kachinas stop dancing. On the other hand, if no one recognizes you, you must return home to us for ever." These were the instructions that the children received.

After that the twins were taken back to Oraibi by their antelope father again. Back home now they too, like the rest of the villagers, waited for the time of the night dances to arrive. Finally, the time came. The two were filled with anticipation. However, deep down they did not exactly have the desire to return home to Nuvatukya'ovi.

Soon it was the morning of the special event. People were looking forward to watching the dances and were talking about nothing else. Sure enough, when night fell, the twins went with their mother to see the dances. All kinds of kachinas were performing, going from kiva to kiva. Brother and sister did exactly as instructed. The dances were not yet concluded when they expressed a desire to go home. Their mother complied and took them to their house. Their father arrived a little later. The woman said to her husband, "They wanted to go home, so I brought them, even though it is not over yet. When they are in bed, you can watch the dance and check on them in the intervals."

The husband agreed at once. "Sure, I can watch from the top of the kiva and keep an eye on them. The dance will be over soon."

The two children appeared to fall asleep quickly, and their parents returned to the kiva to watch the dance. The children, of course, had only pretended to be asleep. They were waiting for a visitor. Before long he arrived and said to them. "All right, don't tarry now. The dance is nearing its end. Get up and come here. I need to dress you up."

The children obeyed and got up. As they approached the visitor they saw that it was their antelope father who had taken them to Nuvatukya'ovi. He now costumed them in every detail as Antelope kachinas. The little boy had a small wig with long flowing hair and bangs from a piece of strung-up hair. His face was decorated with stripes from the bridge of his nose across both cheeks. A cluster of eagle down was tied to the top of his head and he wore a red-hair kilt. In addition, he carried the ceremonial talavayi stick in one hand and a small blue-green rattle in the other. His sister was dressed in the black woolen dress over which she had draped like a shawl the *atö'ö* cape with wide black and red borders. From her hair dangled a prayer feather, and in a little basket she carried sacred cornmeal. When the two were properly costumed their antelope father said,

"All right, in this way you will take part with the others now. The kachinas who own the kiva are about to stage their last performance, so let's go."

All three of them went out and headed to the kiva. Sure enough, that very moment Antelope kachinas were entering it. Once more the twins' animal father spoke. "You know what to do. If someone recognizes you and doesn't let you leave, you will have to remain here in Oraibi. However, if nobody recognizes you, you must return home to us for good. I will wait for you and will know whether they catch you or not." With that he let the twins go.

The two children now entered the kiva with the other kachinas. Sure enough, the spectators were asking each other, "Whose kachina friends are those little ones?" They were anxious to find out, but no one had any idea who they were. Even their mother did not recognize them. Neither did their father. So the children danced there with the others, one of them at the front of the dance line, the other at its rear. All the people's eyes were on them only. Even the kachinas were at a loss as to who they were. They had not been with them during the prior dances.

Then the performance was concluded. The children held their breath waiting, but no one came up to them. They were going to be the last to exit the kiva. It was their turn now and one of them was already approaching the ladder on the way out, when a spectator shouted from the kiva roof, "Hold it!"

No sooner did he utter this command than the little girl and her brother were transformed into real antelopes. They were no longer in the guise of kachinas. They simply leaped up from the floor through the kiva hatch. The spectators on the roof pressed up to them and tried to catch them, but they failed.

The two antelope kids dashed off, running one behind the other down the southwestern side of Oraibi mesa. When they had descended all the away they found their father waiting. "Have you come?" he said.

"Yes," the two replied.

"Well then, let's go!" With that all three of them sped off toward Nuvatukya'ovi. Upon arriving at the mountains they were happily greeted. "All right," the other antelopes said to them, "You had to return because nobody recognized you. From this day on you have no choice but to live here with us. Your human parents, however, will be all alone again. It seems they did not really want you. We gave you to them, but it did not work out. By now they probably understand the whole story. After all, that song said it all."

In this manner the two antelope kids came back to Nuvatukya'o-vi. As was to be expected, their parents at Oraibi were heartbroken. After they returned from the night dances their children were no-where in sight. Thereupon the man said to his wife, "I just had a feeling this would happen. That's why I always warned you. Now we'll have to live without children again. Those antelope kids that emerged from the kiva must really have been our children. Now we sure won't be praying for children anymore." His wife had nothing to say.

This is how that couple lost its children. Being alone they had time to think about everything. Soon they began to long for their children. They would not even get up from bed anymore. They were totally unkempt from grief. The antelopes observed them from their abode at the San Francisco Peaks. Finally, they said to the twins, "Go visit your human parents one more time. At least, wake them up from their depression."

The twins did as bidden, but this time they traveled to their parents in the guise of snipes. The parents were lying out in the open on the rooftop of the upper story. Arriving in bird shape they flew up to them. Following the ridge formed by a stone wall they hopped around, constantly chirping. Eventually they went near their parents, who expressed delight at the sight of the snipes. "How cute! Who are you?" they exclaimed.

The twins in the form of the birds landed next to them, and as they did the man and his wife kept grabbing for them. In this way the children succeeded in getting their parents up again. Having accomplished that they returned home for ever.

This is how that couple got to be without children again. I guess they still live there alone.

And here the story ends.

Wren and Bullsnake

Aliksa'i. People were living in Oraibi. Not far from the village Wren had made her home, and Bullsnake, too, lived there. So the two always could be found roaming that area. Actually, Wren had built her nest at a steep bluff. One day she laid some eggs and after brooding them, she had six little ones.

Once when the weather was very hot Bullsnake was about. After a while he stopped and coiled up right beneath Wren's nest. He had done so because he suffered from the heat. As he lay there, Wren kept staring at him. Suddenly, she began singing a song that was directed at the snake.

Bullsnake, bullsnake
Is starving, is starving.
Bullsnake, bullsnake
Is starving, is starving.
But you can't climb up to me.

Then the bird flew off, only to perch again. This went on and on. All day long Wren kept teasing the snake from her nest.

In time, Bullsnake became annoyed and said to Wren, "You keep saying that I can't get up to you. Just wait, I'll climb up there and then I'll eat all your children."

Once again Wren made fun of the snake. Each time she ended her song, she mocked the snake, "But you can't climb up to me." And then she flew way up in the air. The bird kept up this behavior.

Bullsnake really turned angry now and replied, "Rest assured, I'll make it up to your nest." With that, he slithered up to the base of the cliff and tried to climb it. However, he only managed to climb up a little distance before he fell back down. He kept doing this, but in spite of several attempts he failed to reach the nest. Still, Bullsnake persisted. He was really determined now to reach the nest. And slowly but surely, he managed to slither up the bluff.

Once up there, he entered the birds' nest. The poor babies were chirping pitifully, but Bullsnake devoured all of them. He simply swallowed them, the way they were. The birds were so tiny, they were no match for the snake. He gobbled all of them down. When he was done with his meal, he coiled up and made himself comfortable in the nest. Soon he fell into a relaxing sleep.

When Wren returned she found Bullsnake coiled up in her nest. Upon realizing that all her children had been eaten, she became furious. Shooting up into the air she exclaimed, "Oh no, you killed my poor babies!"

"Well, why did you keep saying I couldn't get up here?" Bullsnake retorted. "It's your own fault that you're now without your children."

"I'll get even with you. You can bet on that," Wren shrieked at Bullsnake.

"No way, you can't get even with me. What's more, I'll eat you up too," Bullsnake hissed back.

Instead of replying Wren flew up and rose into the air. Higher and higher she flew, all the way to the sky. Up there was a great deal of snow, some of which Wren loaded on her wings. Carrying the snow in this way she descended to the world below. Upon reaching her nest she shook the snow off of her wings right on top of Bullsnake. All day long the bird traveled back and forth doing this. In this manner she piled a large amount of snow on the snake. Since the weather was hot that day, at first the snow quickly melted whenever it was dumped on the reptile.

Wren, however, was persistent, and eventually Bullsnake began to feel the cold a little. Wren continued throughout the day and finally had Bullsnake completely buried under the snow. Now the wretched creature really did begin to feel the cold. Being packed in the snow, he actually froze to death.

Wren now sang once more:

Bullsnake, bullsnake
Is starving, is starving.
Bullsnake, bullsnake
Is starving, is starving.
But now you can't devour me.

Then the bird flew up in the air, just as before. Bullsnake, poor thing, by this time did not stir any longer. In this way he died.

And so it was that Wren avenged the death of her children. I guess she is still living there somewhere.

And here the story ends.

Appendix I: Glossary

Aliksa'i (story opener)

A storyteller usually begins with *aliksa'i*. In reply to this formulaic introduction the listeners utter "*Oh*." As the narrator continues with his story, we keep acknowledging his story with this same response. But not all Hopis begin their tales in this manner. We who trace our ancestry to Oraibi follow this custom, while some living in the distant villages of the other mesas commence by saying "*Ituwutsi*," which means "It is my story."

All-Night Vigil

When kachinas are "closed in" during a night dance, that is, when they are asked to hold a day dance later in the year, people set a date for the occasion. Once the date is announced, they move along toward it. Upon reaching the set deadline for the dance, the kachinas who were "closed in" do not sleep on the eve of the dance, but hold an all-night vigil. Then the following day they perform in the plaza.

The same is true when children are initiated into the Kachina society. On the eve of the event, at night, they sleep only for a little while and then go watch the Powamuy kachinas. Then they too hold an all-night vigil. Also, each time social dancers intend to dance, they keep an all-night vigil the night before the event. To help them stay awake, groups of social dancers from other villages typically visit them in their kiva and entertain them with dancing.

Angwushahay'i

Angwushahay'i is a kachina. Her first appearance is during the early morning hours of Powamuya, the "Bean dance." Over a woolen dress she wears a ceremonial cape that is embroidered along the top and bottom borders. In an open container, usually a wicker plaque, she carries fresh bean sprouts and corn plants. Each time a person sprinkles her with sacred cornmeal, he helps himself to a bundle of sprouts from her tray.

As Angwushahay'i comes along, she sings about little girls and little boys. It is still gray dawn in the early morning of *totokya* as she arrives. After she has departed, the kachinas emerge from their kivas, bringing plaques and bows and arrows for the little boys and girls. Upon receiving the plaques, the little girls go around with cornmeal on them, among their aunts and grandmothers. The little boys in turn, upon getting their bows and arrows, go hunting jackrabbits for their aunts and grandmothers. That's what Angwushahay'i's song is about.

Angwushahay'i and Angwusnasomtaqa, "Crow Mother," are
slightly different in appearance. Crow Mother is an ill-tempered
woman with little eyes that are round and yellow. She is the mother
of the two Whipper kachinas that she brings with her when children
are initiated into the Kachina society. These kachinas, known as Hu'
kachinas, whip the initiates. The Crow Mother actually encourages
them as they do this. While Angwushahay'i usually wears wedding
boots, Angwusnasomtaqa wears blue moccasins.

Ant

There are many varieties of ants native to Hopiland. Some are
yellow while others are red, and some are tiny while others are huge.
Hopis believe in leaving ants unmolested and not destroying an
anthill. People claim that, as a consequence of disturbing them in any
manner, they will build their nests in a person's body. Even though
we knew this as children, we would still take a small stick and poke
into the opening of an anthill of yellow ants. After removing the stick,
we would shake off all the ants clinging to it and then lick the stick,
which had a pleasantly salty taste.

Antelope

Antelopes inhabit an area far from Hopiland in the vicinity of
Nuvatukya'ovi, the San Francisco Peaks. Once they were creatures of
Hopiland, but for some reason they no longer dwell there. Long ago,
a man who possessed the endurance to run down an antelope did so
till the animal was fatigued, whereupon he bagged it and carried the
meat home.

Because an antelope always gives birth to two fawns, the twin
offspring of a Hopi woman are referred to as *tsöviwhoyat*, "little
antelopes." There is also an Antelope kachina. A society known as the
Antelopes performs in conjunction with the Snake society during the
Snake ceremony.

Apoonivi (place name)

Apoonivi is a peak that lies somewhere southwest of the Oraibi
mesa and slightly to the northwest. Of whitish appearance, it is an
important place for the Hopi. When someone dies, he first ascends
this peak and then, after making his descent to the northwest side,
continues his journey to Maski, "Home of the Dead." There are steps
leading up to Apoonivi, two on the southeastern and northwestern

flanks of the elevation. At its very top is a house. Only the deceased can see this house.

Applying Cornmeal to Skin

Grinding corn is a very arduous task. Small wonder then that a woman perspires when engaged in this work. For this reason a woman prone to perspiring takes a little bit of cornmeal and daubs it on her face so she does not feel so hot. As a rule, any woman grinding corn smears corn flour on her face, for with it she keeps herself cool.

Corn flour is also used on the twentieth day after the birth of a child when the female who is attending the newborn and her relatives hold a naming ceremony. On this occasion they wash the infant's hair and pat its face with white corn flour. In addition, they rub some on the baby's back and on the chest over the heart area.

Arrow

To manufacture an arrow one first needs to collect the necessary wood. Desirable branches are very straight and very strong. Apache plume is said to make beautiful arrows, but men going after this plant generally have to travel far. Others use greasewood or cliff-rose to construct their arrows. As a first step, the wooden shafts are straightened out as much as possible. Next, one end of the arrow receives a point, while on the opposite end a groove is cut across the top. Into this groove the bowstring is inserted, which, when drawn, projects the arrow. Directly below this grooved end, three split feathers are firmly attached with sinew wrappings. The other ends of the feathers are also bound to the shaft with sinew. Should a person intend to decorate his arrow, he does so, of course, prior to mounting the feathers.

The arrow that comes with a child's bow is painted red at the lower end. The portion where the feathers are mounted has its own distinct decoration, and the bottom tip is painted blue-green. The very first arrows a baby boy ever receives are fashioned from a small reed. One arrow from this first bundle is set aside for his umbilical cord, which is tied to it and then stuck into the ceiling at the home of his birth.

In former days the Hopis used to coat their arrows with rattlesnake poison. When such an arrow was shot at a foe and penetrated his skin, the poison would spread within his body and bring on a quick death. During those times, when the arrow was one of the few Hopi weapons, the Hopis also used shaft straighteners to align their crooked shafts when necessary. This implement was made from some hard material and had three or four perforations. Exactly how it was employed, however, has been forgotten.

Badger

For the Hopis, the badger is a great medicine man. They also have him as a kachina. Therefore, at times when a person is suffering from some malady, he prays to the badger to heal his ailment. The badger is also the clan ancestor of some Hopi.

Bean Dance Ceremony

During the Powamuy or "Bean dance" ceremony, people are being purified. That's the reason it is called Powamuya. The purification is carried out by the Powamuy or Bean dance leader. He purifies people of everything, especially of the desire to dance in social dances. During this month the kachinas harvest bean sprouts and bring them to the children on the morning of *totokya* or "ceremonial eve." That same night there are kachina dances in the kivas that uninitiated children are not permitted to watch.

Bear

Hopis have been familiar with bears for a very long time. It is well established that black bears still roam the forests near the San Francisco Peaks. More than one person has spotted that species there. For some Hopis, the bear constitutes the clan ancestor. Traditionally, the *kikmongwi* or "village chief" comes from this clan. Some medicine men, too, derive their powers from bears and use them as ceremonial fathers when they treat people. Bears are also part of the Hopi kachina pantheon. There are two kinds: the White Bear and the Black Bear. Because this animal is considered a powerful being a kachina will have its paw depicted on his face.

Bee

As it is easily seen that bees store honey in their abodes, people used to gather this honey in the olden days. First, one needs something that can serve as a swatter, for as soon as one digs into the hive underground, the bees become aware of it and, emerging in large numbers, attack the pilferer. Now is the moment to use the swatter and strike at them. Once in a while when a bee manages to get under one's shirt, one really suffers, because even though one strikes after the bees, one of the bees is bound to succeed and sting a person.

Eventually, however, people manage to take the honey out, where-upon they distribute it among themselves. Occasionally, they return home with a big eye and their face all swollen up.

Bees are believed to be powerful beings, so people go and deposit sacred cornmeal along with a prayer feather for them at certain shrines. Whenever they do this, they take some honey along on a piece of corn husk. After the whole offering has been deposited, one dusts oneself off. After that one gets into a standing position, puts some of the honey into one's mouth, and sprays it into all six direc-tions: first into the northwest, then toward the southwest, the south-east, and northeast; after that, toward the heavens and then the earth.

Blanket

Hopi blankets are manufactured by the Hopis themselves. As a rule, the men and boys do the weaving. They also carry out the spinning. They always spin a white yarn, and if a weaver wants to create a blanket with colored stripes, he dyes the yarn. Then he weaves it in different colors. Normally a blanket is woven in narrow consecutive bands. These bands are usually black and white, but occasionally a blue-green stripe is also part of the weave.

Body Paint

Whenever a Hopi is involved in a ceremony, body paint is a pre-requisite. According to the ceremony in question, the participants are distinguished by their own individual markings. For example, the members of the Snake society share the same characteristic body painting. Some kachinas whose bodies are most elaborately painted are colored after the Powamuy kachina. Others are daubed with paint in only a few places. The Tseeveyo kachina from the Third Mesa vil-lage of Oraibi, for instance, is smeared only with kaolin on certain areas of his body. The body paints assigned by tradition to a particu-lar person or kachina are never varied. There is quite an assortment: kaolin, soot, and red ocher are naturally available whereas yellow, red, and blue pigments are manufactured body washes.

Bullsnake

We Hopis include bullsnakes in our prayers for rain; for this reason we also dance with them. Whenever a person comes across a bullsnake, he does not molest it, but ushers it to the side of the trail if the snake lies there stretched out. We hold bullsnakes in high regard, just like rattlesnakes. Rattlers, however, are of an angry disposition. That's why they warn people to leave them alone.

It is also held that if one steps over a bullsnake's tracks, one's legs will hurt and one will get skinny around the waist. When spotting a bullsnake, one is therefore supposed to drag one's feet across the snake's tracks and not step over them.

When a bullsnake wants to kill a cottontail or jackrabbit, it roams far and wide. Upon spotting one, it hypnotizes it as if by inhaling. In the same fashion the snake is calling out for rain: it draws in the cloud's juice.

They tell people that a bullsnake normally does not come into a village. Once in a great while, however, a bullsnake is seen inside a house. When that happens, people kill it, for that bullsnake is believed to be a sorcerer.

Butterfly Hairdo

When a girl reaches a marriageable age, her mother styles her hair in a fashion called *poli'ini*. First she brushes her hair thoroughly before parting it in the center. Then, using a wooden hoop for support, she fashions a whorl on each side of her daughter's head. When the girl's hair is long and luxuriant, she will inevitably have large whorls. A girl wearing her hair in this fashion is most attractive in the eyes of the Hopi. The similarity of the whorls in the girl's hair style to the wings of a butterfly account for its being called *poli'ini*, "butterfly hairdo."

Preadolescent girls, on the other hand, have a hairdo referred to as *naasomi*. The *naasomi* is worn on both sides of the head above the ears and is not as large as the *poli'ini*.

Cat

Some Hopis claim that a cat will roam about at night without uttering a sound. Therefore, in order not to be recognized, sorcerers travel about the villages in the guise of a cat when they intend to harm a person.

Chicken Hawk

The chicken hawk is an excellent hunter that hunts around for cottontails and jackrabbits. Long ago, some Hopis used to have a lot of chickens. Whenever a hawk started killing them, it would not let up. The bird's wing is shaped like a rabbit stick. That's why one story explains how the Hopis received the rabbit stick from the chicken hawk. One of the Runner kachinas comes in the guise of a chicken hawk.

Chipmunk

Chipmunks have their homes along the edge of the mesa and in rock piles. Whenever people have bountiful peach crops, chipmunks try to get to them first. That's why people set traps for them. After all, they simply waste the peaches. They split them open to get at the seeds in the peach stones. And that is wasteful.

One of the Runner kachinas comes in the guise of a chipmunk. He has a white stripe running vertically down his face.

Cicada

The cicada is supposed to know how to produce warmth. This is why the Hopis hold it in high regard. It is said that when the cicada plays its flute, warm weather arrives. Members of the Flute society pray to the cicada, among other things, when conducting their ceremony. Long ago, when the Hopis had not yet come to their destined land but were still engaged in their migration, the owners of the Flute ritual reached the northernmost spot on earth. They tried in vain to melt the ice there, using their knowledge of producing heat, before they arrived in Hopi country.

Clouds

The Hopis ask the clouds for rain, for only when it rains do they have water. Also, when people plant, somebody's father is usually engaged in ritual smoking. He does this day after day, and the purpose is to bring rain.

According to Hopi belief a person is transformed into a cloud at the time of his death. During planting season the clouds then say, "Let's go check on the plants of our relatives. Maybe they're coming up. We should go water them." For this reason, when kachinas hold a dance and the women go feed them at noon, one of the kachinas secretly takes a pinch from the food, goes to the edge of the kachina resting area, and offers it up to the clouds. The following words are spoken at that occasion: "Here, please eat. Let it rain hard."

Not all clouds are the same, so they have different names. For example, cirrus clouds are stretched out across the sky, and cirrocumulus move along in little balls. Cumulus clouds are grayish in color and stacked up high. *Heyapaw* clouds travel along really low, almost touching the earth. Billowing thunder clouds are really dark. It is from them that the rain falls.

Whenever cumulonimbus clouds are towering somewhere and a person stares at them, someone will say, "Don't keep looking at them or you will get a cataract."

Corn

Corn is ever present in the life of a Hopi. At birth, a perfect ear of white corn represents the symbolic mother of a child. From corn a variety of items are made: food, sacred cornmeal, flour. Wherever a special event is going on, corn or its byproduct is never missing. Corn is so precious that whenever it is incorporated into a Hopi's song, it is spoken of as his mother. At death, a path of cornmeal is made along which the deceased travels wherever he is destined to go.

Corn Mother

A *tsotsmingwu* or Corn Mother is considered a person's mother. When a person is initiated into a society, he brings one along as his mother. Consequently, a Hopi says, "I have corn as my mother and the sun as my father."

A *tsotsmingwu* is not just ordinary corn. Nor is it just any color. It is always white. Once in a while it will have its tassel attached, or it may also lack it, but the tip of the corn never shows, that is, it is completely enclosed with kernels. Also, it usually has the little stalk at the bottom of the ear. Otherwise, it is not the perfect Corn Mother.

Cottontail

Long ago cottontails were quite abundant in Hopi country, so the Hopis went about hunting them. At that time, when sheep did not yet exist, cottontails and jackrabbits were the Hopis' only source of stewing meat. Hunting was done either alone or with a partner. Communal rabbit hunts were also announced for specific dates in those days. When a set date was reached, everybody went out to hunt. Frequently, people went out hunting in winter, immediately after a snowfall, because then the animals' tracks could be readily seen. People also used to fashion snow boots for themselves out of cottontail skins.

Coyote

A Hopi has no use for the coyote whatsoever; therefore, he does not prize him. It may be that the ancient Hopi benefited from him somehow, but no one has ever mentioned anything along these lines. In many stories Coyote believes everything he is told. As a result, he gets into all sorts of predicaments, and people laugh at him. Any person, therefore, who is equally easily duped is labeled *ihu* by the Hopi, which denotes both "coyote" and "sucker." Coyote also has to imitate everything. In other tales he gets himself into sticky situations because of his lecherousness. Once in a while, however, he will do something beneficial for people.

Farmers certainly do not appreciate the coyote. After all, it roams their fields destroying their watermelons and muskmelons. Thus, long ago people used to organize coyote drives to get rid of these pests. However, neither its pelt nor its meat was ever used.

For some Hopi the coyote constitutes a clan totem. Consequently they refer to themselves as belonging to the Coyote clan.

It is in the coyote's nature to waste things. So, if people have watermelons somewhere, he just takes a bite out of them and lets the rest go to waste. People are upset about that. And because he is like that, many are angry with him, especially a person who has plants. In this sense the coyote is also bad. Also those who have sheep are mad at the coyote. Once in a while he has a habit of stealing an animal from their flock, especially a lamb. The coyote pelt is not worn ceremonially, and we have absolutely no other use for him. No one has ever said anything to the effect that we Hopi eat coyote meat. We only hunt cottontails. jackrabbits, and good-tasting game for meat.

Coyote Hunt

When people go on a coyote drive, the one in charge of the hunt fashions prayer feathers. Usually he makes one with a long breath string and one with a short breath string. The one with the short breath string is for the coyote. Thus, when the hunters have flushed out a coyote, he will not run very far because he has short breath; therefore, he can be killed without much effort. The one with the long breath string is, of course, for the hunters. When they are long-winded they will not tire so quickly.

They say that a coyote's snout is his weak spot, If someone hits his snout with a stick he dies instantly. For this reason the hunters aim for his snout when they try to hit him.

Cricket

When the weather turns warm in summer, crickets chirp after sunset. Occasionally the insect will enter a house. Then one can hear people say, "There's a cricket inside. Make sure you kill it, for this creature causes cracks in the walls." When people search for it then, they often can't find it right away. Its chirping will be emanating from a particular spot, but when people get there, the sounds are heard from another place again. Thus, it takes quite a bit of time to get rid of a cricket.

Crier Chief

In the past the person in charge of public announcements came from the Greasewood clan. Whenever the *kikmongwi* commissioned him to make an announcement, he would do his bidding. If a date had been set for a certain event such as the Niman ceremony or if there was to be a hunt, the *tsa'akmongwi* would announce it publicly. After he had been instructed as to the announcement, he would carry it out verbatim. If the *kikmongwi* cleared his voice at a certain spot or coughed, the crier would do likewise.

Crow

In the eyes of the Hopi, the crow is a completely useless creature. The farmer, above all, wants to be rid of it. He detests crows because they feed on his crops. Thus, in the past, when someone killed a crow, he hung it up in the midst of his field to discourage other crows from flocking there.

Occasionally, the Hopi will also accuse the crow of being a witch. They claim that witches use crows as a mode of transportation and profit from them. Once in a while when one rises early in the morning and goes about, one will discover some crows flying in from the east. At other times, a crow will come flying from that direction some time after sunrise. It is then that people say, "This wretched creature got up late. That's why it is only coming home now, that darn witch crow. This guy did not beat the sunrise, that's why he's returning just now." According to Hopi tradition the sorcerers gather in large numbers somewhere in the east at a place called Palangwu to practice their witchcraft. For this reason a crow that comes flying in from the east after the sun has been up for a while is tagged as a witch crow.

Two kachinas, the Angwusnasomtaqa and the Angwushahay'i, adorn the sides of their heads with crow's wings. Moreover, Angwusngöntaqa, one of the racing kachinas, wears crow feathers as a ruff.

When a Hopi learns about the arrival of the racing kachinas, he comes into the house and announces, "The crow is flying about in blue moccasins." As children when we heard this we usually ran outdoors and looked around. But when one of us actually spotted a crow flying about it never wore blue moccasins. Many things are still unrevealed to an uninitiated person and it was only later, after a person had grown older, that he figured out why this peculiar saying was used. This was the way of signaling the women to begin preparing foods that the racing kachinas would then bear as gifts.

Daughter-in-Law

Mö'wi is a kinship term reserved for the female who marries a man who is related to her clan-wise. Thus, the wives of the men of a certain clan are *mö'wi* to all members of that clan and the phratry it belongs to. When a son marries, his wife is also a *mö'wi*. But in this case only the father and his male clan relatives consider her as their *mö'wi*.

Because a *mö'wi* is generally very revered, we do not address her by name. However, if someone mentions her by her given name, he is said to be taken along by the setting sun. Why this saying exists, no one knows.

Deer

Deer live in the forest near the San Francisco Peaks. In times past, when a Hopi slew one he would invite his paternal aunts to feast on its meat. One had to be a good hunter to kill one in those days because firearms did not exist then. The Hopi also have a Deer kachina.

Deer Mouse

In the eyes of the Hopis deer mice are endowed with supernatural powers. For this reason they treat people medically in stories. In one such narrative a man who broke his leg comes to their abode. The mice cure him and can therefore be regarded as bone doctors.

Long ago, the Hopis also trapped deer mice because they would eat their corn plants.

Directional Cloud Chiefs

In the Hopi view of things the sun rises in the southeast and sets in the southwest. In addition, the Hopi know of a northwest and northeast. The Hopi further believes that the Chiefs of the Four Directions reside in those four zones. Thus, when someone composes a song and the song incorporates clouds as a subject, a different color cloud comes from each of those directions. First a yellow cloud is mentioned as coming from the northwest. It is followed by the blue cloud from the southwest, the red cloud from the southwest, and finally the white cloud from the northeast.

Directions

Whenever a Hopi intends to do something with the different directions, he always begins with the northwest. Then follow southwest, southeast, and northeast. These directions based on the sun are supplemented by the direction up, or zenith, and down, or nadir.

Every direction is associated with a specific color. The northwest is yellow, the southwest blue, the southeast red, and the northeast white. Up is gray and down is black.

The same is true for the flowers. Each particular direction is linked with a flower. Thus, the mariposa lily goes with the northwest, larkspur with the southwest, Indian paintbrush with the southeast, and evening primrose with the northeast. The sunflower is associated with the zenith and all kinds of flowers with the nadir.

The crops, too, have their established places in the sequence of directions. Corn goes with the northwest, beans with the southwest, watermelon with the southeast, and muskmelon with the northeast. Squash is reserved for up, and the gourd for down.

From the realm of birds the yellow warbler belongs to the northwest, the bluebird to the southwest, the parrot to the southeast, and the magpie to the northeast. The little sparrow hawk is the bird of the zenith, the canyon wren the bird of the nadir.

Finally, there are corn ears for each direction. Yellow corn relates to the northwest, blue corn to the southwest, red corn to the southeast, and white corn to the northeast. Sweet corn is reserved for the zenith and the purple corn for the nadir.

Of course, the Hopis have names for all these directions. Thus, *kwiniwi* refers to the northwest, *teevenge* to the southwest, *taatö* to the southeast, and *hoopo* to the northeast. And if a person wants to tell someone an object's location, he uses the directional terms to point out the place. The same holds for locations inside the house. For example, if someone can't find his blanket, he asks, "Where is my blanket?" "There, inside, along the northeast side, it is draped over the hanging beam," comes the reply.

Drum

The drum is one of the musical instruments the Hopi has employed for a long time. Whenever a Hopi performs a ceremony that requires a drum accompaniment, he beats the drum. During the month of Kyaamuya (approximately December) there must not be any drumming. According to Hopi custom, pounding a drum at this time would signify to those living in the underworld that there is life here above.

Drums are usually fashioned from cottonwood trunks. Being hollow inside, each open end is covered with horsehide, which is believed to give the drum a loud "voice." Occasionally cowhide is also used. Long ago, of course, when hides from horse or cow were not available, other animal skins were employed.

Manufacturing a drum also requires creating a heart for it. Since the heart is located inside the resonator it is not visible. The heart consists of a piece of sinew stretched across the inside of the drum with a turkey feather attached in the middle. Just before closing up the drum, the kiva member reputed to have the deepest bass inserts his voice into it by coughing or clearing his throat into the resonator. That done, the drum is considered to possess a deep tone. It is held that at times a drum may easily get chilled. For this reason the drummer will first place it adjacent to the stove and not use it until it has warmed up.

Naturally, a drum must also have a drumstick, which is occasionally referred to as its "husband." Perhaps the drumstick is labeled this way because it is always together with the drum and actually resembles a penis. As a rule, drums are also given a name, usually that of a female.

Elk

The elk shares its habitat with the deer. But the elk is much larger than the deer. Its antlers are huge, and when it moves about it does so with its head raised since its antlers place a lot of weight on its back. Like antelopes and deer, elks are easily excited. Because elk hide is extremely thick the old people fashioned shields from it.

Fields

Because the Hopis grow all their food themselves, the land is dotted with many fields. Since there are a number of differences between them, all sorts of terms exist for the many types of Hopi fields. As soon as the weather turns warm, the Hopis plant their first crops in fields known as *pömavasa* or "early cornfields." The fields termed *nöngavasa*, "drift sand field," are also called *pisavasa*, "dune sand field," because they are located in an area where windblown dune sand has collected in drifts. Another type of field is the *munvasa* or "flood field," which lies in the path of a dry wash. After a rainfall the runoff water floods through the wash and in the process irrigates the plants. A real downpour, however, can ruin the entire crop of such a field. Another field is known by the name of *yongivasa* or "warm field" because it is found in a location that is relatively warm and safe against strong winds. The *nayavasa* or "clay field" is situated in a loamy or clayish area. The *tsivokvasa* or "silt field" originates wherever new sediments are deposited after a flood. By damming up a stream the same type of ground can be created. Highly desirable as a sowing area is the *halasamvasa* or "moisture-holding field," considered the most attractive ground. It is so moist that the plants pierce the soil in no time and without any difficulties.

Firepit

Within a kiva the firepit is always situated just beneath the entrance ladder. It is in the area northwest of this firepit that most activities take place. The ancient firepits were usually square and slightly dug into the floor. Their side walls consisted of flat rocks. The fuel was always kept underneath the ladder. The person who looked after the fire was known as *tsoylan'aya* or "fire tender."

Flood

The Hopis have met with floods from time immemorial and are consequently fearful of this disaster. Not long after people were first created, they disobeyed the instructions given them by their creator, which caused him to be displeased. Having decided to do away with those who did not heed him and who would not give up their corrupt ways, he got rid of them by means of a flood. The Hopi also know by tradition that several settlements were in the past destroyed by floods. One good example is Palatkwapi. Again, people had become so incorrigible that their father, the village chief, could not control them any longer and had to instigate a flood himself. Since this flood was caused by the Water Serpent, it affected only the villagers of Palatkwapi rather than the entire world population.

Flute

The Hopi flute is made from a bamboo reed. At its far end a small gourd is attached that flares out, thereby forming a lip. The reed itself has several holes, but I'm not sure how many, maybe four. At the near end where the mouthpiece is the flute has a slightly larger hole. Through this the flutist blows. Only members of the Flute society play this instrument.

Flute Society Members

Long ago, the members of the Flute society used to entertain the people in Oraibi with their ceremonies. There were two groups, the Gray Flutes and the Blue-Green Flutes. In Oraibi they performed every other year, taking turns with the initiates of the Snake society. Some of the Flute members used to play a flute with a broad rim at the end. They were usually the ones walking along the outer sides of the group as it made its procession into the village. They were beautifully costumed, dressed in kilts and embroidered kachina sashes, and wore a *pavayoykyasi* or "moisture tablet" on their back.

Frog

When a tadpole reaches maturity it changes into a frog. Frogs live underground, not too far from the surface. They are considered pets of the clouds. That's why Hopis include them in their prayers for rain. Each time there is a really good rain, the air is filled with the croaking of frogs.

Gopher

The gopher is a pest. Found wherever corn grows, this animal actually drags the whole plant underground and then feeds on it. Since a gopher's burrow has multiple exits, it is not easily caught in a deadfall stone trap.

Greasewood

In the eyes of the Hopis greasewood is a hard wood that has many uses. Men fashion planting or hunting sticks from it. The curved rabbit stick is also made out of this wood, as are women's stirring sticks and tools to stir coarse cornmeal. For these tools, several small greasewood sticks are tied into a bundle which the women then use to stir their lightly roasted coarse cornmeal.

Grinding Bin

A Hopi woman uses corn flour on a daily basis. Consequently, in the past it was a must for her to possess her own grinding bin or metate. There are two types of grinding stones. One is a coarse-grained slab, the other is a fine-grained one. Sometimes the coarser metate is equipped with two hand stones or manos with which the grinding is carried out. Generally, the woman first shells her corn, then grinds it down to the proper size in the coarse grinding bin. By repeating this process she produces flour with a coarse texture. After she removes the flour from the bin, she dries it in a hot kettle. Next, she places it on the finer stone slab where she regrinds the entire amount two or three times.

The metate proper is an enclosure with four sides of thin flat stone slabs. In the front of the grinding stone is a narrow channel referred to as *matavuva*. A similar channel runs along each side. These channels, about equal in width to the front one, are sloped upward. Along the top there is still another channel that is also termed *matavuva*. Overall, the top end of the metate is positioned somewhat higher than the bottom part, so that the person grinding is compelled to make downward strokes only. The place behind the grinding bin where the grinding is carried out in kneeling position is referred to as *mataptsö*, "metate corner."

As the process of fine-grinding the corn goes on, the finished flour is placed into a pottery vessel where it is firmly packed down. Not all the flour can be removed from the slab, however; a small amount always remains. So the person grinding takes a brush, licks it in order to moisten it, and with spittle removes the small amount remaining by touching it with her brush. In this way all the flour is cleaned off the metate.

People are told not to step inside the grinding bin. Should someone do so, according to a saying, one's colon will protrude from one's anus.

Grinding Corn

When a woman or girl intends to grind corn, she first shells the amount of corn she wants and then winnows it so that the chaff and worm-eaten kernels can be separated. Next, she puts the corn kernels into the coarse grinding stone and there begins to crush them, coarse-grinding everything. This done, she brings the corn back up in the slanted metate and grinds it repeatedly to make it finer. Finally, the corn becomes cornmeal, and when it is the desired texture, she scoops it from the grinding bin. Next, she builds a fire under a roasting pot and dry-roasts the cornmeal until no trace of moisture is left. Then she places the corn in a finer metate, spreading it out there to cool off, at which time she fine-grinds it. This accomplished, she sifts the cornmeal to remove any remaining chaff and, if she wishes, grinds it once more.

Hahay'iwuuti

According to Hopi belief Hahay'iwuuti is the mother of all kachinas. Appearing only at special ceremonies she accompanies, for example, the So'yoko ogre group and also comes during the performance of the two Sa'lako puppet girls. She has her own peculiar song that she keeps singing over and over. Characteristically, she has a very high-pitched voice in which she both talks and sings. She always carries a small water vessel and a perfect ear of corn. From the vessel she pours a small amount into the palm of her hand and pats it on people's heads. With this gesture she symbolizes the hair washing ritual.

A female infant always receives a flat Hahay'i as her first kachina doll. A new bride is also presented one on the occasion of the Niman ritual. The doll she slides down her body for the purpose of bearing many children.

The Hahay'iwuuti who appears in Oraibi wears a *nasomhoya* or "little knotted hairdo of the non-marriageable girl" on each side of her head, whereas the one appearing in the villages of the other mesas has a *torikuyi* or "braid," a married woman's hairstyle. The front of Hahay'iwuuti's forehead is adorned with a fluffy eagle breast feather. In addition, she has bangs of red hair. Each of her cheeks is marked with a circular red spot. Her mouth is painted in the fashion of an upside-down crescent moon with a black dot directly above it. The configuration of the eyes is exactly like that of the mouth.

Hee'e'wuuti

Hee'e'wuuti is one of the many kachinas in the Hopi kachina pantheon. She is extremely brave. Once, way back in time, when her mother was fixing her hair in the traditional hairdo of the prepubescent girl, enemies suddenly appeared. Right away the girl shouldered her quiver, grabbed her bow, and rushed out to meet the foe. They say she killed a great many. From that day on quiver and bow have been carried by Hee'e'wuuti. Also, on one side of her head her hair is still wrapped around the U-shaped hair frame and not folded in properly. She is clad in the standard black wool dress of a woman, which is decorated with star designs made of husk. Hee'e'wuuti only comes at the time of Patsavu and the Powamuy ceremony, or "Bean dance," when she escorts the kachinas, her children, through the village.

Hopis

We Hopis settled here ages ago and we are still here. But the land is not ours. We are here only as tenants. We made our emergence from the underworld at the Grand Canyon with all sorts of other people and from there migrated in all directions. The being who first inhabited this upper world gave us certain instructions, and we are the only people that still live in some ways by these instructions. Tradition has it that at first we undertook a great migration before arriving here in Hopiland. Along the way we left many ruins that still exist. It is as if we marked the territory that is ours in this way. Some of those who went through the migration are Hopis just as we, but when they arrived at certain locations, they settled there permanently for some reason. Yet our destination was a place called Tuuwanasavi or "Earth Center," and only after reaching this place were we to settle for good. These were our instructions though they were not followed by the others.

It seems as though a Hopi does not do any evil, thus the name Hopi. But some of us are evil.

Hotooto

The Hotootos are kachinas who always come as a pair. Their appearances differ, however, in that one is yellow, the other blue-green. Both are equipped with bow and quiver, but their songs are not the same. The melodies vary slightly, but both end their singing at the same time. They normally come during the Powamuy ceremony and are only accompanied by Hee'e'wuuti on their rounds.

House Mouse

The house mouse lives in people's homes. There it urinates and defecates on the corn stacks. Of course, it also feeds on the corn. Building nests from material like cotton, this mouse usually gnaws on people's clothes.

Hu' Kachina

There are two Hu' kachinas who, at the time of the Powamuy ceremony, come to whip the children that are to be initiated into the Kachina society. They always arrive with their mother, Angwusnasomtaqa, who is a mean-spirited woman. The kachinas use tied yucca for whips with which they beat the children. That's how they initiate the children. When they are done whipping the initiates, they first strike each other with the yucca and then their mother. Then they leave the kiva. The cries the two kachinas utter are "*Huu, hu,*" hence their name. They end their cries with, "*Ko'aha.*"

Huk'ovi (place name)

Huk'ovi is a butte southwest of Oraibi. There is a ruin there. It seems to be windy there all the time. For this reason the location is referred to as Huk'ovi, "Windy High Place."

Hunting Stick

The Hopis have possessed the *putskoho* or "flat hunting stick" for ages. The name *putskoho* is derived from the fact that it is broad and flat. Long ago it also had a design painted on it. The prairie falcon is believed to have given this weapon to the Hopis. When this bird is out hunting and is about to make a kill, it will swoop down from the sky upon its prey without flapping its wings. As it dives from the sky in this manner, its wings very much resemble this flat hunting stick. One gets the impression that the bird hurls its wings at the prey to knock it into a daze before it returns to slay it. The Hopis make use of this stick when hunting cottontails and jackrabbits. It is thrown at them after they are flushed out of their hiding places. If the animal is struck just right, the stick will break its leg, thereby preventing it from making a getaway. The hunter then walks up to his prey and kills it.

In the eyes of the Hopis a scorpion appears to be toting about a flat hunting stick by the manner in which it scuffles along with its stinger curved upwards. Named after the scorpion is Putskoomok-taqa, a runner kachina, who actually carries the flat hunting stick with him. In addition, there is one kachina called Putskookatsina who has this hunting stick depicted just above his snout.

Jackrabbit

The jackrabbit is as skittish as the cottontail but is quite a bit larger. Jackrabbits were eaten by the Hopis, so they were hunted for their meat. Sometimes a person will go out stalking them alone. On a communal hunt, however, everyone goes out hunting for all the animals that have good meat. Such a hunt was formally announced by the crier chief with specifics as to place and time of the venture. When a jackrabbit was brought home, a female member of the hunter's household would roast the prey and bake a special cake of cornmeal called *sowitangu'viki* for this occasion. Blankets were made from jackrabbit pelts.

Journey Food

In the old days, when a man went planting and wanted to spend the whole day at the field, he would take some journey food along. As a rule, the old people took along only piki sheets that were folded in half and *kwiptosi*, "fine-ground corn." In addition, they would bring some water in a little canteen. The food was then wrapped into a little boy's blanket, tied up, and attached to the waist. Once in a while people also trekked along with these things slung over their shoulder.

Kachina

A kachina is something very special to a Hopi. Although the kachinas live unseen, they appear in person when one calls them in Hopiland. At that time they are visible. Upon their arrival, they entertain us all day long. They visit us with the intention that everything will be good. They bring us gifts that consist of foods prepared by their sisters. At the conclusion of their dances we present them with prayer feathers and pray to them that they will take our messages into every direction so that we may be constantly visited by rain. But a Hopi does not pray solely for himself, he prays for everyone who is thirsty, including animals and plants. He prays to the kachinas for rain for all things.

The kachinas inhabit a variety of places. They reside where springs surface. They travel about by way of clouds and that is the mode they use when they visit us.

Way back in the past the Hopis did not carry out the kachina ceremony on their own. At that time it was the real kachinas who came to the Hopi. Because some Hopis were evil, however, and began to show disrespect for the kachinas, the kachinas abandoned them. But before they departed, they turned over their secrets to the Hopi. From that time forward the Hopi had to carry on the kachina cult on their own. As a result, they endure hardships whenever they do so.

Kachina Initiation

Hopi children must all be initiated. Once a child has become a member of a secret society, it can assist its mother or father when kachina dances are performed. At noon a girl will help her mother haul food to the kachina resting place. In turn a boy can clean up when the kachinas have finished their meal.

Some of the children, both young girls and boys, get initiated into the Powamuy society. In return they are privileged to take care of the kachinas during a dance and make offerings of sacred cornmeal to them. In summer, they are the ones who will bring water to the Niman, or "Home dance," kachinas. A few of the little girls and boys are inducted into the Kachina society. At this occasion they are whipped by the Hu' kachinas. As a result, they may not take care of the kachinas like the Powamuy initiates. Once a child is introduced to the privileged knowledge of these societies, it knows that the kachinas are really its relatives.

Kiisiwu (place name)

Kiisiwu is a spring somewhere northeast of Oraibi, quite a distance away. People say that kachinas live there, so a Hopi will direct his prayers for rain to this spring also. In the summer, pine branches are retrieved from Kiisiwu for the Home dance kachinas. The same is true for the pine tree that is planted on the plaza during this ceremonial occasion. In preparation for these activities, prayer feathers are fashioned for the kachinas which are then deposited at the spring. Only after praying to the gods there are the pine branches taken. In this manner the Hopis trek to Kiisiwu in search of spiritual rebirth.

Kiva

Many different kachinas hold their dance performances in the kivas. But they are not the only ones who make use of the kiva. When the initiated members of a secret society are to hold their ceremonies, they also assemble within these underground structures. For example, the men stage their religious activities here during Wuwtsim. In addition, the Powamuy, Flute, and Snake societies, to mention only a few, congregate here for their secret endeavors.

Since women too have rituals of their own, the Maraw, Lakon, and Owaqöl societies also carry out their ceremonies in a kiva. So these religious chambers are not occupied solely by men. Social dancers also use the kivas to practice. In winter men and boys occupy the kivas, engaging in whatever activities are assigned to them. Thus, one may bring his weaving to the kiva and set up a loom there. For Powamuya, kachina dolls, bows and arrows, and other items of this nature are manufactured. A kiva is off-limits only to uninitiated children. It is not until the month of Paamuya and the night dances following the Powamuy rites, that these children, accompanied by their mothers or grandmothers, are allowed to witness the dances. On these occasions they watch the dances, together with the women, from the raised area to the southeast of the kiva's interior. At one time even young girls who are initiated were not permitted to witness dances unaccompanied. The same was true when they went there to practice for a social dance.

The ancestors of the Hopis all lived in kivas once. Thus, in the eyes of the Hopis, the kiva is also a home. However, it was not like the dwellings we inhabit today; it was simply a hole dug in the ground with a cover on top. Entering the kiva was, therefore, only possible by descending a ladder.

Kiva Hatch

The only hole a traditional kiva has is at it rooftop. This hole is known as *kivaytsiwa*, "kiva opening" or "kiva hatch." A ladder sticks forth from it, and it is through this opening that people enter and exit. There is a covering along one side of the hatch. Usually this covering is kept rolled up, but when necessary it is used to close up the kiva opening. This covering is fashioned from bundles of grass that are strung together. The grass used is sand grass, which has a reedlike quality.

Kooyemsi

The Kooyemsi is a kachina for both the Hopi and the Zuni people. His head is painted with reddish-brown ocher; small globes are attached in place of his ears and on the top and back of his head. This accounts for the name Tatsiqtö or "Ball Head" that is occasionally applied to him. From the balls hang turkey feathers. The kachina's mouth and eyes can take on various shapes. Around his neck some sort of cloth is usually tied. For a kilt he wears a folded woman's dress and his waist is adorned by a silver concho belt. On his legs and feet he wears footless black stockings and brown (sometimes white) moccasins. At times he may also go barefooted. In his right hand the Kooyemsi carries a rattle that has its own distinctive style, and in his left hand he holds an eagle wing feather with which he motions while dancing. A second feather is tucked into his kilt on his back.

A Kooyemsi can fulfill more than one function. While not considered a clown, the kachina will perform in funny ways similar to a clown. In the past he acted in this role only during dances performed by kachinas called *taqkatsinam*, or "powerful, manly kachinas," such as the Hoote, Hooli, and Tsa'kwayna. Today, he no longer clowns for the *taqkatsinam* in any of the villages. Only at Zuni does he still carry out this function. Whenever a kachina group requires a drummer, the Kooyemsi will also take on this task.

In the days when Hopi men still herded sheep, a sheep herder participating in a kachina dance might once in a while not have the time to prepare for the event. He would then simply join them as a Kooyemsi. So sometimes he would be a Kooyemsi-Long Hair kachina or perhaps a Hoote. The dancer would be dressed exactly like the other kachinas, but would be a Kooyemsi only at the head.

There are occasions when a large group of Kooyemsi will sing as a chorus for the other nonchanting kachinas. Also, each time clowns are part of a kachina plaza dance, a few Kooyemsi always act as *kipokkatsinam* or "Raider kachinas." Hence they are named *kipokkokoyemsim* or "Raider Kooyemsi." Also in the past they used to arrive in the village during the month of Ösömuyaw (approximately March) to challenge the girls to all sorts of guessing games in the dance court. Occasionally, they would also come during kachina nighttime performances for this same reason.

Kwaatoko

The Kwaatoko is a gigantic bird, much larger than the eagle. I guess it used to live once in Hopiland, but nobody has seen one anywhere for a long time.

In ancient times, when a Hopi set out on the warpath and killed an enemy, he used to put the blame for the slain warrior on this bird. He would say to the slain, "It was Kwaatoko who killed you. So don't seek revenge on me." By shifting the blame onto the bird, a Hopi does not get sick from worrying about the act of killing.

Ladder

Long ago, when doors in the modern sense did not yet exist, the only way the ancient people entered their homes was by means of ladders. In those days, therefore, one had to ascend to the rooftop first either by way of steps or on a ladder and then climb indoors, again, by using another ladder. But now that the Hopis have acquired doors from the white man, they enter a house only through them. Even for kivas this entrance mode is the preferred one today.

Leader

A *mongwi* is the person in charge wherever an activity is taking place. But he is not like the white man's leader. He does not tell the others to do things just for the sake of it. Nor does he ask others to do his wishes. But people must have a person overseeing them in any endeavor and that is the reason he is in charge.

Leenangwva (place name)

Leenangwva, "Leenangw Spring," lies southwest of Oraibi. It was the main spring where the old residents of Oraibi went to fetch water. Apparently, there was a constant supply of water there. Way back when the members of the Len, or "Flute," society were going through their rites in Oraibi, they did something important there on the final day of the ceremony or the day before; thus that spring is named after them. Also, at the time of Nevenwehe, unmarried girls used to congregate there along with men and older boys. After proceeding from the spring, the boys and men gathered wild greens.

Light-Complexioned Person

Because in the past the Hopis carried out most of their activities in the sun, their skin was usually dark pigmented. Hence, when a person had fair-complexioned skin, he or she was usually admired because of it; this is especially true of a female. Light-colored skin, therefore, enhances the beauty of a Hopi girl or woman.

Louse

Whenever a person gets lice, he notices it right away, for his head itches. The itching is caused when the lice suck blood from a person's scalp. As soon as a child gets afflicted with head lice, his mother picks the lice from his hair. When they are all removed, one is cured again. Once in while, however, if someone is not deloused, the lice multiply. As one scratches then, the skin gets infected with sores. Such a person people refer to as *atu'ya*, "one with a head full of lice."

Medicine Man

There is more than one type of Hopi medicine man. One is the bone doctor who treats or cures only maladies of a person's bones. Another is the herb doctor, knowledgeable in the use of all medicinal plants, who performs his remedies by means of them. The last is the crystal gazer or shaman who has his own method of treatment. Looking through his crystal, he diagnoses the ailment of a person and then instructs him in the appropriate treatment. At other times he will remove the object causing the sickness. For instance, he may draw out a thorn or a shell implanted in the patient by another person. Moreover, if the shaman detects that someone has unknowingly violated a taboo or committed some other wrong act, he will enlighten the person and instruct him in the remedy to apply. These shamans no longer exist, and with them has died the knowledge of their practice.

The Hopis also perceive Badger as a great healer. Medicine men in general rely on some animal as they serve their patients. Sometimes a medicine man may choose a powerful being such as Bear to be his symbolic father to help him practice his skills.

Mishongnovi (Second Mesa village)

When the Mishongnovi people arrived here, they first settled on the southwest side of Kwangwup'ovi. In due course, when they expressed a desire to become integrated members of the village of Shungopavi, they approached the *kikmongwi* to ask his permission. Tradition has it that they were very loquacious and that they spoke quite aggressively. Whenever the *kikmongwi* said something they were quick to give a negative reply. But the *kikmongwi* of Shungopavi spoke to them as follows: "There is no way that you can live with us here in Shungopavi. We have become quite numerous here. If your heart is indeed set on living here with the Hopis, build your own settlement at that butte off to the east. There I have my seed stored. If you really want to settle here among us go to that place, establish a village, and guard my seed." The Mishongnovis consented and did exactly that.

Mockingbird

The mockingbird is one of the small birds referred to as *tsiro*. It knows the characteristic sounds of all living beings. In stories the mockingbird is said to speak the languages of all peoples.

Once in a while, when a child does not begin to speak right away, people kill a mockingbird, bring it home, and place the bird's beak in the child's mouth. As a result, the child learns to speak. The mockingbird also comes in the guise of a kachina.

Moencopi (Third Mesa village)

In the days when there was no village yet at Moencopi, "place where there is water flowing," some of the Oraibi people had their fields there. Because there is an abundance of water there, things grow profusely. A farmer who had crops growing at that place would go to that site by foot all the way from Oraibi, tend to his field, and then return. Today there is a community inhabited by some Hopis. Actually, two villages are situated there, one above the other. Those who reside in the lower one are known as *atkyavit* or "down-people" while those living in the upper one are called *ooveqvit* or "up-people."

Mumurva (place name)

Mumurva, or "Marshgrass Spring," lies on the southwest side of Oraibi, a little distance away from the mesa in the open.

Navajos

The elders tell of the Navajos as having arrived only relatively recently in the Hopi area. They say that long ago Navajos used to live farther northeast, but they started migrating in this direction. Moreover, the Hopis claim that Navajos are such thieves that they are certain to pilfer something from one's field on their way home. When we were children our mothers and fathers warned us that if we were badly behaved they would trade us to the Navajos. They also said that Navajos would kidnap people. So it is small wonder a Navajo is feared when he comes into the village. Ever since the Navajos arrived in this area the Hopis and Navajos have been enemies. As a result, more than one Hopi lost his life to them. It has only been in more recent times that the Hopis and Navajos have become friendly toward each other.

North Wind

The Hopi dread *kwingyaw*, "the northwest wind," because it is a malevolent wind that freezes the crops and peach orchards. This wind always comes from the northwest and is ice-cold.

Number Four

A Hopi always does things four times or in multiples of four, for example, eight or sixteen times. Thus, when a group of people are engaged in a ceremony that is planned to run its entire length, they will be in session for the full sixteen days. At other times they may go on for only eight or even four days. By the same token, when a Hopi seeks a response to his inquiry, he will ask only four times and then quit. At that point he will be given an answer if he did not receive one right away. Thus, there is not a single thing in Hopi culture that does not require the number four as a determiner. Likewise, the creator has now purified us thrice. If he cares to repeat this purification and cleanses us once more, thereafter we will live as we should.

Nuvatukya'ovi (San Francisco Peaks)

The mountain range to the southwest of Hopiland is known by the name of Nuvatukya'ovi. We go to that place during ceremonials such as the Niman and also occasionally during Powamuya to gather evergreens. Since there are shrines at that location, those who go to gather these evergreens deposit paho at these sites. In our belief the San Francisco Peaks are one of the homes of the kachinas; therefore, there is a kiva on top of one of its peaks. Nuvatukya'ovi is also one of the boundary markers of Hopiland.

Old Spider Woman

Old Spider Woman is a personage who is extremely talented in all creative arts. For this reason, whenever a Hopi girl or woman wishes to acquire a certain skill, she turns to her in prayer. For example, one may want to learn how to make piki or to become skilled in pottery making or wicker plaque weaving. On each occasion one prays to her. Since she is the grandmother of the Pöqangw brothers, Pöqangwhoya and Palöngawhoya are just like her, versed in many things. In stories Old Spider Woman helps anyone in need. Thus, she has ways of doing away with a person's enemies. Also she always gives a person advice on what to do.

Oraibi (Third Mesa village)

According to some, the Hopis first settled at Shungopavi. There the *kikmongwi* and his younger brother are said to have differed over some matter. As a result, the younger brother left, headed north, and started his own community at Oraibi. However, not everyone shares the same version of this event. Some others say that the Hopis, after their emergence at the Grand Canyon, first embarked on a migration before they established their first settlement at Oraibi.

Then, in the more recent past, the people there clashed again due to different views regarding the white man's way of life, in particular, schooling. This led to the banishment of those who rejected the Anglo way of life. In turn they established the village of Hotevilla. After renewed differences there, some people settled at Bacavi. Next, several of those who wanted the way of the whites and had remained at Oraibi moved below the mesa and founded another village where they worked for the government. Today that place is known as Kykotsmovi. Yet others for some reason migrated to Moencopi where the Oraibi people had been going on foot for a long time already because they owned fields there. Thus, as a result of the banishment, several villages now exist northwest of Oraibi.

Owl

As children we were told that an owl can devour us. Therefore, an obnoxious child is threatened with the owl to stop his bad behavior. When a mother sings a lullaby to her child at night, the song tells of an owl consuming the child.

The owl is thought of as a harbinger of bad news if it hoots in broad daylight. During a public kachina-day dance the Owl kachina, therefore, calls on the clowns in broad daylight, letting them know that they are destined to meet a bad end. Also when some member of a family is seriously ill, an owl will drop in on them at night to upset them.

From the owl's downy feathers paho are fashioned for peach orchards so that they may bear an abundance of fruit. At night, while hunting in these orchards, the owl perches on the peach trees. Because owl feathers retain warmth, paho made from them prevent the peach trees from freezing when the bloom.

Long ago, when the Hopis went on the warpath, they used the cries of the owl and the whippoorwill to communicate with each other at night.

Paired Feather Arrangement

A *hurunkwa* or "paired feather arrangement" altogether consists of four wing feathers that are tied together in pairs with the string that is typically used for making prayer feathers. In this fashion a kachina attaches this arrangement to his hair. It creates the effect of four wing feathers extending forward from the forehead. Hewto and Tsa'kwayna, for example, wear these two-clustered feathers on their heads.

Palöngawhoya

Palöngawhoya is one of the grandsons of Old Spider Woman and the younger brother of Pöqangwhoya.

Paternal Aunt

In Hopi society, all the female relatives of one's father are considered a person's paternal aunts. Such an aunt is fond of all her nieces and nephews. She "hates" the wife of her nephew and once in a while gives the husband of her niece a hard time. When a nephew marries, his paternal aunts "raid" the bride, that is, they come with muddy water and regular water and pour it over the groom's female relatives as well as his real father and his kachina godfather.

Pavayoykyasi

They say that very early in the morning Pavayoykyasi walks about sprinkling the crops in the Hopis' fields. And, indeed, just as one arrives at his field, there are drops of dew clinging to the crops. People describe Pavayoykyasi as a handsome youth who is always dressed very nicely.

The term *pavayoykyasi* is also used to mean a "moisture tablet" which is worn for example on the back of an Eagle kachina. A member of the Flute society also carries one.

Pik'ami (dish)

When a woman wants to make *pik'ami* pudding, she shells white corn. After removing the desired quantity she washes the kernels in water and strains them through a yucca sifter. After the water has drained off, she lets the kernels dry in the sun for a while. When they are dry, she first coarse-grinds them, then fine-grinds them. Now the corn flour can be sifted and all the chaff can be removed.

As a next step, the woman prepares hot water, or maybe she makes a fire first in the stone-lined earth oven. Once the fire is going inside it, she must watch it. As soon as it burns down, she adds more fuel. Now the oven gets hot, as indicated by the white color that creeps up along its stone walls. As the white heat reaches the top of the pit, the woman makes a batter out of her corn flour. As the hot water comes to a boil, she dumps the flour into a large pottery bowl and then pours the boiling water into it. Next, she stirs it with a stick. When all the flour is soaked, yeast is added. All of this is stirred again. Now the whole mass gets liquid and turns into the desired batter, which needs constant stirring.

After the batter has cooled off a little, a box-shaped container is lined with corn husks, first on the bottom and then on all four sides. It's almost like building a house. Next, some batter is poured in. As it reaches the side walls of the container, more husks are added. Once again, batter is poured in and husks added until the container is full. Now, the top, too, is closed off with husks. This done, the squarish can is placed into the earth oven. Finally, a flagstone is placed across the opening, and cracks around its edges are sealed with mud.

After this is accomplished, the woman makes charcoal and places it on top of everything. Wood is added to the charcoal and then lit.

This fire stays there all through the night. The following morning the ashes are removed and the oven opened. After peeling off the husk, the contents of the oven are stirred first before they are taken out and put on a sifter. The result is *pik'ami* pudding.

Piki (dish)
Piki is an ancient food of the Hopi. When a woman plans to make it she begins by heating up her stone griddle. She then boils some water and pours it on blue flour. That accomplished, she adds wood ashes mixed with water, which gives the batter its hue. As soon as her stone griddle is hot enough, she spreads ground melon seeds over it and allows them to burn into the stone. Then she makes her first piki, stacking them next to her. As she continues with the process removing each piki sheet, she spreads a new layer of batter over the griddle. The previously baked piki is next placed on top and becomes moist from the steam of the new batter. The completed piki can then be rolled up for storage. From that point on she continues rolling and stacking one piki on top of another.
It is said that Old Spider Woman is skillful and talented in many things, so someone eager to learn to make piki prays to her. Old Spider Woman also resides somewhere southwest of Oraibi. Thus, whenever a girl wishes to learn the art of piki making, she takes some wood to Old Spider Woman's abode and leaves it there for her along with some sacred cornmeal.

Piki House
The piki house is a small house that does not take up a lot of space. One only needs to build a chimney in the corner of a room and dig a fire pit underneath it for the piki griddle. After placing the griddle over the fire pit, one can make piki on it. That's what a piki house is.

Piktotokya (ceremonial day designation)
Piktotokya occurs two days before *tiikive*, the "day of the public dance performance." *Piktotokya*, in turn, is preceded by the day *suus qa himu*, "once nothing day." On *piktotokya* the women are traditionally busy preparing piki, hence the name *piktotokya*, or "*piki totokya*."

Pinyon Nuts

The Hopis used to eat pinyon nuts as part of their diet. They would therefore watch the pinyon trees, and when they found an area where the trees were laden with cones, they kept it in mind. Then they paid attention to their corn plants. As soon as they produced fresh ears and the corn began to ripen, people would go roast pinyon cones. They headed out to the place where the nuts were plentiful and first collected wood. Next they dug a large pit at a desirable spot and built a fire. Only then did they go out to pick the pinyon cones. After a while, when a lot were amassed, they hauled them to the fire and piled them up next to it. As soon as the fire had burned down and hot embers were in ample supply, the cones were placed on top of the embers, and everything was buried with sand. Now another fire was lit on top and left there for a while. When it looked as if the cones might be done, they were dug up and put into a sack. Back home, people then spread them out on their rooftops. As they dried in the sun the cones popped open, releasing the nuts.

Later in the year, when the pinyon nuts were actually falling out of their cones, people went out once more, this time to pick up the nuts on the ground. After bringing them home they dry-roasted them in a kettle usually reserved for parching corn. Once in a while they also mixed some of the nuts with corn kernels. This mixture was then roasted and eaten. At other times people placed the dry-roasted nuts into a metate and mashed them into a paste. The result was pinyon nut paste, which was consumed with piki.

Pitch

Pine trees have a lot of pitch that people collect by scratching it off with a little stick. It is then placed into a little storage vessel or carried on something flat like a pottery fragment. In this way the pitch can be brought home.

Hopis employ pitch as medicine. Occasionally, if what was collected is really pure, a person's grandmother or mother will take a little pinch and swallow it in the morning. Also, when someone breaks a little bowl that he treasures, he plasters the pieces with pitch and puts them back together. Whatever oozes out is burned off. In this way the crack is mended with pitch.

Plaza

The plaza is usually situated somewhere near the middle of a village, hence it is used as the dance court if a ceremonial activity is taking place, for example, and kachinas have come. Various other dances are also performed in the plaza. The Snake, Lakon, and Kwan societies, for instance, carry out their dance performances there.

Houses are erected on all four sides of the plaza, and alleys lead into it. In the past, when certain items were to be traded, someone would make a public announcement on behalf of the vendor, who would then sell his things at the plaza.

Pocket Mouse

Pocket mice clearly live in fields and therefore get their food from the plants there, especially watermelons. For this reason people have to set up deadfall traps to catch them.

In narratives this mouse is usually referred to as *tusanhomiitsi*, "dirty pocket mouse."

Pöqangwhoya

Pöqangwhoya is one of the grandsons of Old Spider Woman.

Prayer Feather

A *nakwakwusi* is fashioned to the accompaniment of a prayer. Then it is also smoked upon. This type of prayer feather has more than one function. It can be the symbol of a path laid out, but it can equally well be worn on the head. It also serves to symbolically represent the breath of life. A *nakwakwusi* is produced from the downy breast feather of an eagle together with hand-spun cotton twine.

Prayer Stick/Prayer Feather

A paho, or prayer stick or prayer feather, is made not only from a variety of items but it is also fashioned in many different ways. While it is never made from the breast feather of the eagle, it can be made from turkey feathers. Pahos can be found hanging from the ceilings of kivas. For example, when kachinas are to return to their homes, they are given pahos. The members of the Kwan, Al, and Wuwtsim societies each fashion their own unique pahos. A great diversity of pahos are made at the time of Soyalangw. It is said that those for whom the paho is intended are elated upon receiving it. A paho carries with it a person's most intense wishes and prayers. A medicine man who has treated you takes what ails you along with a paho and goes to deposit it. In fact, there is nothing that the Hopi does not make a paho for. He makes it for the sun, the moon, those that exist unseen, and all the other beings that he relies upon for his existence.

Public Announcement

When a Hopi wished to inform his fellow villagers of certain things, he would petition someone to make a public announcement on his behalf. At other times, a formal announcement could be made by the *tsa'akmongwi*, or official "crier chief." To broadcast his message, the crier always climbed on a rooftop. The opening formula of his announcement usually sounded as follows: "Those of you people out there heed my words." The conclusion was equally formalized: "This is the announcement I was instructed to make known to you. That's about it." Whenever the crier shouted out his announcement, he typically drew out the last word of each sentence.

Qa'ötaqtipu

Qa'ötaqtipu is a ruin somewhere on the northeast side of Bacavi. Burned corn was discovered there, hence the name Qa'ötaqtipu, "Burned Corn."

Rabbit Hunt

A man who intends to sponsor a rabbit hunt goes to the crier chief and asks him to announce the event publicly. He tells him exactly where the hunters are to leave the village, where to assemble, and what their destination will be after they have gathered. The crier chief then shouts this information out from the rooftop.

The following day those who decide to participate in the hunt dress and then head out to the agreed meeting place. They say that upon getting there the sponsor already has a fire going. He first ritually smokes with all the men and then purifies their hunting sticks with juniper smoke. This is to ensure that they will fly accurately.

After that the group departs. The men now form a circle and go along striking on the bushes with their hunting sticks. In this fashion they flush out the cottontails and jackrabbits. Immediately upon flushing them out they hurl their sticks at them. If a man is in luck, he brings down the rabbit.

Upon arriving home with his prey the hunter brings it inside the house. His wife now takes a handful of blue or white corn flour and lays the rabbits out in a straight row. Then she feeds them by sprinkling little pinches of flour into their mouths.

The pelts of the rabbits are not thrown away. Rather, they are draped over something, and when they have dried, people make blankets from them, so-called rabbitskin blankets. A rabbit pelt can also be used to whitewash the walls of a house.

Rabbitskin Blanket

On the old days the Hopis used only rabbitskin blankets for quilts. Whenever hunters killed cottontails and jackrabbits, women carefully skinned them and saved their pelts. Once they had accumulated a good quantity, they made quilts from them. At first, yarn had to be spun. When a lot of yarn was ready, the warp was set up on the loom. Next, the rabbitskins were cut into oblong strips. These were wrapped around the warp strings of the loom and then tied together with weft strings.

Long ago Hopis also used rabbitskin blankets to close their entranceways.

Rain

The Hopis are forever praying for rain. By drinking the moisture of rain-bearing clouds their plants will grow. With the resulting crops the Hopis sustain themselves. Whenever a serious ceremony is conducted, longing for rain is always on the mind of the participants. Also, whenever the kachinas are about to return home, prayers for rain are uttered so that they may carry these petitions with them.

Rattle

Rattles are fashioned from gourds. They contain small pebbles that give them their voice. Whenever a Hopi dances, he carries a rattle. This applies to both kachina and social dancers. Kachinas, as a rule, have unadorned rattles. However, should a kachina wish to have a painted rattle, he usually colors it a uniform blue-green, or occasionally white. Sometimes the rattles of social dancers and kachinas have flowers depicted on them. Almost all the kachinas' rattles are flat on each side. Only the Kooyemsi have round ones. However, once in a while a kachina or social dancer will carry a small round rattle. The members of the Antelope society carry white roundish rattles. In former times some rattles were manufactured from the scrotums of antelopes or other game animals. Normally, the women used these rattles when putting their infants to sleep.

The rattles given to children at the occasion of Powamuya are not at all decorated in the same manner. And while a little girl ceases to receive a rattle at a certain age, little boys will always get one during Powamuya. The small rattle given to an infant is painted blue or green and decorated with bird tracks. Together with the rattle, a little boy annually receives a bow until the time he is initiated into the Kachina or Powamuy society.

One of the rattles he may receive has a blue-green mark in its center and a white background. The blue-green marking consists of a fairly large spot that is said to represent the earth. After all, when it rains for a long time, the earth is green throughout just like this color. In the middle of the rattle and radiating out from the navel of the gourd into the four cardinal directions are four lines with hooks. Some say they symbolize the migratory routes the Hopis took before arriving at Oraibi. After this migration, they claim, the Hopis gathered back at Tuuwanasavi, the "Center of the Earth." The blue-green patch is encircled by a black line decorated with dashes of white. From the top of this configuration little red crooked lines that are supposed to represent the sun branch in a multidirectional pattern. Around the edge of the rattle dividing the gourd in half is a design resembling barbed wire. It is said to depict the Milky Way. At the top of the rattle is attached a bunch of eagle down feathers, all of them sticking upward, except for one that dangles down and resembles a prayer feather worn on the head.

Rattlesnake

A Hopi is afraid of the rattlesnake, for once in a while when coming across one it will really be angry. A person will then not go near it. When a rattlesnake is angry it will jump at a person, bite him, and inject its poison. As a result, a swelling rushes through the victim. Occasionally the swelling gets so bad that it reaches the heart. The person then dies. For this reason the Hopis fear rattlesnakes. The person who got bitten may go to a member of the Snake society who usually sucks on the wound. Once in a while he succeeds in extracting all the poison in this way. The person is then healed.

In the past, when the Hopis were still being attacked by enemies, the Hopis smeared rattlesnake poison on the tips of their arrows. With these they then shot at the enemies.

A Hopi who spots a rattlesnake that is not aggressive prays to it for rain by casting a pinch of sacred cornmeal at it. When the members of the Snake society are in session, they hunt for rattlesnakes, and everyone who chances upon one captures it. With these the Snake initiates then dance for rain.

Red-Tailed Hawk Kachina
The Red-Tailed Hawk is one of the many Hopi kachinas. He may stage a dance performance at any time. The kachina has long hair from the back of which a fan of red-tailed hawk tail feathers hangs. In addition, the kachina is equipped with a rattle and a bow. To the front of the head he wears a *hurunkwa* or "paired feather arrangement." His calls mimic that of the red-tailed hawk.

Reed Case
The reed case is made for a *mö'wi*, or daughter-in-law. At the time when she is to return home after the wedding ceremony, the small bridal cape and the wedding sash are wrapped in it for her. The receptacle, consisting of reeds strung together, is made at the same time as wedding garments are fashioned for the *mö'wi*.

Ritual Requiring Initiation
Whatever religious practice a Hopi is initiated into by means of a hair-washing rite constitutes his *wiimi*. The Hopis engage in many rituals, and no one Hopi is familiar with the esoteric practices of all of them. Some rites are exclusively for men; others are only for women. The first exposure to a *wiimi* takes place when a child is initiated into the kachina cult. Thereafter, a Hopi can learn about the ritual of another society. Usually, it is the society that is affiliated with one's kachina godfather or godmother.

Long ago people were involved in a great variety of rituals conducted by special societies, some of which have become extinct. For example, the Nakya rites and the clown ritual no longer exist. Also the Momtsit do not carry on their ritual anymore. Only the initiates of the Powamuy, Wuwtsim, Soyal, Al, Kwan, Taw, Snake, Antelope, Flute, Lakon, Owaqöl, and Maraw societies still conduct their esoteric practices in some villages.

Rooster

The rooster wakes up the Hopis in the morning. I guess, in former days Hopis kept chickens and roosters as pets and paid attention to them in the morning to determine what time it was. When the rooster crowed for the first time, they would say, "They just crowed for the first time." By then it was usually gray dawn. After keeping quiet for a while the roosters crowed again. After a good length of time they crowed a third time. Finally, after a lengthy interval, they could be heard once more. By this fourth time it was then daylight.

Runner Kachinas

Runner kachinas typically come during the month of Ösömuya (approximately March). As a rule, they appear without anyone's prior knowledge. They bring all sorts of gifts with them as they proceed to the location where they plan to challenge people to a race. Some of the kachinas' kiva partners know about their arrival, of course, and dress up in fanciful ways. They then go in this guise to where the Runner kachinas are and challenge a Runner kachina to a race. But the kachinas, too, pull in spectators if one of them fancies one to run with him. Taking his victim to a line, the spectator usually dashes off as soon as he stops at the line. The kachina then sets out in pursuit of him.

There is a great variety of Runner kachinas. They all have different names. Tatsiipölölö, for instance, throws his ball at the loser, and Tsöqaapölölö metes out his punishment with balls of clay. Tsilitos-moktaqa, upon catching up with his victim and grabbing him, force-feeds him chili powder. The Kwitanono'a, on the other hand, feeds his victim excrement. Aykatsina, or "Rattle kachina," whips the loser with yucca strips. Nahoyleetsi'ytaqa does the same. The Kokopölmana, finally, flings her victim on the ground as soon as she catches him. Then she flattens out on top of him and thrusts her pelvis into him several times.

Sacred Cornmeal

Sacred cornmeal was once used by the Hopi on an everyday basis. Each morning as he went out to pray toward the rising sun, he made it a habit to pray with *hooma*.

The kachina father, that is, the man who tends the kachinas, also uses it as he takes care of them during their dances. When the kachinas are to change dance positions, the father makes a cornmeal path for them. He ceremonially feeds them with the cornmeal, whereupon they commence dancing. In the evening, at the conclusion of their performance, sacred cornmeal is again an ingredient in ritually preparing the kachinas for their journey home.

On the occasion of a wedding, after the ceremony is completed and the bride is to return home, a cornmeal path once more is marked on the ground for her. Again, when there is a ritual in progress and prayers are being conducted, cornmeal is involved. On *astotokya*, the climactic night of the Wuwtsim initiation, a member of the Kwan society seals off the paths leading into the village with cornmeal. Finally, when one goes to deposit a paho one always takes cornmeal along. Before the paho is deposited, one first prays to it using the cornmeal. This accounts for the expression *hom'oyto*, "he is going to deposit cornmeal."

Sand Cricket

The sand cricket is normally buried in the mud somewhere. Or it lives under some rocks where the soil is wet. The insect has a large forehead which is shiny. That's the reason for its name, *qalatötö*, "shiny bug."

Sandsnake

A sandsnake is usually buried in a sand dune where it is moist. Once in a while when people push aside the sand they uncover this snake.

Shinny

When we were children and wanted to entertain ourselves, we would do so by playing shinny. There were many of us and we always had two sides. We had two leaders who would choose whomever they wanted on their team. A goal was made at each end of the playing field. The object of the game was to get the ball into the opponents' goal. To start the game a hole was dug in the middle of the field and the ball buried in it. Then two players were selected to strike the dirt with their shinny sticks in order to uncover the ball. As soon as the ball was extracted from the hole, we all joined in to play shinny. Before the game it was also decided how many times a team would have to put the ball into the other side's goal to be declared the winner.

Shungopavi (Second Mesa village)

Shungopavi lies approximately southeast of Oraibi. According to the traditions of some, the Hopis established their first settlement there. But they did not settle on top of the mesa then. To that location they migrated much later. Tradition also has it that two brothers, the *kikmongwi* and his younger brother Matsito, had differences of opinion that resulted in Matsito moving to Oraibi. He took some people along and founded Oraibi. For some unknown reason the people of Shungopavi and the people of Oraibi do not speak the same dialect, even though they are both Hopis.

Smoking

Long ago a Hopi prayed every day, and while he did this he always smoked a pipe. Also, whenever the *kikmongwi* had a caller, he had to offer him his pipe. Likewise, when one plans to participate in a kachina dance and goes to the kiva from which the kachinas will come, the person in charge of the ceremony must first offer you a smoke before you can join in. When a ceremony is in progress, there is a round of smoking at the beginning and end of the ritual. As soon as your neighbor has finished, he hands you the pipe. You now take a few puffs and address him in the manner according to which you are related to him. If he is your father, you would say "my father." When his turn comes to reply he would say "my child." In the past all people knew how they were related to one another. If one is not familiar with one's neighbor and that person happens to be older than you, you may address him as "my father." And if he is not much older than you, the proper form of address would be "my elder brother." If one does not wish to use this expression, an alternative form of address is "Companion of my heart."

The person smoking first prays fervently from his heart that things will turn out beneficial for him and prosper before he exhales the smoke. This smoke then carries one's prayers to those who are more powerful. This is what ritual smoking means to a Hopi. Thus it is little wonder that whenever he is engaged in a certain endeavor, tobacco and pipe are ever present.

Snake Kilt

The Snake kilt is made out of leather and is normally brown. On it is painted a bullsnake. The bullsnake in turn is decorated with Pöqangw tracks, or "warrior marks," and bird tracks. Along its bottom edge the kilt is fringed and equipped with tin cone clinkers.

Snow

Snow is very important to the Hopis. Each time it snows a lot they are happy about it, for this assures that there will be moisture for the fields at the beginning of the warm season. Also, in the old days, water was always scarce. There was no flowing water close to the houses. Therefore some people filled their water vessels with snow following a heavy snowfall. After it melted, they drank the water. The Hopis also used to bathe their children in the snow. This was to make them strong and give them skin that would not get prematurely wrinkled.

People are advised not to eat the first snow of the season, because disease is believed to come with this first snow. Anyone eating it gets sick right away.

Since there are so many different kachinas there is also one that relates to snow. His name is Nuvaktsina, "Snow kachina."

Social Dance

The Hopis perform kachina dances as well as social dances. Some of these social events have their time in the winter, others during the warm season. Thus, Buffalo dances are typically staged during the month of Paamuya (approximately January). Social dances featuring Butterfly dancers, Navajos, Paiutes, and Havasupais, on the other hand, always take place in summertime. The Nalöq Butterfly dance, however, which consists of four pairs of male-female partners, is scheduled in winter.

Society Standard

Each time the Hopis are in the kiva for a secret session of their society, they signal this to the other people by means of a *na'tsi*, or "society standard." Society standards have a variety of forms, and each society puts up the one that it considers its own. Thus, the Snake society members have a bow to which woven hair is strung. This bow is placed across the top of the ladder that sticks out from the kiva opening. The Maraw initiates in turn, who use the wings of a sparrow hawk for prayer feathers, have several of them tied to a stick, which serves as *na'tsi*.

Söhönasomtaqa

The Söhönasomtaqa is a kachina that has galleta grass tied to both sides of his head. This accounts for his name, which literally translates as "one who has galleta grass attached to himself."

Songs

When a Hopi does something, he usually does this to the accompaniment of a song. For example, long ago a man would go to the fields singing. The reason for the singing was to alert his crops of his approach. He wanted them fully awake before his arrival. And as he walked about his plants, he also sang. Likewise when a woman or a young girl grinds corn, she does it to the tune of a song. That is a grinding song. With the accompaniment of a song her work is not so tedious; therefore, she sings while grinding. Whenever a woman puts her child to sleep, she also sings it a lullaby. When we were playing as children, we did so while singing a song. Also while we swam, there was still another song.

Even an evil person has a song at hand, a song that makes you go crazy. With it he causes a person to go wild when he desires that person sexually.

All rituals are complete only with song. Thus, the members of the Wuwtsim and Maraw societies, the kachinas, the social dancers, and even the clowns all have their individual songs. There is also the Snake dance song, the Flute ceremonial song, and the Kwan song.

People who played the guessing game *sosotukwpi* also had songs of their own. Players sang as they competed against one another.

At times when women are weaving wicker plaques, they weave while singing the Owaqöl, or "Basket dance" songs.

Finally, it seems that folktales generally included a song, but some of them have been forgotten. It is said that the Hopi is a mockingbird. That is why he composes songs using the languages of many other people. Thus, one song might be in the Zuni language, another in Navajo. As a matter of fact, songs always include words from other Indian groups. Some are so ancient that the meaning of the words is completely obscure.

When Coyote sings in a story, he always does so in a very deep voice. He never sings in a high-pitched tone. He bellows the song out.

Spring

Ages ago, when the Hopis were still on their migratory route, it was customary for them to take a water vessel along. Each time they intended to settle at a site, they buried the vessel in the ground, whereupon a spring emerged, giving them a source of water. When they finally arrived at Hopi country, they established settlements at places situated close by springs. As soon as they became familiar with the springs in the area, they gave them names. Thus, the discoverer of a newly emerged spring would name it according to his clan totem.

Some springs are inhabited by kachinas, so the Hopis go to these sites to deposit prayer feathers to ask for rain. Obviously, water is most precious to the Hopis. For this reason they conduct communal spring-cleanup parties that take place every year.

The elders also remind children that Paalölöqangw, the Water Serpent, inhabits every spring and that one should therefore not play around these locations. The Serpent is said to make his appearance there exactly at noon. When someone wants to drink from a spring, he should not do so by bending over it. Instead, one should ladle the water out. If a ladle is lacking, the cupped hands should be used to take a drink. A third taboo relating to pools of water forbids sexual intercourse in or near the water. A consequence of breaking it is that the girl will be impregnated by the Serpent.

Stone Axe

A stone axe is fashioned from sharp rock that is extremely hard. Around its middle a groove is made, and it is then equipped with a handle in the form of a forked stick. The edge of the forked stick fits flush in the groove on both sides. The handle is tied on with strips of cowhide. They hold stone and handle tightly together.

Tick

According to the Hopis a tick will crawl into a person's ear. Itching is a clue that a tick is inside. To remove the tick one is advised to crush some alkaline salt and pour a little into the ear. If the ear is then plugged up with cotton, the tick will be dislodged.

Totokya (ceremonial day designation)

The ceremonial day *totokya* occurs on the day before *tiikive*, the day of the public dance performance. Occasionally, a particular ceremonial event actually takes place on *totokya*. For example, during the post-Powamuy season of kiva night dances, the kachinas stage their dances on totokya, that is, the eve of *tiikive*. In the event of a day dance in summer, those involved keep an all-night vigil on *totokya*. Also, when a person elects to undertake a certain activity at a particular time, the preceding day is spoken of as if it were his *totokya*.

Tuuwanasavi (place name)

Tuuwanasavi, or "Sand Center," is a place slightly southwest of Kykotsmovi.

Twins

Once in a great while a woman gives birth to twins. The Hopis call these *tsöviwhoyat*, "little antelopes." Twins have greater than average powers, for they are not ordinary children. As a rule, twins are endowed with the knowledge of a medicine man. Thus, when a woman or a man gets a urinary infection, they usually consult twins. They will advise their patients to smear saliva along their groins. As a result, they can urinate again.

In times past a woman who bore twins did not raise both of them together. Who knows why, but that was the custom, and so twins were given to different aunts. When this was done, both of them would survive.

Upper Story

The *tupatsa* is a structure erected on the ground floor of a house. Older Hopi residences occasionally had one or more additional stories. The bottommost structure housed the living quarters but featured no entranceway of its own. In order to enter, therefore, it was necessary to climb to the rooftop first by means of a ladder or stairs; only then could one descend to the ground floor. The upper story, as a rule, held the corn stacks, the grinding bins, and also a firepit. In the olden days it was customary for girls to grind corn on this upper story.

Vent Hole

The ancient dwellings were never without vent holes. Because the Hopis did not have windows in those days, vent holes were there for the same purpose. In summer, when the weather was hot, it was through this opening that a cool breeze entered the house. Then it was not so hot in the interior. The room where a person ground corn was always equipped with this opening. Through it a suitor talked to his girlfriend while courting her.

Village

Whenever the Hopis established a village, they settled there with the intention of staying permanently. As soon as some sort of disaster struck the community, however, they usually moved on in search of a place with better living conditions where they could found another village. Unlike some other Indian groups, the Hopis, therefore, were not nomads. Homes were built using only stone and mortar, except for the roof, which was constructed from log beams covered with brush and mud. Wherever a village was erected, a village center or plaza had to be part of it. In general, the northwestern end of the plaza was occupied by members of the Bear clan, who constituted the Hopi elite. The three remaining sides of the plaza were open for any-one who wished to build there. Within the village were several rows of houses that were often multistoried. They consisted of rooms built especially to store corn and other crops, a chamber where piki was made, and of course an area that served as living quarters.

Village Chief

The *kikmongwi* or "village chief" of old came from the Bear clan. In a given village he is supposed to be the father to all. Therefore, in the olden days, he was the first to rise in the morning and the last to retire at night. The *kikmongwi* never gives orders. He does not think of only himself when he does things. On the contrary, his only concern is that as an end result his children will benefit. Therefore, he is not alone when he takes on a task. He seeks advice from his fellow leaders as he works on it. Obviously, a white man's "chief" and the *mongwi* of the Hopis are not synonymous.

Vulture

The vulture is a big bird that gobbles up anything that is decayed. A vulture's wing feather is employed to discharm people. As a rule the person who does the discharming places ashes on the feather. If he uses a discharming song while carrying out his ritual, he sings it as he loads the ashes on it. With this feather he then motions, holding it in his left hand. When he comes to the fourth name in the song, he carries out the discharming act by moving the feather in a circular motion. Next, he brushes the ashes off it. Then he takes some more ashes and repeats the whole procedure four times.

Walpi (First Mesa village)

Walpi is an old village. The people of Walpi may have settled at this location about the same time as the people of Oraibi and Shungo-pavi, but one cannot say for certain where they came from. Just as the Shungopavi residents, they used to live below the mesa. But due to the constant raids of enemy groups they moved to a site above the

original settlement where they were better off. In time, some relo-
cated to a place northeast of Walpi and founded another village,
which is known as Sichomovi. Finally, people from a Rio Grande
pueblo arrived and settled at the northeasternmost end of the mesa,
just southwest of the Gap. That village is referred to as Hanoki by the
Hopis.

Wedding Boots

When a Hopi prepares wedding garments for his female in-law,
he also makes wedding boots for her. They are fashioned from tanned
buckskin and cowhide. Cowhide is used for the soles and the uppers
are produced from a piece of supple white buckskin. It takes a while
to put these boots on. The uppers are usually quite long, so that the
woman putting them on must wrap them around her legs several
times. Extremely long uppers almost reach up to the knee and wind
around the leg in several coils. But these boots are not for everyday
wear.

Although termed wedding boots, they are worn by women other
than brides. On some occasions teenage girls, and even little girls,
also wear them when they participate in a ceremony.

Wedding Robe

The *oova* or "wedding robe" comes in two sizes, one being quite a
bit larger than the other. The large one is woven for the bride so that
she can journey to Maski, "Home of the Dead." As the robe constituted a married woman's vehicle to make her descent to the underworld, she was not supposed to sell it. In previous times when the
oova was never sold, the woman would sometimes fashion a sack
from it. People also used the garment as a sitting mat. It was also not
supposed to be decorated. Embroidery would have added weight to
it and not permitted the dead woman to ride it down the Grand
Canyon on her way to the underworld.

The bridal robe is further said to function as a water sieve. With
its help the clouds sift their moisture to produce the very fine rain. In
Hopi belief, upon one's demise a mortal is transformed into a cloud
personage, and whenever a woman checks on the people she left
behind, she employs the *oova* as a sieve. By using the *oova* to sift the
rains, a fine drizzle is produced instead of hail. Hail is dreaded by the

Hopis because it ruins the corn crops and smashes holes into musk-melons and watermelons.

One of the corners of the wedding robe is embroidered with six-teen stitches of red yarn. They symbolize a young woman's menstrua-tion. Also attached at this corner is a corncob. This corncob is not a real cob but is made from multicolored yarn. However, it closely resembles a corn.

Weeds

Whenever a Hopi farmer has sowed and the plants start coming up, he checks on them regularly. As weeds also sprout, he hoes them away. Since weeds suck most of the water from the ground, a Hopi watches out for his plants. He cuts away the weeds so that they don't grow too quickly.

Whipsnake

The whipsnake is another kind of snake. It can really run fast. The Hopis pray to it for rain just like the other snakes.

Wren

According to Hopi tradition the rock wren belongs to the *tsiro* class of birds and is believed to possess the power to make a girl go sexually wild. Therefore, it was once said that if a man desired a female he should fashion a *nakwakwusi* or prayer feather using the middle section of the wren's tail feather and place it outside the girl's house. That was all that had to be done. The prayer feather was then supposed to cause the girl to submit to the man's desires. Some claim that the girl in question actually came to the maker of the prayer feather of her own volition.

Wrist Guard

Hopis have been wearing wrist guards for a long, long time. Whenever someone goes hunting he must wear one around his wrist so that the bowstring does not injure him as he releases the arrow. And since nowadays Hopis don't hunt with bow and arrow anymore, it is the kachinas that wear wrist guards as part of their clothing.